the Arctic Monkeys

Whatever People Say They Are...
That's What They're Not

the Arctic Monkeys

Whatever People Say They Are...
That's What They're Not

Ben Osborne

OMNIBUS PRESS

London / New York / Paris / Sydney / Copenhagen / Berlin / Madrid / Tokyo

Cover designed by Fresh Lemon
Picture research by Jacqui Black

ISBN: 978.0.85712.859.1
Order No: OP54901

Exclusive Distributors
Music Sales Limited,
14/15 Berners Street,
London, W1T 3LJ.

Music Sales Corporation
180 Madison Avenue, 24th Floor,
New York,
NY 10016,
USA.

Macmillan Distribution Services,
56 Parkwest Drive
Derrimut, Vic 3030,
Australia.

Printed in the EU.

A catalogue record for this book is available from the British Library.

Visit Omnibus Press on the web at www.omnibuspress.com

Many are owed gratitude, so I apologise to those not mentioned by name in this truncated acknowledgement. You are not forgotten. Thank you to my literary agent, Sarah Such, and David 'Baz' Barraclough, Charlie Harris, Paul Woods and all at Omnibus who made this book possible. To everyone who shared their stories, contacts and insights and all the music people, journalists, publications, radio stations, websites, fans and everyone who has supported, and all who continue to support, good music. Thank you to Dad and Mum, who indulged my noisy passion; likewise to, and in memory of, Liz. To all my friends and family, old and new, and, with love and gratitude for all, to C and L, to whom this book is dedicated. Finally, thank you Arctic Monkeys for the songs.

Finally, thank you Arctic Monkeys for the songs and remember that there are bound to be many different versions iof something as epic as the Arctic Monkeys' story. I have triedto be inclusive and balanced, accepting that people will have different memories of the same incident.

Contents

Prelude: Potion Approaching

CAUGHT in the densely packed mops of dripping hair, shiny sweat-drenched faces, smiles and happily chanting voices, a brief snap freeze-framed the storm that had left everyone hot and soaking. There were faces in this room that had travelled miles to get here, friends and strangers who had become family. And onstage, grinning because at moments like this it was impossible not to, were four friends who'd been pinching themselves, disbelieving their luck for a year now.

In a brief moment, the frontman with the winsome pixie-like quality, the human Slinky New Yorkers had dubbed 'Harry Potter', had raised a lone index finger in the air to signify that the next song, which everyone was about to sing so loudly he wouldn't be able to hear himself, had got to number one in the singles chart.

What he didn't know yet was that, by this time tomorrow, their debut LP would unassailably top the album charts on its first day of sales.

But right here, now, tonight, as he raised his finger and people realised what he meant, a thousand tiny shivers simultaneously swept down a thousand sweat-drenched spines.

In the next moment the crowd would start singing; the chords would slow; a collision of guitar, bass and drums would slam together with pin-point precision. And after that, all hell would break loose.

1

The View From The Afternoon

IN 2002, a group of suburban school friends walked out of their last exam and, wondering what to do next, decided to form a band. One of them already had a guitar, as did his next-door neighbour, while another had acquired a bass and a fourth was allotted the drums.

Before they played a single note together they agreed a name: Arctic Monkeys. It was given to them by the second guitarist, James Cook – although no one can quite remember why.

From this off-the-cuff start, the band would go on to create the fastest-selling UK debut album by any band ever. They would also be recognised as the first act to be broken by the internet and, after racking up four number one albums, would headline the 2012 Olympics opening cere-mony alongside Sir Paul McCartney, in front of 27.3 million people.

Not bad for a group of boys who walked out of their last exam barely capable of playing their instruments. As they would one day recall, they'd only wanted to form a band to play cover versions of Strokes songs for their mates. Somehow it had all got a bit serious.

But then their tale is a very familiar British rock'n'roll story – the journey of a group of teenagers travelling from a small-town backwater to global glory.

Before rock'n'roll, the United Kingdom had not made that great a con-tribution to music. To be sure, there were outstanding composers in the classical tradition – Elgar, Purcell, Vaughan Williams, Britten – and the music hall had thrown up performers such as Flanagan & Allen. But for a nation that had created the furthest reaching empire the world had known, its influence on global music had been disproportionately slight. Russia, France, Italy, Germany and the Austro-Hungarians could all look down their noses at Great Britain with some justification.

When North America exported the homogeneous culture of the twentieth century, with the sounds of the swinging Twenties morphing into jazz and movie musicals, Britain's musicians increasingly fell into line behind the US screen stars.

By the time rock'n'roll had sent the first wave of youth culture crashing around the world in the Fifties, the UK was already in thrall to American music fashions. Just as the French created Johnny Hallyday in the image of Elvis, so the Brits fashioned Cliff Richard and Billy Fury into neutered rock'n'roll heroes that Fifties mums and dads were happy to listen to.

The Sixties changed all that. Liverpool, London, Manchester and further flung reaches of the UK found their voice. They gobbled up US influences and spat them back with a distinctly British twang. They took distorted guitar lines that owed as much to Bo Diddley as Buddy Holly and restructured them into English power chords. The Beatles and The Rolling Stones led the way, but, once the secret was out, a new mix of multiple musical heritages bubbled to the surface.

Rather than being the processed music of popular culture, it was a raw sound inspired by the downtrodden of America, taken from the delta and urban blues traditions of Leadbelly, John Lee Hooker and Muddy Waters.

For more than two decades the UK continued to provide the world with genre-defining artists as diverse as The Kinks, The Bee Gees, Led Zeppelin, Deep Purple, Pink Floyd, David Bowie, The Clash and The Jam. The list goes on. Coming from the little-known housing estates, minor suburbs, ancient university seats, small market towns and obscure corners of England, they sprang onto the world stage and defined new forms of popular music.

In the late Eighties it was Sheffield's turn to unleash a global movement, as the first of a clutch of new wave synth-pop acts emerged from the city. The Human League paved the way for the glamour of the 'New Romantics': London-based Culture Club, Birmingham's Duran Duran and others who spearheaded a new invasion of the USA by British bands.

By the turn of the twenty-first century, however, Britain's musical lineage had started fading. The big bands of the Nineties had made less of a global impact than the home-grown hype had anticipated. More importantly, the whole recorded music industry had gone into crisis, as the commercial value of music was terminally undermined by the internet.

Against this background, our group of friends in a small northern English suburb, inspired by a new wave of American rock'n'roll, decided to form a band.

In common with many of Britain's greatest acts, Arctic Monkeys were brought together by geography. This simple fact is no small detail. It represents the cavernous distance between them and the contrived boy bands, manufactured pop groups, groomed pre-teens and TV competition entrants who clutter contemporary popular music.

It's often asserted The Beatles were the first boy band, and there's no doubting they were skilfully managed and nurtured by Brian Epstein. But Lennon and McCartney had already formed their songwriting partnership before Epstein and George Martin fine-tuned it; Paul and George had gone to school together, and, even if Ringo had come sliding in at the last minute, it was Liverpool – not a manager, TV mogul or brand executive – that had drawn the band together.

The geographical accident that brought Arctic Monkeys together was the Sheffield suburb of High Green.

As its name implies, High Green is a distant, almost rural, area at the northernmost point of the city. Located eight miles from the city centre, it has no local rail station. The nearest is in Chapeltown, an adjacent suburb separated 20 years ago from High Green by greenbelt open spaces. Recent building expansion has seen the two suburbs merge into a continuous con-urbation, but the area remains strikingly green for a suburban environment. From the centre of High Green on Wortley Road, the horizon to the east ends in Mortomley Park, High Green Playing Fields and hills rising in the distance towards Hesley Wood, while fields and countryside lie beyond Westwood New Road to the west.

In the centre of High Green are reminders of the area as it once was: late Victorian and early twentieth-century terrace houses built alongside a narrow two-lane roadway that would have been a main access route into and out of the city.

Many of the buildings that constitute the modern High Green are more recent, built postwar or post-Sixties and planned with neatly mapped-out gardens and parking spaces arranged around cul-de-sacs, connected by footpaths and open spaces – ideal places for young kids to play in.

The local high street, Wortley Road, has a smattering of shops: Kevin

Williams' Quality Butchers; a local NISA supermarket; a betting shop; a drop-in barber's; the Huang Lou Xing Chinese takeaway; a furniture and upholstery store; two doctors' practices; a dentist; and a few local pubs, thoughtfully arranged within crawling distance from each other.

Jamie Cook, Matt Helders, Nick O'Malley and Alex Turner came from the side of High Green that backed onto Blackburn Brook and Thorncliffe Wood, opening up into the greenery to the north of Wortley Road. Their streets were a short walk west of what would become their local pub, The Packhorse – not strictly the nearest watering hole but their regular, tucked down a side lane and close to the green open spaces.

None of them lived far from each other, although Jamie and Alex were probably the nearest neighbours with Matt just around the corner. Nick, the last member of the band to join in 2006, was only a little further up the road and you could walk between all four houses in under 10 minutes.

High Green doesn't have its own secondary school, so local teenagers usually go to Ecclesfield, Stocksbridge or Notre Dame schools. All are at least a two-mile bus journey away. The journey into Sheffield itself takes nearly an hour and, not surprisingly, buses feature heavily in young people's lives in High Green – as reflected in the Arctic Monkeys song 'Red Light Indicates Doors Are Secured'.

As a breeding ground for angst-driven rock'n'roll, High Green is typical of great swathes of the UK. Small-town conurbations that spawn volumes of venom-ridden anthems and whimsical pop classics – diverting youths such as Paul Weller, Syd Barrett and Ray Davies into often acerbic and frequently fanciful lyrical outlets.

This scratching at the suburban scab has made a crucial contribution to Britain's musical heritage. The need to escape the claustrophobic cul-de-sac is at least as fierce a motivator for the UK's finest songwriters as the desire to bust out of the ghetto has been for US rap stars.

The suburban confinement of stifled creativity was concisely described in the late Seventies by punk band The Members, and their 1979 chart hit 'Sound Of The Suburbs', penned by singer Nicky Tesco (born Nicholas Lightowlers). Tesco would later write for *Music Week* at the time Arctic Monkeys first broke. For reasons that will be obvious, he felt an immediate affinity with their lyrics and was, perhaps unsurprisingly, among the first journalists to pick up on the band.

The son of a Yorkshire man, Tesco grew up in Camberley, a small Surrey town south-west of London. His memory of being a teenager, surrounded by mind-numbing suburban life, and the effect it had on him and his band is still vivid.

"We'd grown up somewhere where nothing happened. It was really tedious. If you went near a nightclub you'd get beaten up!

"So it was small town, small minds, being run by people who . . . didn't give a fuck. And it was drinking, soft drugs and having sex underage.

"That aspect of provincial, suburban life hasn't changed in this country. You've still got the small towns run by the same kind of arseholes with tight little minds. It makes you just want to shout and scream – I recognise that in the Arctic Monkeys."

Tesco says that forming a band has become a default reaction to growing up in small-town Britain: "There's this line that runs from Ray Davies, The Beatles, The Jam – the ability to make the minutiae of suburban, provincial life almost beautiful; almost a political statement," explains Tesco. "Many of the same things are at play with Turner – his lyrics, his acute observation and use of colloquial northern language.

"Alex and his mates knew people who had formed bands, so they formed a band. It's like forming gangs, but without the guns and knives – and it's a far brighter and better way of doing stuff."

The potential for the less 'bright' way of doing things is also present in Arctic Monkeys' youthful experiences, for example when Turner recounts a game of chase between youths and the police in the song 'Riot Van'.

Turner's ability to pen lyrics that stand easy comparison with British icons such as Ray Davies is present in the earliest of the band's recordings. But it wasn't only the quality of Alex's songwriting that made the Arctic Monkeys stand out. It was also the pent-up energy released in the band's interpretations of Turner's songs, combined with an ability to churn out new tracks at astonishing speed.

Music journalist John Harris has argued that this frustrated genius, created by small-town claustrophobia, is an essential ingredient in British songwriting.

Harris identified in a *Guardian* article "a very English genre: rock music uprooted from the glamour and dazzle of the city, and recast as the soundtrack to life in suburbs, small towns, and the kind of places . . . held up as bywords for broken hopes and limited horizons. The lineage began with Ray Davies's compositions for The Kinks. Later on, it took in The Jam, and Coventry's Specials, as well as scores of half-forgotten punk and new wave bands . . ."

2

Little Monkeys From The Suburbs

IN many ways, Arctic Monkeys were the classic boys next door done good – having risen from normal backgrounds to do something extraordinary. "We don't look like superstars," Andy Nicholson later commented to *Blender* magazine, as the band were breaking into the limelight. "I think people look at us and think, 'They're just normal people making good music. I'm sure I could do it.' Anyone can do it. We're living proof of that."

And yet, even in their earliest period, they'd had qualities that made them stand out.

Simon Armitage, celebrated poet and Yorkshireman, described this innate 'otherness' when he interviewed Alex for *The Guardian* in 2009: "For an occasionally cocky frontman with an occasional foul mouth and furious guitar, there's an ethereal, almost gravity-defying quality about the man himself, twisting in his chair, floating in his thoughts. Turner exhibits a sort of double jointed-ness of both body and mind, as if he might metamorphose into a puff of smoke or ring-tailed lemur should the notion occur to him. A kind of human Slinky . . ."

Alexander David Turner, the human Slinky, was born on January 6, 1986, the only child of schoolteachers David and Penny, who taught German at Parkwood High School.

Alex's early musical recollections refer to a friend's dad more than his own father: "I used to hang out with my neighbour growing up, and his dad loved classic rock," he would later recall for *Pitchfork*. "He would play Deep Purple on this boombox in their back garden. I can remember playing Batman and Robin to 'Hush' on Saturday afternoons.

"My neighbour was a bit older than me, and he was allowed to chew bubblegum – I couldn't do that as a five-year-old. He was allowed to wear hair gel, too. I wanted to be him a little bit."

Back at home, Alex remembers listening to whatever the family had around: a standard post-World War II soundtrack including records by The Beatles, The Beach Boys and Frank Sinatra.

"The other night we were in a cab in Chicago and that Toto song, 'Hold the Line', came on," Alex recalled. "I knew an alarming amount of lyrics to that tune because my mum used to play it in the car, driving me around in the booster seat. She would always play The Eagles too, so I'm word-perfect on shit loads of Eagles tunes whenever I hear them in restaurants now. I can sing 'Hotel California' all the whole way through."

The first members of Arctic Monkeys to connect were Alex and Matt Helders, at a young age. Matt was born on 7 May 1986, making them within a month of being the same age. They have stayed joined at the hip throughout the extraordinary journey that followed.

While Alex was getting an early introduction to music via West Coast country rock and West Midlands heavy metal, Matt had been receiving a more soulful grounding a few streets around the corner.

A big character with a reputation for charm and warmth, Matt is generally held to be the most outgoing of the Arctic Monkeys. The youngest of two brothers – his brother Gary is four years older – both boys came as a surprise to their parents. While still in her teens, Matt's mum, Jill, had been told she wouldn't be able to have children. So husband and wife had settled down as a childless couple – only to later become, by what must have seemed something of a miracle, a family of four.

The Jill and Clive Helders' story is full of such romantic moments. The pair had been childhood sweethearts who met at the Pathfinders youth club in Hillsborough, Sheffield, when Jill was 14 and Clive three years older. They soon fell in love, getting married when Jill was 18 years old, and have been together ever since.

Both parents have worked most of their lives, despite Jill taking a few years off to be a full-time mum when Matt was born. Clive's career started in the family boiler suit business and, for years, the family's curtains and bedding were made from the same fabric as the factory's boiler suits – which at one point meant they had pink curtains, presumably with matching bed sheets.

During the Nineties, Clive Helders was listed as a director for Barnsley-based clothing company Christy's By Design. He resigned the post by the turn of the century, but the connection with Christy's would come back into play when Matt launched his own clothing line for the Supremebeing label – a subsidiary of Christy's By Design.

Matt's parents also introduced him to beat-driven music at an early age. "We used to play Motown," his mother told BBC Yorkshire in early 2009. "I remember one of the first albums we used to play was Michael Jackson's *Bad* album. We all used to sing along. I dread to think about some of the other stuff we played though."

Gary took to his older brother role immediately, ensuring that Matt had an attentive sibling throughout his early years. But as Matt turned 13, this part of the family unit disappeared.

Gary had finished school and decided to take a gap year before university. He went to stay with his uncle and aunt in the Cayman Islands, working as a diving instructor. The gap year turned into several years and then, after meeting an American girl, he eventually settled there. The couple married in 2006.

For Matt, who'd spent his early years under Gary's wing, this must have been a significant change. For one thing, it removed the influence of an elder sibling at a crucial point in the development of his musical tastes. It also meant that Matt and Alex suddenly had much more comparable home lives, with both now living as an only child.

They also shared family backgrounds that encouraged them to be interested in music. Matt's family, unlike Alex's dad, may have had no formal musical connection but they would be supremely supportive of their son's musical vocation.

For his part, Matt had shown an early interest in playing music. He also demonstrated an innate ability to learn instruments quickly, which would come in handy when, without so much as a lesson behind him, he was suddenly given the role of drumming for Arctic Monkeys.

Matt's first instrument was the keyboard and, at his request, his mum had enrolled him for lessons at Meadowhall shopping centre.

Jill was persuaded to pay £800 for Matt's first keyboard – having been told he needed to practise on the same instrument that he was learning on. It was costly, but it ultimately taught everyone a lesson. When Matt later asked his parents if he could have a drum kit for the band, they went looking for the cheapest kit available.

The investment in the keyboard initially paid off, however. Matt progressed rapidly, passing his first music exam with flying colours. He then promptly lost interest, abandoning his pricey instrument to collect dust until, unloved and unplayed, it was donated to a local school.

★ ★ ★

The friendship between Alex and Matt had begun when they were seven years old. Already close neighbours, they became friends at primary school and it was here that they made their first mutual musical connections, as well as making their debut stage performance in the school assembly.

Among their early influences was Oasis's 1995 album *(What's The Story) Morning Glory?* They'd both been drawn to Oasis by the band's look, knowing that they looked cool but, as Alex later admitted to *Pitchfork*, without really knowing what 'cool' meant.

"With Oasis, it's just that attitude, like it's resistant against everything else that's going on in music. I don't know if you can fully understand that – it's like an impulse, innit? Especially at that age, you don't rationalise, you're just like, 'That looks cool.'"

In the final year of their primary school, it was customary for the leaving kids to perform at their last school assembly. Matt and Alex, backed up by a couple more friends, naturally chose to perform the title track to *Morning Glory*, while a group of girls mimed to The Spice Girls.

Grabbing some tennis rackets and other props, Matt took the part of Liam: "He had the bucket hat on," recalled Alex. "I was the bass player. We were just standing there, doing what Oasis did onstage . . . which was not a great deal. I don't think we got as good a reaction as The Spice Girls."

After leaving primary school in 1997, Matt and Alex moved on to Stocksbridge High School, situated in a small former steel town a couple of miles to the west of High Green. They studied there until 2002. It was during their five years at Stocksbridge that, among other things, the future Arctic Monkeys amused each other by coming up with silly names for bands and fantasy football teams, writing them down on the back of their school folders. It was here that Alex also secretly started writing songs.

The school itself was an unremarkable brick building, surrounded by a playground and car park. The Arctic Monkeys' time might have been similarly unremarkable – were it not for the fact that the school inadvertently paved the way for the band and inspired some of Alex's lyrics.

"Alex was never particularly vocal," his former teacher, Steve Baker, later told *The Guardian*. "But you could sense when some pieces of poetry moved him. One day, I read out a John Cooper Clarke poem, 'I Wanna Be Yours' . . . years later . . . Alex said he'd sat there in class that day thinking: 'Wow!'

"I knew this was someone unconventional, a little bit different, with a brightness and a cleverness that would serve him well. He had a very original sense of humour, as you'd expect . . ."

It was while they were at Stocksbridge that Alex and Matt began to hang out with some of the boys who would form the Monkeys' original line-up. Andy Nicholson, the band's first bass player, was the only member of the band who didn't live in High Green. Like Matt's parents he came from nearby Hillsborough, a sprawling suburb that, by a cruel twist of fate, had become linked to the worst sporting tragedy in British history: the 1989 FA Cup semi-final disaster when 96 Liverpool fans had been crushed to death at Hillsborough Stadium.

But for Arctic Monkeys, Hillsborough Stadium had a happier significance. It was the home of the football team they all supported, Sheffield Wednesday. Alongside school and geography, this was the other bond that had brought the band together and it was through football that the rest of the band's line-up originally got to know Alex's neighbour, Jamie Cook.

All the Arctic Monkeys were keen football players, but Jamie was the most serious – and perhaps the one who came closest to realising his dream of playing pro football. A contemporary of Cook's at Ecclesfield School, Billy Sharp had gone on to play for Sheffield United, debuting for the team in 2007 while Jamie was enjoying the first fruits of musical success.

For a period Jamie Cook would manage to straddle both of his boyhood dreams, continuing to play right back for High Green Villa, the football team at his local boozer, well after the band had broken into the big time. He was still claiming the other players didn't know he was in a band as late as a September 2006 *Soccer AM* interview – although it's likely some of them cottoned on after Arctic Monkeys celebrated their first number one single in the pub.

Born James Robert Cook in Sheffield on July 8, 1985, Jamie is considered the no-nonsense, outspoken, blue-collar member of the band – a perception perhaps reinforced by his dad's job as an engineer. He had been the only Arctic Monkey to go to Ecclesfield School, a secondary school to the south of High Green. Surprisingly, considering his outspoken reputation, his teachers remember Jamie as a quiet boy. But the school had been given 'specialist in visual and performing arts' status while he was there and he doubtless benefited from being in an environment that prized and encouraged creativity.

Cook was always considered the most die-hard indie-guitar fan of the band members. At the time the Monkeys formed, he came pre-loaded with a musical taste that took in bands such as The Smiths, The Strokes and Oasis, and it was Jamie who introduced the rest of the band to acts such as The Coral and The Hives.

3

Here's Three Chords – Now Form A Band[*]

THE mainstream music of Turner, Helders, Cook and Nicholson's formative years had been dominated first by the tail end of Britpop, and then by the UK's dance music explosion of the late Nineties. While Jamie had always liked guitar bands, the young Alex and Matt had been attracted to the more underground side of the club scene. Turner had been a disciple of UK hip hop and bashment acts such as Roots Manuva (aka Rodney Smith), Braintax and other artists on imprints such as Low-Life, the Lyricist Lounge compilations and Rawkus Records.

"There wasn't a lot of guitar music in my world then," Alex later told *Pitchfork* of his early teens. "I'm sure there were great bands at the time, but they just didn't make it to our little village, 20 minutes outside Sheffield.

"We were into hip hop in a big way – we would wear caps and shit, and our trousers definitely fit a lot less snug than they do now. Matt used to shave my head in his kitchen, but he'd leave two stripes on, and then the gap in between those stripes came down and went through me eyebrow. That's the weirdest haircut I've ever had.

"I was listening to . . . Outkast, Eminem, Wu-Tang and all that. But I think the reason why I connected with Roots Manuva's *Run Come Save Me* was probably because he was talking about quite mundane things with a bit of a stoned slant."

Matt's teenage initiation into music had also come through hip hop, something that's often credited for his interest in beats, and he spent most of his early teens listening to rap and UK garage, dreaming about

---

* *Sideburns* fanzine, January 1977.

becoming a DJ. He had already started experimenting with DJing while he was at school, playing UK garage tracks to his mates at 14 years old. Alex remembers him spinning records such as '21 Seconds' by two-step act So Solid Crew.

After mastering the art of sitting-room DJing, Matt had moved onto sampling records, borrowing Frank Sinatra and Motown from his grand-dad and Beach Boys and Carpenters albums from his parents. Having been turned onto dance beats and hip hop, he'd also been drawn, like many a hip hop head before him, to Led Zeppelin's legendary drummer, John Bonham.

Matt Helders had often explained that he only started playing drums because the others had already taken all the guitar positions. But it's also true to say he already had the strongest affinity with beat-driven music. According-ing to Mike Smith, the veteran A&R man who would eventually sign them to EMI Publishing, it was Matt and Alex's hip hop background that made Arctic Monkeys stand out from a plethora of similar-sounding guitar bands. It might not be the most obvious route to guitar music, but through hip hop Matt had honed his natural inclination to pummel the drum kit.

Meanwhile, Alex would learn to sing in a rapid-fire lyrical flow that would lead him to sound like an unlikely cross between proto-punk Howard Devoto and The Streets.

In a different era, Alex may have stayed with grime and Matt may have continued down the path to DJ stardom. But by the year 2000 the raw, edgy subversion of early dance music had been replaced by a lucrative money-making machine. Massive DJ fees and ticket prices for Millennium Eve parties left punters disillusioned. The media turned against the bloated genre with a wolf-pack intensity as a new generation of young teens looked elsewhere for a less tainted, more dynamic scene.

The backlash against dance music ushered in a paradigm shift that the *NME* dubbed the 'New Rock 'n' Roll Revolution'. A new wave of young guitar bands surged onto its front cover and into the psyches of the nation's youth.

At the forefront of this explosion of guitar rock was a group of young New Yorkers called The Strokes. Their sound was reminiscent of the New York Dolls/Richard Hell school of early American punk. The Strokes' backgrounds hardly fitted into the lineage of UK punk (and their life experience was certainly a million miles away from life in High Green). All the same, their music was fired with a testosterone-fuelled energy that resonated loudly with the up-and-coming early teen genera-tion of British suburbia.

The Strokes were not alone in ushering in the new music. Amongst others there was New Zealand's The D4, who also had a transformative influence on the four mates in High Green. When The D4 played a free gig at The Leadmill in Sheffield on November 29, 2002, the quartet of friends made a pilgrimage to see them. The following day, Matt Helders, until recently a wannabe UK garage DJ, rushed into Barnsley HMV to buy their limited edition LP.

As the boys approached their GCSEs, all four had become ensnared in the excitement of a new wave of explosive rock'n'roll. It could only point in one musical direction.

At this point Matt was probably the only future Monkey who owned a musical instrument – and even that was a keyboard gathering dust in the corner. But that was a small detail. It was going to be only a matter of time before they formed a band.

★   ★   ★

According to Alex Turner, the idea of forming the Monkeys came to them all quite late. The epiphany came in 2001 when, according to well-worn legend, Alex and Jamie both asked for electric guitars as Christmas presents. Given Alex's recent conversion to (and Jamie's long-standing love of) guitar music, this pattern of events is less coincidental than it sounds.

The oft-repeated story describes the two neighbours teaching each other to play their new instruments. (Why Turner was left by his dad to teach himself guitar remains an enigma.) But with Andy Nicholson playing bass, three-quarters of the band was formed.

Matt Helders, of course, had a background in keyboard playing, but this was more in tune with an earlier generation of Sheffield music. So he ended up on drums – "that was all that were left," he would later patiently tell reporters. "They all had guitars so I bought a drum kit."

As his earlier keyboard lessons had demonstrated, Matt was lucky to have parents keen to support his musical interests. But Jill had already forked out £800 on his rapidly abandoned keyboard, so she decided on a more modest £200 investment on Matt's first kit. It was enough to get the band started and soon they were practising at the Helders family home and in Alex's garage around the corner.

Matt Helders would turn out to be as natural on the drums as he had been on the keyboard. Within a few years of starting to play, he would be garnering praise from international hip hop star Kanye West, while being personally invited to drum for Puff Daddy's band.

"It was just kind of something to do," Matt told *Prefix* of the genesis of the band. "At 15 or 16, some of our friends were in bands that we used to go and watch, and we kind of thought it looked like an interesting thing to do. You see people in bands and you wonder how you get into that industry – it looks like a lot of trouble. But it's really quite easy to start a band up. So we knew that it could be done, and we just decided to start."

At this time Clive and Jill Helders were working together at a warehouse which had a spare, unused mezzanine room. The space was turned over to Arctic Monkeys as a rehearsal studio, so the band moved in and began using it as their regular practice space – as well as making use of the warehouse's gaming facilities.

"Three nights a week we used to run them out there to practise," Jill recalled to BBC Yorkshire. "We just used to leave them and then pick them up a couple of hours later. If they knew you were there they would just stop [playing], so we had to sneak in really quietly so we could sit and listen. They used to play a lot of covers, like The Strokes. Half the time, though, they were playing table tennis."

The original line-up of the band consisted of Alex and Jamie on guitars and backing vocals, Matt on drums and backing vocals, Andy Nicholson on bass and backing vocals, and Glyn Jones on lead vocals. Although Jamie and Alex had received their guitars at Christmas and had started learning to play together, it had been classmate Glyn who Turner had at first turned to as a writing partner.

Turner and Jones started working on songs together the day they'd finished their last GCSE. "We felt a bit stupid playing, so we would write rubbish that didn't mean anything and just mess about," Glyn later recalled for *The Sun*. "I suppose the way we wrote then was similar to how Alex writes now . . . about real things that happened to us, things people relate to."

Despite writing the songs, Alex didn't want to be the singer. The only trouble was that neither did anyone else. At first Alex had managed to persuade Glyn, but he was reluctant from the start and never really settled into the role.

For his part, Glyn recalls these early days as being just a gang of mates messing around in a garage – largely because there wasn't much else for them to do. Similarly, Alex remembers that their initial ambitions were limited to playing a gig to a few mates and keeping out of trouble.

"We weren't like yobbos," Turner later told *The Guardian* of their behaviour at the time. "We wouldn't have got an ASBO," Helders agreed. "Maybe borderline ASBO. You might hang around with people who break into houses, but it doesn't mean you do."

But Cook had always perceived a bigger future for the Monkeys and soon the rest of the band's vision started to expand. While Glyn had been happy enough to hang out with his mates and do a bit of singing, he started to have doubts as things began to take a more serious turn. Soon he decided to leave the band.

After he quit the Monkeys tried, but failed, to find a replacement singer. Eventually it fell upon Alex, as chief songwriter, to assume the role of lead vocalist.

"Lyrics were a dark patch," Alex later recalled for the Leeds Music Scene website/*NME*. "Nobody wanted to admit they wrote them, so we kept trying other singers so they'd do it for us. But I'd secretly been writing since school and I enjoyed it. I'd just never told anyone, because I didn't want to have the piss took out of me!

"You couldn't be creative at school. Even when we started the band, lyrics were an area that we were ashamed to talk about . . . But I'd always write things down in secret and one day I just thought, 'Fuck it!'"

Despite this timid start, once Alex's singer-songwriter role was accepted, his enormous capacity for composition kicked in. Soon the songs were pouring out with a Prince-like rapidity that has barely paused since.

"I think they would have come through at any point. There was something about them," Nick Tesco observes. "They weren't a band of some strutting wannabes, they just got on with it. Maybe that's their northern attitude. I do think that being from Sheffield had something to do with it.

"I mean, when they won the Mercury Award they said, 'Someone call the police, Richard Hawley's been robbed!' They were genuflecting to Richard Hawley [also from Sheffield]. But there's Hawley, Cabaret Voltaire, Human League, Heaven 17 . . . The list of great Sheffield bands is endless; far bigger than other places. It's a fucking good city."

4

Forged In Sheffield

ALEX Turner has often said that a major catalyst for Arctic Monkeys was being surrounded by mates in local bands. At the time the Monkeys formed, Sheffield's scene was certainly going through a purple patch, sprouting a crop of young bands such as The Harrisons, Bromheads Jacket, The Long Blondes and Milburn – who would soon be dubbed, alongside a similar scene in Leeds, the 'New Yorkshire' movement.

"Where we grew up there were these other kids that had a band, and they used to play in one of the pubs, and we started hanging around with them," Alex later recalled for *Pitchfork*. "We'd go and watch them and drink cider and be stupid and chase after girls. Then, sitting around chatting on a Friday night, we were like: 'We should form a band!' Just desperately looking for something to do. None of us could play anything . . . It was just based on this idea of seeing these other kids whose only ambition was to play a show in the pub."

In Sheffield's relatively small and interconnected music community, the bands on the circuit were often friends. Acts such as Milburn started playing when they were only 13 or 14 years old; they were already gigging before Arctic Monkeys formed and clearly influenced the 15-year-olds. Having local mentors made the process of performing seem less mysterious and more attainable.

But it wasn't only the current bands surrounding them who gave the Monkeys the confidence to climb onstage themselves. The enormous historical heritage of Sheffield's music scene was equally important, demonstrating that bands really could rise from the streets and conquer the world.

Arctic Monkeys were following an established DIY cultural heritage. Rock'n'roll music had been coursing through Sheffield's bloodstream since the music had first arrived in the UK and, throughout their formative years, the Monkeys were surrounded by great Sheffield bands.

With a proudly separate identity to London, Sheffield's music scene had played a global role over the last three decades. Its past was awash with seminal clubs, labels, bands, DJs and musicians. Although the city's contribution to Eighties synth-pop would cement its place in cultural history, Sheffield first began to make its mark on British music in the mid-Sixties, when clubs such as Club 60, Black Cat, The Esquire and King Mojo opened. These attracted the defining acts of the period – The Yardbirds, The Who, Stevie Wonder, Pink Floyd, The Hollies and Jimi Hendrix – and it wasn't long before the city began to produce its own stars, most notably Joe Cocker and local blues guitarist Frank White.

By the late Seventies and early Eighties, Sheffield had developed its own distinct music scene with a new wave of post-punk electronic acts at its core. Amongst them, a band called The Extras first took to the stage in 1977; held by many to be the band that kick-started the Sheffield music scene proper, they epitomised the punk movement's DIY aesthetic.

The band themselves were typically self-deprecating in a characteristic Sheffield manner. In the documentary film *Made In Sheffield*, The Extras summed up the difference between themselves and The Human League by describing the original League as "avant-garde", while The Extras were "'aven't a clue". Although large-scale success eluded them, The Extras were partly responsible for the generation of Sheffield acts that followed them.

In the late Seventies the post-punk and post-disco new wave culture of New York began to filter into the UK. Artists started mixing black music and German electronic sounds, and this post-industrial urban soundscape found a natural home in the city.

Central to this period of Sheffield's musical development was The Crazy Daisy Club, a late-night venue run by Webster's brewery and, later, from 1978, Tetley's. Opening on the premises of The Beer Keller in 1973, the club was situated in the basement of an Art Deco building on the corner of York Street and High Street (currently home to a bank and some shops).

The club's place in history was cemented when Phil Oakey, lead singer of The Human League, spotted two schoolgirls, Joanne Catherall and

Susan Ann Sulley, dancing there in October 1980. The Human League had imploded on Oakey earlier that night, when the original line-up had walked out on the eve of an international tour. He was drowning his sorrows as he watched the two schoolgirls dance, which led to him immediately recruiting them without a single audition or rehearsal. Within four days they'd been whisked out of school and onto a hectic tour schedule that was followed by a meteoric rise to international pop stardom.

The rest of the Eighties saw electronic synth-pop explode out of Sheffield to become an international phenomenon. Cabaret Voltaire, Heaven 17 (Martyn Ware's successor group to The Human League), ABC and, later, Graeme Park, LFO and Warp Records became global pioneers and international stars, forming a new British musical invasion of the USA. They also inspired a rapidly evolving nightclub scene in the UK that would launch acid house and lead the world into a new era of electronic music.

The city's influence on early electro-pop alone had given it a status of Detroit or Dusseldorf proportions in the history of techno and dance music. Despite the international dance crossover success of The Human League, Heaven 17 and ABC, however, its scene had remained fiercely independent – with a long line of indie bands later rising from the Steel City's streets.

The Crazy Daisy had turned into Legends by the mid-Eighties, but by then The Leadmill and The Boardwalk had begun to take up the city's musical baton. Parallel to electronica, Sheffield also helped shape a new wave of indie guitar and British heavy metal bands – the city's most notable rockers being Def Leppard.

The Leadmill opened at 6–7 Leadmill Road in the autumn of 1980, against the backdrop of the decline of Sheffield's mainstay steelworks industry and the Thatcher government's determination to move Britain away from smokestack manufacturing. Situated in part of a derelict flour mill, it wasn't the first time the building had been repurposed as a music venue, having previously housed the legendary Esquire club.

Starting life as a performing arts venue, with a booking policy that included jazz, pop, theatre, workshops, club nights and artist spaces, it quickly became a magnet for Sheffield's burgeoning post-punk electronic acts – as well as attracting local art-minded guitar band Pulp.

Like The Hacienda in Manchester, The Leadmill not only brought in and supported local, national and international acts but also inspired its regulars to form their own bands. In September 1982, The Leadmill reopened after a significant refurbishment. Later that year a little-known Jarvis Cocker wrote and directed a Christmas pantomime for The Leadmill, drawing on a pool of Sheffield guitar bands as his cast.

Throughout the early to mid-Eighties the city's key acts were permanent fixtures in the UK charts, but by the late Eighties synth-pop had lost its shine. The advent of house music, which began to be played in British clubs from 1986, was soon reviving Sheffield's fortunes as veteran DJs such as DJ Parrot became pioneers of the new sound.

In 1988 a new club night, The Steamer, with resident DJ Graeme Park, started at The Leadmill. Park had been one of the first DJs to play house music and the night soon became one of the leading acid house venues in the north, alongside The Hacienda.

The two venues arranged a swap between The Steamer and The Hacienda's seminal Wednesday night acid house session, Hot. Hosted by Mike Pickering and Jon Dasilva, the exchange introduced Graeme Park to Madchester and cemented him, alongside Pickering, as one of the fathers of house music in northern England.

The city's position at the centre of electronic music continued to thrive into the Nineties, when the Yorkshire bleep and bass movement saw Sheffield acts such as LFO, Sweet Exorcist and Autechre redefine dance music – with the innovative Sheffield-based record label Warp leading electronic music in new directions. Warp was founded in 1989, by Steve Beckett, Robert Gordon and Rob Mitchell, while they were working at the FON record store. Gordon was responsible for their first release, Forgemasters' 'Track With No Name', while the second single, Nightmares On Wax's 'Dextrous', sold some 30,000 copies and launched Warp's first star act.

For its next release Warp recruited Sweet Exorcist to the label. The act consisted of two of the city's most iconic figureheads: Richard H. Kirk of electronic pioneers Cabaret Voltaire and Richard Barratt, aka DJ Parrot, the venerated club DJ and member of All Seeing I and I Monster. With Warp increasingly representing the city's new music scene, the duo helped define Sheffield's "bleep" techno sound.

By its fifth release, Warp scored its first Top 20 hit, with LFO's epony-mous single 'LFO', which sold 130,000 and peaked at number 12 in the UK singles chart. This was soon followed by Tricky Disco, another Warp act, hitting number 14 in the national charts.

From here the label's influence became embedded in the story of UK techno, with local and international acts added to its formidable roster – including Aphex Twin, Autechre, B12, Black Dog, Richie Hawtin, Andrew Weatherall, Antipop Consortium, !!! and Battles among many seminal acts.

As with earlier Sheffield luminaries, the success of the label was eventu-ally followed by relocation, and in 2000 the label moved south to London. By this time co-founder Robert Gordon had parted company with the label and, tragically, co-founder Rob Mitchell was diagnosed with cancer in early 2001 and died later that year.

Just as Warp had become a watchword for left-field electronic music, in the late Nineties Moloko became the respectable face of commercial dance music. In the 2000s producers such as Oris Jay and Toddla T were to rise from the Steel City to push dub step and grime into new directions, while the city's Niche club gave rise to the bassline genre – stretching Sheffield's involvement into every facet of electronic music.

Meanwhile, Jarvis Cocker and his band Pulp had become figureheads of the mid-Nineties Britpop era, alongside Oasis and Blur. Their long rise (they formed early in the previous decade) heralded the growth of a new spate of Sheffield-based guitar bands, with The Longpigs also achieving Top 20 success by the mid-Nineties.

However, The Longpigs' most memorable musical legacy was their guitarist and songwriter Richard Hawley, who went on to work with Jarvis Cocker on his Relaxed Muscle electro project and to play on Pulp's *We Love Life* album, before establishing himself as a successful solo singer/songwriter. Hawley's solo career took off in earnest in the period leading up to Arctic Monkeys' rapid ascent. In 2006, his LP *Coles Corner* was nominated for the Nationwide Mercury Music Prize. As we've seen, when the prize went to Arctic Monkeys, Alex Turner famously accepted the award by saying Richard Hawley had been robbed; their recognition of his place in Sheffield's musical history could not have been made clearer.

"Richard Hawley's always believed you don't have to leave Sheffield to be a success, so there's his influence keeping the Arctic Monkeys attached to Sheffield," explains Kate Linderholm of BBC Radio Sheffield. "And it's a scene where the music of other acts rubs off on each other. If you talk to a successful musician in Sheffield they'll almost certainly mention someone else they're going to see; they find ways to support other local bands."

It was artists such as Hawley who paved the way for Milburn, Bromheads Jacket, Reverend & The Makers, The Long Blondes, Champion Kickboxer and Arctic Monkeys themselves. By the time the Monkeys were breaking through, all of these bands had been namechecked by the *NME* for leading a new musical movement dubbed the 'New Yorkshire scene'.

As Nick Tesco says, Sheffield was indeed a "fucking great city" to call home.

5

What's In A Name?

IT might have taken the four mates a long time to get around to forming a band, but they at least managed to avoid the usual month-long battles over what it was going to be called. There is little agreement about where the name came from and absolutely no consensus whatsoever about what it means. But everyone agrees it was arrived at rapidly and stuck quickly – despite most of the band thinking it was rubbish.

One strand of Arctic Monkeys legend has it that the name came from Glyn Jones, who then promptly scampered off into the bushes to admire his handiwork from afar – an easy cop-out for the remaining band members, but probably not true.

Another legend holds that it was bestowed randomly on them by a tramp after a gig, while other early reports suggested they named them-selves after Matt Helders' uncle's (or even father's) old band. An extreme version of the latter suggests the name was passed down from father to son in the Helders family.

When a journalist from US magazine *Prefix* repeated these rumours to Helders in 2005, he dismissed it all as a lie: "We made that up 'cause we got so many people asking us – every interviewer asked us about that. So we just started making stories up. We made so many up that it was hard to keep track."

The real story behind the Arctic Monkeys' name is likely to be far less entertaining. Both Matt and Alex eventually attributed it to Jamie, who had, for reasons known only to himself, apparently insisted on Arctic Monkeys as the band's name from the start.

"It is just a name that Jamie Cook came up with at school before the band existed. He just always wanted to be in a band called Arctic Monkeys," Helders explained.

"Our guitar player was always going to have a band called this," Alex admitted to New Jersey magazine *The Aquarian* some years later. "I guess he used to think about band names when he was in school. It's a pretty terrible name. It makes no sense to me . . . If he does know where the name came from, he's keeping it a secret from me!"

★   ★   ★

In the months between taking up their guitars and forming the band, Jamie Cook and Alex Turner had started playing together in their bedrooms, picking up chords and songs, and prodding each other through a rapid curve as each tried to outdo the other's learning capacity.

"It got to March and I'd only learned a few chords, but [Cookie] could already play all the Bond theme," Alex later told *NME*. "I realised I had to step up my game."

In many ways, it's surprising it took them as long as it did to form a band. They were already a close-knit group of mates who shared the same taste in music and lived in each other's pockets, hanging out together day and night at school and home.

"I didn't think stuff like that happened to normal people," Matt later recalled for *The Guardian*. "You'd look at a band and think, I wonder how that happened? Then you realise your mate's in a band, so you think it's not that hard, is it?"

But once they'd started they leapt straight into rehearsing, barely giving themselves time to learn their instruments. After Glyn Jones left, the remaining four spent the rest of the summer of 2002 holed up in Matt's mum and dad's warehouse, Alex's parents' garage, or the Helders' front room, learning Strokes songs, other cover versions and Alex's early compositions. Having only just finished their GCSEs, with all the revision that entailed, it was hardly a slacker's option. But it established the pattern for the next 12 months, as the four friends set about refining their sound in preparation for the first gig.

Towards the end of the summer, further education and new day jobs kicked in; despite these extra commitments, however, Arctic Monkeys continued rehearsing. Matt and Alex moved on through the education system together, starting two-year courses in music technology and art at Barnsley College in the autumn of 2002.

As with their earlier education, both continued to be diligent students; Matt particularly took to photography, which he carried on practising after he left the college. Their A-level music course complemented their formative work with the band, with the college's music tutor, Richard Tolson, later recalling how the boys used its studio facilities to record cover songs with the Monkeys as part of their coursework.

This segue between education and band rehearsals appears to have worked well. Arctic Monkeys had already started playing gigs at The Grapes and The Boardwalk when they were halfway through their A-level course – and they clearly had parental approval, as Mr and Mrs Helders willingly fell in as the band's initial roadies.

Nonetheless, Matt and Alex both made sure they finished their sixth form courses – an expedient move on both their parts. Having shown educational commitment to his teacher parents, Alex was now given permission to suspend his education and devote a year to the band. It wasn't an open-ended deal, but he had a full 12 months to try to make it work. If, after this time, the band hadn't succeeded, he was expected to go back into education and take up his university place.

Whether Alex really would have gone back into full-time education is open to conjecture, but he evidently took his pledge seriously. Even after the band had scored two successive number one hits and were on the eve of releasing the fastest-selling debut album of all time, Alex could still be heard telling journalists he'd resume his education if things didn't work out.

Jamie Cook was equally sanguine about the band's chances of success. At the very moment they were about to break, he was still holding onto everything that would help him drop back into a normal life. He'd been taken on as an apprentice bathroom tiler – a job he would keep until the eve of the band hitting the big time.

Andy Nicholson, on the other hand, had begun working alongside Alex behind the bar at Sheffield's famous Boardwalk venue – although he would later tell journalists he was on the dole at the time the band signed to their label. Like Jamie, Andy had also been keen to stay close to his former lifestyle after the band took off. When the Monkeys returned to The Boardwalk for a sold-out show, Andy yanked on a staff T-shirt and ducked behind the bar to serve pints. After later leaving the band he would open a bar in Sheffield called The Bowery, in partnership with Matt Helders.

In the meantime, the college course and relentless rehearsals were start-ing to pay off. Alex Turner would later recall how it took the band a year to find their sound. But in 2003, they had already begun to gradually stumble towards finding their own voice.

They were nearly ready to show themselves to the world. Before playing their first gig, however, they moved up a grade: from rehearsing in the garage to the Yellow Arch Studios in Neepsend.

Finding their voice was both a metaphorical and literal mission. For Alex, it meant coming to terms with being the band's singer, not just a guitarist and songwriter. He'd easily fallen in love with the guitar but had never regarded himself as a vocalist, only reluctantly taking on the new role after failing to find anyone else who would do it.

Alex later explained that this was why the band's earlier songs had been overly wordy, with only a passing concern for melody, though this was only half the story. Most of his formative vocal influences hadn't been songwriters, or even singers, at all, and even though a legion of music critics would greet Arctic Monkeys as part of an English songwriting tradition, Turner's early songs had as much affinity with hip hop as they did with Ray Davies. He would later come to describe his style as balancing on a knife edge between Mike Skinner (The Streets) and Jarvis Cocker (Pulp); he certainly had the storyteller's prowess of both.

Speaking to *The Guardian*'s Dorian Lynskey in 2006, the band freely admitted their early attempts to write and perform were less than melodic. Still unsure of his vocal style and under the influence of The Strokes, Turner sang in a generic transatlantic drawl. In order to have anything to sing at all, he penned meaningless words.

But as they progressed and found their confidence, Alex started to adopt the techniques and sounds of the artists he admired, mimicking both their lyrical style and delivery. As already noted, he'd been influenced by Roots Manuva and The Streets, but he also took note of artists such as Mancunian punk poet John Cooper Clarke, all of whom based their words on the everyday things they'd experienced.

Turner soon developed a detached, observational approach of his own that enabled him to tackle subjects without them becoming too personal or awkward for him to sing about. "Even the songs that are more personal are done in that observational way because it's not as close to the bone," he explained. "People can't get at me and say, 'Who's that about then?' It's a bit like you're hiding behind something. Sometimes when you write summat and you come to sing it first time in practice, instead of 'I' you [sing] 'he', without even thinking about it."

Alex had also continued to draw inspiration from hip hop, especially the way that rappers could pack an extraordinarily high number of words into songs. But it was his ability to transform the everyday occurrences of his suburban youth experience into poetic passages that marked him down as someone worth watching.

"We live in Sheffield and we write about the things we see here," Alex would tell the Newcastle *Evening Chronicle*. "What else is there to write about?" Gradually, his finely crafted lyrics about nights out ('Dancing Shoes'), the frustrations and results of having nothing to do ('Riot Van'), failed nights out and irrational bouncers ('From The Ritz To The Rubble'), moody girlfriends ('Mardy Bum'), perverts and prostitutes ('Scummy'/'When The Sun Goes Down') would emerge as a distinct Turner style. He was becoming – as Simon Armitage, celebrated British poet and Professor of Poetry at Sheffield University, would write – the "most poetic" of lyricists.

Back when their sound and songs were taking shape in embryonic form, all that the band needed was the right venue. They already had a connection with The Boardwalk, thanks to Andy and Alex, so it must have seemed the most obviously attractive place to start. But for their first outing they were wisely booked at a smaller, more forgiving venue.

Among the places they'd approached for gigs was a city centre venue on Trippet Lane called The Grapes. Although it still features music, today it has reverted to being mainly a pub, having been taken over by the landlords of a nearby Irish hostelry. The last gig of its life as a regular music venue was on Saturday, November 27, 2010, with Thomas Truax, musician-cum-instrument inventor, headlining. In the lead-up to this last concert, Truax described the venue to the *Daily Star*: "It [was] a small room, frequented by friendly musically open-minded and attentive regulars, with the bar being located downstairs, so it's not distracting from the acts onstage, The Grapes epitomised the idea of the perfect 'intimate' venue."

Arctic Monkeys made their public debut on June 13, 2003. One passer-by who called in for a drink described them playing in a dingy upstairs room with a small bar at one end and the band at the other. The gig was by no means packed. The set consisted mostly of cover versions and they received a total fee of £27.

It was a modest debut. But breaking into the live gig circuit immediately upped their game. Until now they had been all about practising and rehearsing, but, spurred on with an extra dose of confidence earned by venturing into the real world, the Monkeys started to become a real band.

Reports of their sound during this period describe them as unpolished and raw, but nonetheless showing promise. "They were rubbish really," friend and Reverend & The Makers frontman Jon McClure later recalled. "They did cover versions – The White Stripes, The Vines, Jimi Hendrix . . . But you could tell they were onto something."

Even at this rough early stage of their music, there was a quality in the white heat of their energetic delivery – a raw power in their performance – and an attitude that made them stand out. This sense of latent potential was made all the more promising by the band's precocious age. Early recordings of 'Ravey Ravey Ravey Club' ably demonstrate the attraction, revealing a sound hauntingly reminiscent of the Howard Devoto-era Buzzcocks, as testified by mid-Seventies bootlegs of that proto-punk band.

At the same time, the band were becoming increasingly integrated into Sheffield's music network, with Alex even making a solo appearance at Laid Back Sunday at The Point, an open-mic hang-out frequented by local musicians.

The Monkeys' second gig was booked in at The Pheasant in Sheffield, where they made their first real breakthrough. It would be an astonishingly rapid advance by anyone's standards.

In the audience that night was a local recording studio owner named Alan Smyth, who Alex had recently met and invited to the gig. Out of curiosity, Smyth had gone along.

Although the band were raw and unpolished, Smyth saw enough potential to recommend them to a friend working as a talent scout for Wildlife – the London-based management company that had launched the careers of Craig David, Travis and The Brand New Heavies.

The friend who Smyth recommended the Monkeys to was a Sheffield-based stalwart called Geoff Barradale. Within the space of two gigs, it looked as if Arctic Monkeys were on the verge of landing a management deal that most artists might spend a lifetime dreaming about.

The pace at which they would move from being complete novices to signing a major management deal is, in retrospect, dumbfounding. But as would soon become clear, Arctic Monkeys were in the habit of doing things at astonishing speed.

6

Under New Management

GEOFF Barradale was a veteran of the Sheffield scene. If things had a habit of moving quickly for Arctic Monkeys, then success had come a lot more slowly for him.

Barradale had been an established figure for decades before he'd taken on the Monkeys. He'd started his career as lead singer of early Eighties synth-pop act Vitamin Z and had started playing Sheffield's venues while the city was still enjoying its Eighties hype.

His band had attracted major label interest quickly and, after releasing a few tracks through Polygram, signed to Phonogram in the UK and Geffen in the US. Their debut album, *Rite Of Passage*, was released in 1985 and featured guests such as heavyweight vocalist Peter Gabriel, Adam & The Ants percussionist Chris Merrick Hughes and Blancmange guitarist David Rhodes.

The band secured the support slot on Tears For Fears' England tour and scored a dance hit in the UK and US with synth-pop ballad 'Burning Flame'. But in a lesson that no doubt served Barradale well as a manager, Vitamin Z's second LP became entangled in a dispute over production. A legal battle followed but, despite considerable efforts to resuscitate the album, it failed to make an impact and, not long after its release, the band broke up.

Barradale was bruised but not defeated. In 1987, he appeared on the Alan Parsons Project LP *Gaudi*, and in the mid-Nineties started working with another long-serving member of Sheffield's music community, Alan Smyth. Their band, Seafruit, quickly secured a record deal with Global Warming, a small Essex-based independent imprint, in 1998. An album was scheduled for release the following year, with the first single, 'Looking For Sparks', released in late March 1999.

But the album was frustratingly delayed. Another single, 'Dirty Washing', was followed by two more, 'Hello World' and 'What If Everyone You Ever Loved Wasn't There', before the LP finally came out in October 2000. Despite securing notable tour slots alongside Drugstore and Headswim in late 2000, and licensing the LP in Germany, the band struggled to take off.

By the time Alan Smyth set up 2Fly Studios, Seafruit was limping towards its demise. The band had, however, gained support from an unexpected source. Barradale had grown up in the era of the creative promo video and, in the delayed build-up to Seafruit's LP being released, Geoff had made a video for their single 'Hello World'.

Without the resources to get it onto television, the band had put it online and the video attracted more fans through online channels than they were getting through traditional media. As the Seafruit chapter of his career was drawing to a close, Barradale was still learning valuable lessons that would come into play when it came to managing the Monkeys.

The demise of Seafruit would leave a diverse legacy: Seafruit's manager, Graham Wrench, would go on to manage Richard Hawley; Smyth would start his own studio and record Arctic Monkeys' unofficial first LP; Barradale would shift his talents to management, after he was taken on by the successful London-based management company Wildlife.

Geoff recalls his first meeting with the Monkeys in August 2003, when he had been so impressed that he'd signed them there and then – in the process taking over from Matt's parents as chief roadie. Barradale had taken to the band's exciting raw energy immediately and described the process of making the management deal as the two parties taking each other on, rather than the more usual management speak of *him* picking *them* up.

"We toured up and down the northern corridors of the UK in my battered Saab, and played to a handful [of people]," he later recalled in a rare interview for Cubeweb. "The word of mouth spread via the internet and the gigs got fuller and quickly, thereafter, rammed. The guys also write quickly, so we recorded their best songs with Alan Smyth at 2Fly Studios. We never did anything else. This was a two-year process which we dovetailed around their A-levels and apprenticeships."

This was a somewhat modest assessment of Barradale's own role in the

Monkeys' rise. It barely hinted at the two years of relentless, energy-sapping effort that he and the band put into touring the north of England, Scotland, Wales and the South Coast, building a fanbase while noticeably avoiding the traditional fast route to fame via the music and media hub of London.

As we shall see, the management deal with Geoff Barradale had already given them a substantial connection to the very top of the UK music industry. Had they wanted to take the pop route to market, the options would have been open. In fact, there is no doubt that Barradale immediately started to work on his London connections, such as Anton Brookes of PR agency Bad Moon, to help build the band's profile.

But Arctic Monkeys were no boy band and there is nothing to suggest Barradale would have wanted to take them down the pop-idol route. It would soon transpire he had a quite different, far less glamorous option in mind. The Monkeys had a formidable management team behind them, but before that came into play they had to rely on their own hard work and the power of their music to attract an audience, building a reputation of their own.

The management deal did bring immediate benefits, such as improved facilities and reasonable quality recordings. But it still took the band another four months before they got a gig at The Boardwalk – which they finally played with Milburn on October 23, 2003.

"The first band gig I did with them was in October 2003 at an unsigned night at The Boardwalk," confirms local producer/promoter Barney Vernon, "with Milburn and Tommy Vinx. At that time they were still just a band within the city." The Boardwalk was followed a month later by their last gig of 2003, at The Deep End.

With two core members still studying at college, the New Year was slow to kick in. Their first gig of 2004 saw Arctic Monkeys return to The Boardwalk in March, followed by Sheffield University in April.

Summer brought with it the end of Matt and Alex's Barnsley College course and, with a less constrained timetable, Arctic Monkeys spread their net wider. They played their first gig outside of Sheffield at the Shed in Leicester on September 7, followed by Hull University during fresher's week on September 27. Then came two gigs at Certificate 18 in York, with the first on October 1, followed by The Vine in Leeds, on October 14,

The Angel in Nottingham, on December 1, and The Attic in Manchester, on December 6. All the time they were cultivating their live fanbase by distributing CDs.

Things were starting to take off. By February 2005 the band had played The Garage in London. Rather than months separating their appearances, they had started playing a gig every few days in ever bigger venues and further flung places. Before long, Glasgow, Wigan, Nottingham, Middles-brough, Bristol, Edinburgh, Southampton, Newcastle, and Wakefield had also been notched onto the Monkeys' bedposts. Meanwhile, they were careful to make frequent returns to Sheffield venues to cultivate their home crowd.

In the meantime the band hooked up with Timm Cleasby, who would go on to become their tour manager. Timm had been sound engineer at The Leadmill and had worked with Graham Wrench, who had been the booker at The Leadmill and had managed Geoff Barradale's last band, Seafruit.

When Timm joined Arctic Monkeys he'd been working with The Darkness and had just returned from a US tour. On the way back from America he'd decided to find work nearer to home and his family. Hearing Barradale needed a sound engineer for a new band he was manag-ing, he gave him a call.

Geoff's first reaction was that he couldn't pay Timm enough for it to be worth his while, but he dropped some of the band's music at Timm's house later that evening: a CD of five songs including 'Fake Tales Of San Francisco', 'Mardy Bum', 'I Bet You Look Good On The Dancefloor' and 'When The Sun Goes Down'.

Timm spent a night listening to the music. He had plenty of reasons to hesitate at taking the work, not least that he was an internationally recog-nised engineer who'd just finished touring with one of the biggest acts of the year – and Geoff Barradale could afford to pay him only £30 a gig.

But in truth, Timm later admitted, he knew he was going to take the job as soon as he heard the first track. After meeting the band, he came away certain that they were worth gambling a low starting salary on.

Cleasby started work on February 2, 2005, engineering for the band as they played a support slot for up-and-coming electro-pop act Tom Vek at The Fez in Sheffield. The venue had sold out, but Timm noticed it was packed from the start of the night – rather than just filling up for the main act. It was also abundantly clear from the audience reaction that more people had come to see the Monkeys than Tom Vek.

Given that Vek was the current big news amongst tastemakers and on the verge of releasing a much-hyped LP, this in itself was impressive. But when the Monkeys conclusively stole the show, it left Cleasby in no doubt that he'd made the right decision.

Adding to the legend of that night, when Tom Vek announced a national album tour later that year there was no mention of a Sheffield date. Jubilant Monkeys fans flooded onto music site message boards, taunting that he didn't want to suffer a second humiliation at the hands of their local heroes.

Cleasby's second show engineering for the band, at The Forum, attracted an even bigger crowd of fans. But the next gig he had been booked for was at The Barfly in Glasgow, where Cleasby feared the band would be given a wake-up call.

Not having a tour van, the band pooled cars to get themselves and their gear to Scotland. Cleasby drove up alone with the equipment, expecting an audience of three people and a dog. To his amazement it was packed with 300 fans all screaming the words back at the band.

By this time the New Yorkshire scene had taken shape; while most of the bands were friends with each other, friendly rivalry between them had occasionally started tripping over into something less amicable.

Mark White of The Harrisons blogged about an incident at a party in Arctic Monkeys' new practice rooms at Neepsend. The Monkeys had taken over a unit in an industrial estate at the heart of the city's red-light district (considered to be the inspiration for 'When The Sun Goes Down'). They'd converted it into a social/rehearsal space, with pool tables and furniture, and had invited The Harrisons to play a party, as the two bands were about to undertake a series of dates together. There had been a friendly rivalry between their followers, so the party was intended to help break the ice.

The Harrisons duly turned up with a gang of mates, but as soon as they started playing the Monkeys' supporters began shouting abuse. Both bands finished their sets, but at the end a scuffle broke out between the two camps. The following morning saw emissaries sent between the bands, but reports from The Harrisons' camp suggested relations between them remained tense after that.

Local rivalries aside, by early 2005 the band's relentless gigging was paying off. Without officially releasing a record, Arctic Monkeys had started selling out venues such as the 1,000-capacity Leadmill, which, a year earlier, would have been empty rooms.

As Rick Martin (at the time a Sheffield student) would note in the first *NME* article on Arctic Monkeys, when the band embarked on their first headline mini-tour in spring 2005, tickets were already being re-sold at inflated prices on eBay – despite their national media status as complete unknowns.

But there was more to their success than a punishing live schedule. In 2004 the band had started recording demos at the relatively new 2Fly Studios at the Stag Works. Set up by musician-cum-producer-cum-sound-engineer Alan Smyth in October 2001, the studio was by no means a glamorous location, yet the 15 tracks recorded there would become a significant part of rock'n'roll history.

7

The 2Fly Recordings

AS with many narratives, certain chapters in the Arctic Monkeys story have an element of mystery about them – with hazy memories, blurred details and conflicting accounts making it hard to arrive at a single definitive truth. One such mystery concerns how the Monkeys came to record at 2Fly Studios.

What is clear is that studio owner Alan Smyth was already an important character in their story before the band came to record with him: it was he who had recommended the band to their soon-to-be-manager, Geoff Barradale. Smyth had also been a notable figure in Sheffield's music scene in his own right, for decades. Before starting 2Fly, he had played in bands and, as he had a good ear for mixing, picked up extra work as a live engineer. This developed into studio engineering, where his passion for getting the right sound morphed him into a producer. Along the way he picked up early production work with Pulp, but also continued working as a guitarist and songwriter.

It was in his instrumentalist songwriter capacity that he hooked-up with Geoff Barradale to form Seafruit. The band were still recording and touring when Alan Smyth opened 2Fly Studios in 2001. Although they were soon to lose their UK label, he and Barradale continued to record together. To fill his studio, Smyth had started to tap into the fiery new rock'n'roll bands that were springing up around the city and soon 2Fly had gained a reputation for producing powerfully raw recordings, amongst them a track called 'The Woods' by Rumpus. It was this production that caught the ear of a self-styled young poet and singer called Jon McClure.

McClure's most enduring band, Reverend & The Makers, would also go on to be managed by Barradale and achieve considerable commercial success, contributing to Sheffield's musical heritage in their own right. But in the summer of 2003, McClure was overseeing a sprawling local band called Judan Suki, which featured Alex Turner and Matt Helders as occasional members – as confirmed by Sheffield promoter Barney Vernon, who recalls a Judan Suki gig at The Garage in London, "where Matt Helders was the drummer and Alex played bongos".

McClure had met Turner randomly on a bus and the two had become friends. Jon had ended up inviting Alex to join his band and, after that, the two had become collaborators and sometime housemates. They co-wrote 'He Said He Loved Me', 'The Machine' and 'Old Yellow Bricks' (from *Favourite Worst Nightmare*) together, and Jon also claimed that one of his other bands, 1984, inspired Turner to pen the line "dancing to electro-pop like a robot from 1984" in 'I Bet You Look Good On The Dancefloor'.

Judan Suki were McClure's first proper band and three of its line-up (McClure, Ed Cosens and Laura Manuel – the future Mrs Jon McClure) would go on to form Reverend & The Makers. McClure always claimed he saw it as a bit of a joke, but in 2002 the band had been successful enough to headline and pack out The Boardwalk.

At any rate, Judan Suki were serious enough for McClure to want to record some of their songs. After hearing the 2Fly recording of 'The Woods', he decided to book his band in to record in the summer of 2003.

Alex was moonlighting on rhythm guitar and Smyth remembers that the session was going well. Halfway through, Turner mentioned his own band, Arctic Monkeys, telling Smyth they were about to play their second gig and wanted to make some recordings.

Smyth was interested enough to follow up on the conversation and go see the band the following week. The group clearly had work to do but he'd been impressed by what he'd seen. They played nine songs, of which six were cover tracks, but Smyth hadn't been able to tell which were which – which he took as a good sign. He also liked Alex as a frontman.

A few days later, Barradale turned up at the studio, saying he'd started a new job as a manager/A&R scout and asked Smyth if he'd seen any promising bands. Smyth suggested the Monkeys and put them in touch. By the time of their third gig (their debut at The Boardwalk), they'd been signed by Barradale.

Once signed, the band had the funding to record a demo and the obvious recording venue was Seafruit's old studio – which also happened to be the only studio in which Turner had recorded to date. If Smyth's story is accurate, it was also the connection that had got the band signed to a prestigious management company.

For his part, Alex Turner has a simpler version of events: "Our manager knew the bloke in the studio and that's how we started recording the demos . . . We used to do like three songs in a day or over two days and mix it all there and then. It were all pretty fast."

What came first, the manager or the studio, barely matters. What is clear is that all the events happened pretty much simultaneously and Barradale wasted little time getting the band into the studio. According to most reports, the recording sessions took place between late August 2003 and November 2004.

Barradale's own recollection is that he met and signed the band in August and that it was he who paid for the recording sessions – presumably with seed money from Wildlife, his management company. But still, the connection between Barradale and Smyth was fortuitous for the Monkeys. The demos they recorded at 2Fly are what would soon transform them into a massive online phenomenon. The demos also set the blueprint for the band's record-breaking debut LP, changing the fortunes of Arctic Monkeys and, some would argue, the music industry itself.

8

Beneath The Boardwalk

IT's a sign of Alex Turner's songwriting ability that the Arctic Monkeys' material on their 2Fly demos went on to be released (in a refined though intact form) as commercial recordings.

Amongst the 22 tracks recorded and given away on CD at their early concerts were a surprising number of later releases, even if some, such as 'Cigarette Smoke' and 'Riot Van' were substantially revised in recording sessions with producers Mike Crossey, James Ford and Jim Abbiss. The track list from the 2Fly sessions includes 'Fake Tales Of San Francisco', 'From The Ritz To The Rubble', 'Mardy Bum', 'When The Sun Goes Down' (aka 'Scummy'), 'I Bet You Look Good On The Dancefloor', 'Bigger Boys And Stolen Sweethearts', 'A Certain Romance', 'Dancing Shoes', 'Still Take You Home', 'Stickin' To The Floor', 'Curtains Close', 'View From The Afternoon', 'Vampires Is A Bit Strong But . . .', 'Wavin' Bye To The Train Or The Bus', 'Riot Van', 'Ravey Ravey Ravey Club', 'Knock A Door Run', 'Choo Choo', 'On The Run From The MI5', 'Cigarette Smoke', 'Space Invaders', 'Settle For A Draw', '7' and 'Chun Li's Spinning Bird Kick'.

The sessions were paid for by Barradale, but they weren't long affairs. The band would get in, record what they could and master a mix by the end of the session – all in one sitting. They were recorded as close to their live set-up as possible. For practical reasons, Jamie Cook usually over-dubbed his guitar part at the end of the day, as he was the only band member who had a day job, while Alex's vocals were also usually overdubbed.

To help with editing, Smyth would often use a click track to start the band off, but pull it once they'd got into their stride. "The band were still 17 and were pretty ragged if left to their own devices!" he later explained to Justin Morey at the University of Leeds.

The master track would be assembled from a maximum of two or three takes; unsurprisingly, the sessions maintained the Monkeys' urgent live feel. The results were burnt onto CDs and distributed free to fans at gigs, a tried and tested formula for promotion.

As the CDs were being given away, the band were hardly going to object if fans shared them over the internet. The first person to rip and post the tracks online as free downloads was an associate of the Monkeys called Mark 'The Sheriff' Bull. He christened the tracks on his website with the collective title *Beneath The Boardwalk* – a reference to the Monkeys' occasional venue and Alex and Andy's workplace. They hadn't been intended as an album, being recorded and posted online in a gradual trickle over five recording sessions. But Bull's website catalogue gradually began to be regarded as an LP.

Once released online the tracks became calling cards, introducing Arctic Monkeys to new fans who had never seen one of their gigs, or who lived in cities the band hadn't, as yet, played.

The first time the band noticed the effect of the downloads was on their home patch. "We played a gig in Sheffield and as soon as I started singing the entire crowd sang it back to me," Alex recalled for the *NME*.

Suddenly, kids were turning up for the first time who already knew the words. The online demos were not only bringing new fans in, they were making the live shows better as the audience arrived primed and ready to sing the tracks.

It was the start of a spiralling ascent, as the band's demos brought more fans to their gigs, swelling the audience numbers and reactions, which in turn led to more people downloading and more gigs.

The cumulative effect of this word-of-mouth community became obvious when the band played the Reading Festival for the first time, in August 2005. The Monkeys had only just signed a record deal, but they were already too big for the arena they'd been booked to play. And the entire audience, occupying twice as much space as the arena itself, already knew all the words.

"Before they'd actually released the album they turned up at Reading and loads of people were singing their songs," Martin Talbot, head of the Official Charts Company, observed. "That's particularly interesting at a festival, because you've got loads of people turning up, but they're not at the festival just to hear you. But they still knew all the lyrics."

Arctic Monkeys were heralded as the first act to break through via the internet in the MySpace age. How much of this was truly fan-based, how much the band and their team had manipulated the situation, and how much of it was media spin have all been hotly contested ever since.

There is no doubt they owed at least some of their success to the fevered online activity they generated.

In a report to the UK government's independent review of copyright, major label EMI commented: "It is widely recognised that the Arctic Monkeys' breakthrough was in part due to their success at harnessing the potential of the online environment as an unsigned band."

As journalist Nick Hasted noted in *The Independent* in late 2005, Arctic Monkeys had inspired a self-generated community that was effectively distributing their music for them, before a great swathe of the music industry knew the band existed.

Without any of the usual trappings of rock'n'roll promotion – major label funding, mass-marketing or coin-operated media circus – they were somehow filling venues that they had, in Hasted's words, "no right to fill". They were, he continued, "the leaders of an internet-based music community that could turn the conventional industry to dust".

While the traditional industry was fretting over illegal file sharing, Arctic Monkeys seemed to be celebrating it. Whether they had meant to or not, the band had allowed their music to be swapped for free. But instead of destroying the band, the swapping of MP3s on the internet had both deepened and broadened Arctic Monkeys' appeal. Online communities such as MySpace had offered them the opportunity to promote themselves directly to new fans and to build their fanbase in an unprecedented manner at startling speed.

But the Monkeys themselves have always insisted that they were online Luddites, completely ignorant of the internet beyond sending emails. As far as they were concerned, the online furore around them had come entirely from the fans. It was the fans who had built the band's MySpace pages, uploaded songs and started the escalating online buzz. Far from manipulating their MySpace presence, the band had simply been promoting themselves through the traditional routes to the market – constant gigging and giving away free CDs at gigs.

Chris Heath summed up the band's position neatly in his December 2006 article for *The Observer*: "Their demos and concerts had been widely exchanged and discussed over the internet, but anyone who actually used such sites knew that this was a product of the excitement they were generating, and the vehicle through which it was being expressed, not its cause. 'We wrote the tunes and we played them and we tried to push on musically and do something a bit different, and put a lot of thought and work into it,' says Alex, 'so when people pass it off as sort of this internet phenomenon, it right gets under the skin.'"

But the media was hungry for the first band to break through MySpace and Arctic Monkeys appeared to fit the bill.

Inevitably, their online success became the most frequent interview topic, overshadowing the band's music. In interview after interview, an increasingly agitated Turner, Cook, Helders and Nicholson found themselves batting away question after question about the internet.

"It's not like we had a plan," Matt asserted to *Prefix*. "We used to record demos and just burn them onto CDs and give them away at gigs. Obviously there weren't many demos available so people used to share them on the internet, which was a good way for everyone to hear it. It didn't bother us. And it made the gigs better, because people knew the words and came and sang along.

"The other day someone said to us, 'I looked at your profile on MySpace.' I said, 'I don't even know what MySpace is.' [When we went number one in England] we were on the news and radio about how MySpace has helped us. But that's just the perfect example of someone who doesn't know what the fuck they're talking about. We actually had no idea what [MySpace] was."

But even if the band didn't know what MySpace was, it seems their managers and friends did. And before questions about it started to irritate them, they were appreciative of the role the internet played in getting their tunes out and making their gigs better. They also weren't short of acquaintances who were willing to lend a hand. "There were various friends who were doing the IT for them," recalls Adele Bailey, owner of Sheffield's Plug nightclub. "It was very much friends of family helping out."

The person responsible for first uploading the band's music, Mark Bull, may have started as an early fan but by the time he posted the first downloads he was an associate of the Monkeys, orbiting close to the centre of their world. Bull had also taken early photos and film of the band; when the time came for the Monkeys to make their first promo video, for 'Fake Tales Of San Francisco', the job went naturally to him. In many ways it was the least they could do.

"They had a fanbase right across the country because of Mark Bull sharing the songs," explains Kate Linderholm, of BBC Radio Sheffield. She also recalls Bull being charged for the bandwidth fans used for downloading the songs. "He ended up with a bill for thousands of pounds. It was a lot of money. And the band basically played a couple of gigs in order to pay off his bill, which says a lot for them and their integrity – that they were not coming from the usual routes."

As their career developed, Bull would become integral to the band's story and go on to make videos and tour diary films about them, keeping their official website updated and fulfilling other online roles. But in the early days he wasn't stretching any technological limits. On the contrary, music fans had been uploading and swapping music files for close to a decade. Indeed, Mark Bull and Arctic Monkeys were amongst the first generation to grow up with music freely available on the internet, the first generation for which online access to music was not a novelty.

Most of the Monkeys were 13 years old at the time when the infamous file-sharing pirate site Napster was launched. By the time they had formed the band, Napster had been dissolved and reborn as a legally copyright-respecting company.

Even if the band had not been involved in their own online activity, the online music world was in their DNA. They probably guessed that if you gave someone a CD, the first thing that they were likely to do was rip it; the second was share it.

"Things like giving away CDs at gigs was an extension of the attitude that teenage music fans into cutting-edge left-field music and file sharing had at that point," explains Martin Talbot, head of the Official Charts Company. "It was file sharing with a physical product."

Given the timing, it's not surprising that there was a media rush to hail Arctic Monkeys as the first act to break via MySpace. But the more the media focused on this aspect of their success, the more the band expressed anti-internet sentiments. They were adamant that the media had got it wrong.

The website Mark Bull had uploaded the original songs onto no longer exists, but it was his personal site – not a MySpace page. The Monkeys repeatedly reiterated that neither they nor Bull were responsible for the creation of their MySpace page. This, they say, was done on the initiative of fans and was nothing to do with any marketing campaign or PR exercise.

Not everyone was convinced. In August 2005, *Guardian* journalist Alexis Petridis repeated some of the conspiracy theories about Arctic Monkeys:

"Even by the hyper-speed standards of modern rock and pop, this was a remarkable rise, apparently made possible only because the band had posted their songs on their website and thus built up a vast virtual fanbase before even securing a record deal. It may not be as simple as that – rumours persist that their success involved tactics more commonly associated with manufactured pop artists, including employing a 'street team' of die-hard fans to venture on to other artists' message boards and talk the band up."

Online PR consultant Serena Wilson had been working with the Domino Recording Company on a number of their artists when she received a call in early 2005 asking her to look into a new band they'd signed. The label were aware that something extraordinary was happening with the Monkeys online, but according to her they didn't really understand what it was:

"There were all these rumours about them having this massive marketing machine and that it wasn't an accident, but it simply wasn't true. Domino and Laurence Bell don't work like that.

"There was some pushing [of the band and songs]," Wilson concedes, "but not in the way I've seen documented [by the media]. You've got to remember it was a real time of development in social media. Regardless of how many amazing campaigns you had, it was a lot of learning at that point.

"And it wasn't in the same way the majors perform, when they're like 'this has just happened by accident', and you know there's [people] paddling furiously underneath. I've been in those marketing meetings, where they want it to look organic and like the artist has just come out of nowhere.

"We started doing some research into what was going on on MySpace, because it was only MySpace at that time. They were literally doing the old school thing of giving out mix-tapes. They were encouraging people to upload music and encouraging people to share at a time when lots of bands were locking their stuff down. All the major labels were completely paranoid at this point."

As well as creating opportunities for bands, Wilson points out that MySpace had opened up a completely new experience for fans that made them feel closer to a band than ever before. It was this, she believes, that made the Monkeys so attractive – although she stresses none of it would have happened if their songs hadn't been so compelling. "In those days, people actually thought they were talking direct to the band. And a lot of bands had really set up their own MySpace pages – whereas now most of the big bands' MySpace pages are 'worked' by someone to get the messaging right."

Even if the Monkeys didn't realise it, their MySpace presence was connecting them to their fans. And even if they were unaware of it, Wilson clearly remembers how the band's management had kept ownership of the MySpace page: "The band's manager – had control of that. He may initially have had fans running it, but that was controlled by management – the record label didn't set that up."

Simon Wheeler, head of the digital committee at the Association of Independent Music, also believes there was an element of controlled incentive helping to push the band online: "As much as it wasn't a real PR campaign, it wasn't totally 'grassroots-this-all-happened-organically' either. There were definitely some quite informed and quite smart minds at work.

"Some of it would have come from the band, some of it would have come from people around the band, and some of it would have come from the management. But it was done in such a way as it really did feel like the band was talking to you."

Both Wheeler and Wilson are adamant that the root cause of the band's success was their songs. But they also suggest that there were some very astute people helping them on their way.

9

Walking With Wildlife

FROM the start, the individual members of Arctic Monkeys had shown little actual interest in the internet. But in many ways they didn't need to. The band had been managed from their earliest gigs by a team that knew as much about online promotion as anyone in the industry at the time.

The most well known of the Arctic Monkeys' managers was probably Geoff Barradale, while the other main presence was that of Ian McAndrew, a music manager from Bury St Edmunds in Suffolk, who'd risen to become one of the most respected managers in the UK.

Andy Corrigan, a Suffolk-based recording studio owner and tour manager, knew Ian from his early days. He describes a bright, friendly man who seemed motivated by commerce rather than a musical background: "He was a businessperson, quite young but not desperately young, and somehow he sort of drifted into a management company and then they packed it in, so he took it over," recalls Corrigan.

"When I arrived there was no one else involved. It was just him. And he had Russ Ballard, some singer-songwriters and a couple of other bands that didn't do anything. He signed a band called The Blessing. They had a lot of money spent on them (by their label), were great, but didn't really click with the record-buying public. Then he got Tasmin Archer, who was very successful.

"Tasmin was a new, young singer-songwriter who had signed to Virgin Music and needed someone to look after her. And he did a very good job. She got a number one, but the only problem was, in the end, she didn't want to do it any more. But because of that success he got offered other things, and did Bomb The Bass, Brand New Heavies and Travis.

"He's a very careful and a good manager, and a straight, nice guy. When he took on Travis they weren't taken very seriously and when they became successful he was probably as surprised as anybody. But he was very hands on, made the right decisions and had a good relationship with all his acts."

His management expertise has been recognised by a series of awards, including the Music Management Forum's Peter Grant Award for Outstanding Achievement in Management in 2001 and Manager of the Year in 2008.

The third main person in the management team, north London-born Colin Lester, remained very much in the background and departed when his business partnership with McAndrew and Wildlife ceased in 2008. Nonetheless, he had been a major pioneer in the use of online promotion and the use of new technology to promote his acts.

Lester would make his views on the Monkeys' route to success clear in later interviews. "We gave away free downloads with the Arctic Monkeys," he told amarudontv.com in June 2011, "but people got into the band . . . and when we put a record out, it sold in massive amounts. The reason [for this] was we'd created a club within a culture and people bought into that."

Having looked after some of the biggest acts of the period, McAndrew and Lester were among the industry's most creative businessmen. They had been pioneers of the new music industry models and were far from ignorant of the ways in which the internet could be used to promote their acts.

Colin Lester explained their forward-looking philosophy to the Midem music industry conference in 2011. "Management has changed," he told an audience of industry professionals in a keynote address, "in today's new technology world we need to be across more things . . . to represent our acts in a more successful way."

In 1997, Lester and McAndrew had anticipated 360-degree management deals by setting up an in-house label called Wildstar Records. The imprint was a three-way partnership between Wildlife, Capital Radio and Telstar Records – combining artist management and label expertise with a built-in radio outlet. Almost immediately, they scored a series of Top Five hits with Lutricia McNeal, Alda and Fierce. But it was Craig David who took their label to number one, with his debut solo single, '7 Days'. He would go on to sell over 13 million records.

Wildlife had helped make David one of the youngest male artists to reach number one in the UK, gaining huge plaudits from the industry for their use of online promotion. In managing David they also gained experience of developing an artist from scratch in the internet age – having given him seed money to help him record at the start of his career.

"Craig David is the perfect example of artist development," Colin Lester would tell the amarudontv.com blog in June 2011. "We've continued to make records with him, and continued to use social media, and the new technology available to us to stay in touch with his fans . . . and now he tours all over the world, from here to Australia, selling from 1,000 to 10,000 capacity crowds – and that's long-term planning."

Wildlife had also represented and developed the careers of such prominent acts as Travis and Bomb The Bass, while McAndrew would go on to manage I Am Kloot, Stephen Fretwell and Miles Kane, as well as Alex Turner's spin-off band The Last Shadow Puppets.

But by the time that Lester and McAndrew decided to split Wildlife up in 2008, Craig David and Arctic Monkeys had become their biggest assets. Lester, who had been David's hands-on manager, took him with him and McAndrew kept the Monkeys – confirming his role as one of the band's two long-term managers.

All of this had served to give Arctic Monkeys a fully developed in-house team at the start of their careers. The band had top-flight expertise to call on for more or less any project they could conceive of. When, for example, they wanted to self-release their own single, 2005's *Five Minutes With Arctic Monkeys*, they were able to call on their London managers to set up a label: Wildlife fixed the deal between Bang Bang and Cargo distribution – a company that happened to be based next door to Wildlife's office in south-west London.

It also gave Barradale, as a first-time manager, vital support ready to back him with both knowledge and money.

"Young managers today look to partner with people to allow them to do what they need to do and manage the artist," Lester later explained to amarudontv.com. "That's something I'm passionate about, looking for new young managers, giving them a home and central heating, a few quid and get them managing their artist and do what a good young manager should be doing, without the fear of paying their rent and phone bills . . . and [giving] help at the top end with contacts et cetera."

For a leading management company like Wildlife Entertainment, Geoff Barradale, with his industry experience and local knowledge, was an interesting proposition. "We took him on to look for and develop new talent," Ian McAndrew explained to the PRS magazine *M*. "He became a manager partner and he went on to bring Arctic Monkeys to us."

"He was very adept at it," remembers online PR consultant Serena Wilson of her encounters with Geoff. "He was completely on it. It helps to have [his] kind of insider knowledge."

"Geoff's had bad experiences of the music industry," explains BBC Yorkshire's Kate Linderholm, "so he has always encouraged them to be this tight little unit and do their own thing – and not be sucked into the industry's ideas of what you should do. He had a really good perspective and I also think it's rare [when] you get a band that will take advice, which the Arctic Monkeys always did very much from Geoff."

10

Bang Bang Bingo

Arctic Monkeys spent much of 2004 taking the traditional music industry route. In all they played a relatively modest 17 gigs, at first concentrating on building their home crowd in Sheffield.

The year started with the band's appearance at The Boardwalk on March 19, at a Judan Suki headlining gig promoted by Barney Vernon.

This was followed by a gig at The Deep End on April 7, Sheffield University on April 29, The Grapes on May 22 and a return to The Boardwalk on August 21, with Judan Suki headlining. Local writer Tom Common described the latter gig for Sheffield print fanzine *The Sandman* in September 2004: "The Arctic Monkeys are a right bunch of fucking punks. It's like some sort of sixth form milling around beneath the stage, but the kids on it are dead tight and very fast."

Barney Vernon remembers how things really started to change from this point on: "I put them on with Judan Suki and Milburn at The Boardwalk on 21 August 2004 and it was around then the buzz started. The local nights in Sheffield at that time were good fun, and the nights were well attended. But there was a buzz about Arctic Monkeys that there wasn't for other bands.

"They always had 40 to 60 people who would come – and Judan Suki and Arctic Monkeys and Milburn were always good mates, so if you had one of them you always had a venue full of people. It was also their area. The bands that came from High Green had a good following.

"But it wasn't until 2004, and the first demos that Alan Smyth recorded at 2Fly, that it started to get more exciting. It's usually friends and families at these sort of gigs, but other people were now showing up because there was this buzz about them. It was just incredibly exciting.

"That was the first time I met Geoff Barradale and when Wildlife came in and started managing it properly."

By the summer of 2004, Matt and Alex had also finished college. As the new academic year loomed, Arctic Monkeys started spreading their reach to other northern cities.

They played their first gig at The Leadmill on August 18 and brought the year to a close with a gig at The Forum on December 12. It was at this gig that Alex and the band first noticed a change in their audience. "People were cheering from the minute we went onstage," he recalled for the *NME*. "It were a right good gig until this fight broke out between a load of bouncers." It turned out that the security men had been at a Christmas party and things had got a bit lively in the aftermath. But the band's home crowd was clearly growing and they continued to carefully nurture their home support, dotting Sheffield dates between away gigs to keep up the momentum.

As well as making the most of the university towns in the north of England, Arctic Monkeys played on the historical connections between the Sheffield and Manchester music scenes, which had seen club nights and promoters swapping between the two cities.

Having played The Attic at the end of 2004, they repeatedly returned to Manchester throughout 2005, no doubt drawn by the huge number of students at universities in Greater Manchester. Apart from being a natural audience for a fiery young rock'n'roll band, students were exactly the right community to start a file-sharing frenzy around the band's music.

In the beginning the CD giveaways were in relatively small numbers, but, as Matt Helders would recall in a 2006 interview with US journalist Dave Park, the scarcity of CDs only encouraged fans to share them more online.

In allowing fans to distribute MP3s, the band followed the example of the Grateful Dead, who'd allowed hundreds of bootlegs to circulate while still managing to sell official releases and sell out large live events. In this respect, all that had changed was the format. But some fans also spotted an e-commerce opportunity for traditional physical bootlegs – albeit on CD, rather than vinyl as in the Grateful Dead's day. As Arctic Monkeys' popularity began to rise, it wasn't long before 20-track CDRs started to appear for sale on eBay.

In the meantime the band were still honing their skills and widening the pool of influences they drew inspiration from. "It was around that time that I did a John Cooper Clarke gig in Sheffield at The Boardwalk," recalls Barney Vernon. "Alex came down and I introduced him to John." The meeting cemented Alex's admiration for the punk poet.

The start of 2005 saw the band's live activity accelerate. Instead of playing the odd gig every month or so, they started turning over several a week. At the start of January they were back at The Boardwalk, where the crowd singalong became so overwhelming Alex had to stop singing in helpless hysterics. A week later, on January 15, they were at The Rio in Bradford and then back to The Attic in Manchester on January 24. A home gig at The Fez club in Sheffield on February 2, with Tom Vek, was followed by a second packed home gig at The Forum only four days later. On February 12 they played Manchester's Night & Day and by February 18 they made their debut London gig at The Garage. This is where *NME* writer Rick Martin reported Alex Turner expecting an empty room, only to leave after having been carried around on a sea of hands.

London was followed by Roadmenders in Northampton on February 25 and The Barfly in Glasgow on March 4. Then it was on to The Harley in Sheffield on March 7, Bar Fever in Wigan on March 9, and back to Sheffield Forum on March 14. The Old Vic in Nottingham followed and, the day after, The Forum in Sheffield saw the band mobbed by a continuous stage invasion, making it impossible for anyone more than a few rows back to see. This was also the first gig attended by Domino Records' chief Laurence Bell.

Jabez Clegg in Manchester followed on March 17, as did The Arena, Middlesbrough on March 24 and Head of Steam in Newcastle on March 28. An unannounced gig at The Escobar, Wakefield, on April 4 famously ended with the ceiling covered in footprints from crowd-surfers. Timm Cleasby recalled having to rush onto the stage to protect the band and stop the microphone from being knocked into Alex's teeth. A return to The Leadmill on April 24 was followed by The Ritz in Manchester the next day.

In the first four months of 2005, the band had already played more gigs than in the whole of 2004 – and all the while they were giving away the CDs that were fuelling their self-propelled online campaign. By the end of the year they would have played some 89 shows to an ever-growing army of more and more dedicated fans. "We had to run away from fans and get quite aggressive protecting the boys," Cleasby recalled for the *Mixed In Sheffield* video interview series, *Walls Have Ears*.

"Out of nowhere 'Monkey mania' started to take a grip, fuelled by an abundance of top-notch demos whizzing round the internet," recorded Sheffield-based music blogger Denzil Watson for online indie music magazine *Penny Black*. "Suddenly their Sheffield gigs started to sell out with people coming from far and wide and it became increasingly obvious something rather special was happening."

The band also started spotting fans from other far-flung corners turning up at Sheffield gigs. Amongst them was a crew from Nottingham who regularly appeared with unboxed bags of wine, so they could still sip while they crowd-surfed. Meanwhile, fans drinking from conventional glasses at the front started to hurl them into the mosh pit – starting a tradition in beaker bowling that would see Monkeys fans retreat from concerts drenched in beer, cider and various other liquids that had been lobbed through the air.

The relentless touring was expanding their fanbase, spreading their name and tightening their performance. At an amazingly young age and with astonishing speed, the band had honed the explosive power of Helders' drumming, Nicholson's ability to pin down a bass note and strut urgently around the fret board, Cook's feisty combination of power chords, angst-driven chops and plucking, and Turner's abundant song craft: his subtle ability to display angst and fragility, anger and affection, and a whole series of seemingly exclusive personal contradictions within the same four-minute song. Everyone who heard their music wanted more.

Even as they were rapidly jumping into Barradale's and Cleasby's battered tour cars and charging around the country to deliver their music in person, the viral online marketing campaign was overtaking them, zooming up the fast lane and delivering yet more fans at every gig.

The live appearances and the fans' file sharing were working together, each one building the other. Online activity brought bigger crowds to the gigs and the gigs delivered more downloaders to the online communities. Arctic Monkeys were not only bypassing the traditional media, they were reversing the music industry's standard methodology.

Traditionally, a band would tour to promote a new record in the hope the audience would buy their music afterwards. Arctic Monkeys had stood the process on its head: they were playing to new audiences that already had their music and already knew the words to all their songs. If Turner stopped singing halfway through a verse, the crowd would carry on.

Indeed, the band hadn't even released any of their music for fans to buy yet. In effect, they were using their recorded music to promote their live gigs – which, of course, begged the question whether anyone would *ever* buy their records.

There was no doubt that the internet was rapidly increasing the Monkeys' fanbase in a way that had never been seen before. Just as importantly, it was helping to build their profile in the music industry too.

But many in the music industry were highly sceptical about whether Arctic Monkeys could turn their popularity into commercial success. "Everyone was wondering how they would make money off the internet," music journalist Nick Tesco recalls. "But the [Monkeys] made money by putting it up for free and everyone still wanted it when they finally released it commercially – everyone still bought the songs because they were better recorded."

Simon Wheeler, chair of the Association of Independent Music's digital committee, points out that, although Arctic Monkeys were taking risks and pushing things forward, they were doing so in an intelligent and con-sidered way: "I don't think they gave away the album. They might have given away recordings of the songs, but I think that's quite a difference. They were giving away versions for people to hear what a great set of songs they had and what a great band they were. But it wasn't the same as the version they expected people to pay for.

"The news story wasn't that they were giving away music. The fact was the music was really, really good. You had to have a lot of confidence to make the music freely available and still believe people would like them enough to buy them.

"There was a sense of excitement coming out of there. Now digital is part of what everyone does, but it takes moments like that to push up the next bit."

The band's next move once again demonstrated that they not only had raw talent but also good tactical brains around them. By this time the Monkeys had started to attract serious record label interest and had famously started turning record label A&Rs away from gigs – partly because initial introductions between the band and label executives had ended in acrimony. The band had resented the way major label A&Rs would turn up and immediately start telling them what they should do. Tour manager Timm Cleasby recalls sweat-drenched label executives fighting to get into the dressing room to speak to the band, while he was thinking to himself: "You're a 50-year-old man. You shouldn't even be here."

So while record labels were beating at their door, the band retreated into a studio to re-record and release three of their songs by themselves. It was a masterstroke, demonstrating that, far from losing value, the free downloads had increased Arctic Monkeys' worth. Fans were keen enough to buy copies of tracks they'd already been given free. From this point on the band was irresistible. A label scramble duly ensued.

11

Five Minutes With Arctic Monkeys

THE first commercially released Monkeys single, *Five Minutes With Arctic Monkeys*, hit the streets on May 30, 2005. A limited edition, it was released on their own Bang Bang label, featuring 'Fake Tales Of San Francisco' and 'From The Ritz To The Rubble'.

While common in dance music, artists releasing material on their own label was rare in the indie guitar scene at the time. Arctic Monkeys had once again broken the mould. But the choice of name for their record label was also telling: the Bang (singular) label had put out Van Morrison's first solo hit, 'Brown Eyed Girl'. But label boss Bert Berns had fixed a deal that saw Morrison receiving hardly any royalty payments. The song achieved 10 million radio plays in the USA alone but Van barely saw anything from it, something that rankled with him for most of his career.

In choosing Bang Bang, the Monkeys may well have been signalling to a hungry industry that they weren't about to sign away their rights. On the other hand, they may have just liked the name.

The band had registered the record label as a company under the directorship of all four band members. But it helped that their management team, Wildlife, had been involved in setting up the chart-topping Wildstar label.

The fans who had been trading MP3s for last six months were, of course, already familiar with the tunes. But for many in the media and beyond, *Five Minutes With Arctic Monkeys* was their first introduction to Alex's world of teenage lives and the everyday frustrations of small-town living.

The B-side, 'From The Ritz To The Rubble', was easy to identify with: a tale that starts with being refused entry by a tyrannical bouncer. On the A-side, the enduringly popular 'Fake Tales Of San Francisco' used an imaginary band to document the deceits people practise to escape their background, pretending to be something they're not. Alex's famous put-down in the song reminded the pretentious musicians that they were from Rotherham and not New York.

The single was recorded by Mike Crossey, a Northern Irish studio engineer and producer who'd graduated from Liverpool Institute for Performing Arts a couple of years earlier. He'd been working at Liverpool's Motor Museum studio and had seen Arctic Monkeys playing at Manchester's The Attic in December 2004.

Crossey had approached Barradale about making a recording and roped a fellow LIPA graduate, James Lewis, in to help engineer the sound. It was the start of an enduring association between the band and Crossey, who would be asked to record *Who The Fuck Are Arctic Monkeys?* a year later.

A limited run of 1,500 CDs and vinyl singles were pressed and sold out on pre-orders alone, proving fans who already had the downloads would still clamour for new versions of the same tracks. Just as importantly, the quality of Crossey's new recordings meant the band started to garner serious radio play on stations that hadn't played the rough and ready 2Fly versions.

If their first recordings had established their ever-growing fanbase, their debut single saw them jump to yet another level. Even acts signed to major labels, with all of the marketing budget and campaign plans that entailed, would have been lucky to get the reaction Arctic Monkeys generated from their self-released limited edition.

Drowned In Sound, the long-running online magazine, opened its review of the single by observing that even BBC Radio 1 indie guru Steve Lamacq had been unable to get into Arctic Monkeys' recent London gig. " 'Fake Tales Of San Francisco' . . . is three minutes of the Monkeys doing what they do best, namely offering sharp but funny social commentary in a South Yorkshire patois over bursts of punky, poppy, sometimes ska inflected, guitar . . . It's the nearest you can get to their live show without actually being there. One for Mr Lamacq, then. If five minutes with Arctic Monkeys is this much fun, god help us when the little blighters finally get around to releasing an album."

What made their live reputation all the more remarkable was that, at this point, Arctic Monkeys had kept their London gigs to a minimum. Naturally, the scarcity of the band's appearances meant London promoters were queuing up to book them. In the end, the honour of hosting Arctic Monkeys' second live gig in London fell to Club Fandango, at this time resident in London's iconic Dublin Castle venue where, amongst others, Madness had played their debut concert.

Andy Macleod and Simon Williams of Club Fandango had originally thought it would be amusing to put Eskimo Disco and Arctic Monkeys on the bill together because they had similar-themed names. They had already been trying to book the Monkeys for months, but invited them to play on April 5, 2005 specifically because they'd already booked Eskimo Disco to headline. "The wintery/Inuit theme was frankly too hard to resist," admits Simon Williams, the co-promoter that night.

"Eskimo Disco were the more famous band at that moment and being from London, and having done more gigs, they were going to top the bill," explains former Xfm radio DJ and music producer Caspar Kedros, who was sound engineering for his friends the headliners that night. "Then Scott [from Eskimo Disco] got a call asking if he'd mind if Arctic Monkeys played after them.

"There was definitely a buzz, so Scott said it would be a bit weird if they went on before him. But they just looked like a regular group when we were soundchecking. So I sat around and watched them. And my god it wasn't just hype. The guy's voice was just the best. Because I'm a sound engineer, I had this thing that most people don't sound that great over an SM58 microphone. But Alex just had the perfect voice for an SM58.

"Everyone had wanted to see them, so if you were at that gig you were very lucky," Caspar recalls. "We'd done lots of gigs at The Dublin Castle around that time and it was never that exciting."

Andy Macleod, promoter of Fandango with Simon, recalls the mayhem unfurling before the gig: "The Monkeys' manager didn't want any music industry on the guest list, so we took the phone off the hook because it wouldn't stop ringing from A&R and PAs desperate to get their MDs on the guest list. The upshot was that the soundcheck was packed with A&R execs and we had to board up the doors of the venue with a couple of planks of wood to stop them coming in. I think they stuck around and got into the gig in the end . . . It was mobbed, the kids kept invading the stage and it genuinely felt like the band had reinvented the wheel."

"My main memory of that show was the fact the audience was so split between eager MySpace kids at the front and industry faces at the back," chips in Simon Williams. "There was a clear path running direct from the mixing desk to the bar. I never had an easier walk to get a pint in all those legendary Fandango Tuesdays. But the Arctic Monkeys were terrific – indie skills with a real Supergrass buzz!"

As the last beats of Eskimo Disco's set faded into applause that night, the already busy venue had suddenly filled to capacity as 150 of the city's 'it kids' crammed in clutching the hottest ticket in town. What had been a warm venue had suddenly become decidedly hot.

For a band about to break into the big time, Arctic Monkeys were characteristically casual. Wearing ill-advised woolly jumpers, they squeezed their way through the accumulating throng and set about setting up. A few in the crowd knew the band, some having made their way to London from Sheffield. As Arctic Monkeys shifted amps and drums into position, band members paused for a chat with faces they recognised. But for many of first-time fans, the guys plugging in guitars and switching on amps might as well have been roadies.

Alex announced the band's arrival by punching the air and spitting, "I blame the parents!" Taking that as their cue, the band powered their way into 'I Bet You Look Good On The Dancefloor', blasting The Dublin Castle's back room into a frenzied mosh pit.

They played in the same knitwear and jeans they'd just been setting up in – despite the room now being packed to bursting and the temperature going through the roof. Most of the audience had stripped down to T-shirts and vests.

Within minutes the room had joined in the singing and, as the opening chords of 'When The Sun Goes Down' were struck, Alex stopped altogether to let the crowd take over the first verse. When he asked if he could at least sing his own chorus, the crowd answered with a 30-strong stage invasion.

The episode was symbolic of the night. As band and audience exchanged jovial banter, it was more like mates sharing in-jokes than a room full of strangers. Alex and the band may have written the songs, but the audience took possession of them that night. As the band powered out songs such as 'Bigger Boys And Stolen Sweethearts', the audience screamed them back, only contained in the mosh pit long enough for the band to play a short set before bringing it to a halt with a second stage invasion.

As with The Sex Pistols at the Lesser Free Trade Hall in Manchester, there weren't that many at The Dublin Castle that night. But they knew they had witnessed history in the making.

"Everyone knew they were going to be absolutely massive," Caspar Kedros recalls. Within hours the blogs and boards were filling up with messages from people saying they had been there at a significant moment in rock'n'roll history. For the rest of the week, London was humming with the Monkeys.

Having propelled Arctic Monkeys to stardom faster than anyone before, the internet was now celebrating a rock'n'roll legend within minutes of the event occurring. The legend was being written right here, right now, by the fans and the bloggers.

One such, Xan Phillips, blogged later that night: "All bands need fans and the ones that follow the Monkeys were excellent. They knew the words, they sang along and gave the band as good as they got. It was a hot evening, there were stage invasions, there was northern banter. But mainly there were songs about life and that is what pulls the people to the musicians."

Adding to the excitement that was building before the Dublin Castle gig, a rumour had started circulating that the band would be signing a record deal after the gig. It's not as if the offers hadn't already been coming in.

"By this time the major labels all had their chequebooks open and just wanted to know how many noughts they should write," recalls Simon Wheeler.

Amongst the excited teenagers and students who'd been lucky enough to get into The Dublin Castle were label executives and A&Rs, lining up to make the band an offer that, a few months earlier, they'd have been out of their minds to refuse.

But things had changed. Under the careful guidance of Barradale and

McAndrew, the band were not about to sign themselves away on a promise of private helicopters and jets.

To the majors it probably seemed like Arctic Monkeys were playing hard to get. But there were more than financial questions at play. Barradale, the prudent manager, wasn't about to risk the talent under his charge being wasted by an improvident record deal – even if Matt Helders would later recall being quite taken by the idea of helicopters.

All of this put Laurence Bell and the Domino Recording Company in a particularly good light. Bell had been running Domino for 11 years. A fiercely independent and credible force that crossed genres while maintaining a high-calibre roster of artists, Domino had all the critical functions to perform well in the challenging conditions of the early twenty-first century.

Bell was just one of many label bosses who'd caught wind of the young northern band selling out gigs without having released a single record. But Bell had recent experience that had made him a good proposition. He had signed and broken Glaswegian pop-punk band Franz Ferdinand, helping them become a high-profile act even though they'd only been together for a year.

For Bell, the Monkeys must have looked like a similar proposition and an obvious addition to his roster. On March 15, 2005 he packed his bags and headed north to see them play in Nottingham. Impressed, he stayed to hang out with the band for the next five days – during which time the band played a gig on March 17 at the student-friendly Jabez Clegg in Manchester.

It was the start of a comfortable relationship with the band that, according to the label, saw business being done in a no-nonsense manner over a pint in the pub, rather than through lawyers in suits.

Domino had a history of credible signings that went back to when Bell and partner Jacqui Rice had founded the label with a £40 a week enterprise allowance grant from the government in 1993. The label had started by licensing American artists from seminal US indie labels such as Sub Pop and Drag City. Apart from giving Domino street credibility from the beginning, it also meant Domino developed long-term transatlantic relationships that still exist today.

In stark contrast to the Monkeys' rapid rise, success for Bell's label was a long, arduous slog. A steady stream of high-quality signings gave them increasing authority across different genres of music while holding onto their core critical-but-dedicated fanbase. Acts such as Four Tet (aka Kieran Hebden) reached into the electronic music market while Quickspace, Bonnie Prince Billy and Elliott Smith held onto their alternative indie core.

By 2003 the label had survived long enough to celebrate its tenth anniversary. Bang on cue, Bell then made this most adept signing yet. Franz Ferdinand had been formed in 2002 by a group of Glaswegian musicians with varied backgrounds and experience (ranging from a jazz virtuoso to a complete musical novice). Despite their disparate elements, the band quickly formed into a powerful whole strung together by the songwriting skills of Alex Kapranos and Paul Thomson.

Success followed quickly and, in 2003, Bell snapped them up for his label. They were on the verge of self-releasing their debut EP, and so Bell hurriedly released 'Darts Of Pleasure' on Domino instead. The single just missed the Top 40, but it was enough to get the ball rolling. The band soon picked up the Philip Hall Radar Award at the *NME* Awards in November 2003.

In 2004, Franz Ferdinand secured two Top 10 hits as their single 'Take Me Out' and eponymous debut LP, *Franz Ferdinand*, both charted at number three in the UK singles and album charts. By September 2004 the album had been awarded the Mercury Music Prize, starting a steady flow that included an Ivor Novello Award in 2004 and two Brit Awards in 2005. The surrealistic video for 'Take Me Out' earned them an MTV Award and *NME* lauded *Franz Ferdinand* as the best album of 2004.

For both band and label, the period between 2003 and 2004 was a steep learning curve and a step change in their operations. By the end of 2004, Domino had graduated from a medium-sized UK indie label with a strong catalogue behind it to a medium-sized international player which could take on potential chart acts and deliver successfully.

Yet the label was a modest affair, nothing like big enough to allow Bell to be anything less than hands on with all of his acts. Far from being a hindrance, its diminutive size played to Bell's advantage. Arctic Monkeys had been unimpressed by big-shot A&Rs inclined to start telling them how they could improve things on their first meeting. But they reacted well to the head of a label who was passionate about all the acts he'd personally signed. There was no doubt that, if Arctic Monkeys were offered a deal by Bell, it would be he and not one of his employees who was making the offer.

By the time the Monkeys were about to go onstage at The Dublin Castle, the writing was on the wall – if not already dry on the contract.

12

The Domino Effect

BY April 2005, the buzz around Arctic Monkeys had reached into every corner of the music industry. Stories were circulating about A&Rs being turned away from sold-out gigs while flocks of ticket-wielding fans flooded past them.

By May, record label executives would probably have agreed to anything to get their signatures on a contract. The Monkeys were in a rare position, only ever experienced by a handful of bands, of being able to choose which label they wanted to sign to. Domino was the perfect home for a feisty northern punk outfit brimming with chart-topping potential. With hindsight it seems an obvious choice, but at the time it must have been a difficult decision.

For all the hype surrounding Arctic Monkeys in early 2005, there was still a degree of uncertainty. The band members were at least viewing their prospects with greater seriousness, one sign of this being that James Cook finally quit his job as an apprentice bathroom tiler – but only in the run-up to *Five Minutes With Arctic Monkeys*' release. Viewed from the opposite angle, the fact that 'Cookie' had hung onto his apprenticeship for so long indicated how cautious the band still felt about their future. According to promoter Barney Vernon, Andy and Alex had also kept their bar jobs at The Boardwalk going while the band were breaking.

For all the sold-out gigs, torrents of file sharing and rumblings around the music industry, they were still a long way from being a guaranteed success. They had only just made their first appearance in the national press, when journalist Joe Mott described them as the most exciting emerging act of 2005 in the *Daily Star*.

Given the potential mountains of money and other incentives on offer from major labels, there was some internal wrangling going on in the

Monkeys' camp. "We were ready to sign to a different label," Matt Helders later admitted to *Drowned In Sound*. "I was tempted by the money on offer . . . And then Laurence came to watch us. He seemed like a genuine fan. He decides who he signs, rather than some MD. It all seemed just right, so when the rest of the band met him, we signed to Domino right there."

"With a label like that, you're talking to the person who owns it," Alex Turner said approvingly to *The Guardian*. "If he likes us, you can't really go wrong. He's really passionate about his music and that. It just seemed right."

Whether they actually signed when Bell met the band in March 2005 is a moot point. The official story is that they signed for an undisclosed sum a few months later, but there could have been good reasons for not signing immediately. They'd already booked the Dublin Castle gig with Club Fandango and planned a self-released single – neither of which would necessarily have profited from the Domino deal being announced. Nonetheless, rumours that the band had decided on a label were circulating before their prestigious rock pub gig.

The choice of Domino wasn't entirely due to Bell's personality. Being on a smaller label potentially offered greater artistic control, but Domino was also clearly a growing concern. With the right partners and deals they might be every bit as capable of delivering international hits as any major, but with the flexibility of a lean, independent company. Being on an independent not only suited the band's image, in a rapidly changing music industry it probably made more business sense too.

Domino had a meticulously handpicked roster, but it was also rapidly expanding to run its own offices in New York, Berlin and Paris, as well as launching four offshoot labels and establishing an international network of distributors and music services, each with a specialist knowledge of territories across the world. Domino's flexible, multi-partnered approach was itself a product of the internet age.

"They could have signed with whoever they wanted, but they chose to work with an independent. That choice was very acute and very smart," says Simon Wheeler. "If the artist is of a good enough quality, they can sign to a wider range of companies than just a major and still achieve their goals."

As an indie rock band, Arctic Monkeys needed something that would underpin their credibility, especially given their meteoric rise. Domino had a history of successfully releasing uncompromising, high-quality music. The moment the band signed to Domino, they cemented its reputation as the coolest, most credible label in the world – but, conversely, the label also ensured the band would still be seen as a credible indie act.

For some journalists (such as *The Independent*'s Nick Hasted), Arctic Monkeys signalled a return to the glory days of the independent label scene of the Seventies and Eighties. The charts may have been dominated by TV show spin-offs, but good, honest indie rock appeared to be back on the streets of British suburbia.

With the record deal completed, all sides were aware that they needed to start delivering as soon as possible. The Monkeys' next move was to get their publishing contract in place. Conversations with publishers had in fact been taking place for a while, and, by June 17, senior vice president and director of A&R at EMI Publishing, Mike Smith, announced that the band would be signing. Smith was a veteran industry figure and not about to let the Monkeys slip through his fingers. EMI secured them for a long-term, worldwide exclusive deal at a reputed £1 million signing fee, according to *Billboard*.

It came at a cost but Smith was jubilant. "There are more fresh ideas in one song than you'll find in most rock albums at the moment," he enthused. "In Arctic Monkeys you've got . . . the lyrical dexterity that you don't normally get in a rock band, the sort of storyteller approach you might expect from an artist like Mike Skinner, but doing it in a fresh, exhilarating rock band."

Soon after signing, Smith moved on to become an A&R executive at the Sony-owned Columbia/Epic label, leaving Arctic Monkeys in the hands of a delighted Guy Moot, president of EMI Publishing. Within a year the band started to pay off EMI's investment, increasing the publisher's dominance of the music publishing market.

Despite what already seemed like relentless live dates over the last 18 months, the band could now start touring in earnest while simultaneously recording and completing their first LP. Starting at The Barfly in Cardiff on June 4, 2005, their first tour since signing a deal sold out effortlessly. It moved on to their last small London gig at Islington's Bar Academy on

June 6, where the whole of the venue's smaller room was transformed into a mosh pit, and then to Little Civic Hall in Wolverhampton, Jabez Clegg in Manchester, The Brick Yard in Carlisle and The Faversham in Leeds on June 11.

In late June the band took a break to start their first Domino recordings, after being introduced to producer James Ford of Simian Mobile Disco by Laurence Bell. But by July 26 they were back on the road, playing The Birdwell Club in Barnsley at a Barney Vernon-promoted event. "I remember they had all the publisher A&Rs up," recalls Vernon.

Barnsley was followed by a quick succession of gigs at Fibbers in York, The Empire in Middlesbrough, King Tut's in Glasgow on 30 July and The Leadmill in Sheffield, all before the end of the month.

Along with the rest of the tour, the 1,000-capacity Leadmill had sold out in a flash and, back amongst his home crowd, Alex was able to muster a series of massive cheers just by uttering, "Sheffield," into the microphone.

Next the tour headed north to The Cluny in Newcastle and Cafe Nirvana in Wigan. Here Alex taunted some of the crowd who had clearly bought tickets just because of the hype. "Come on, cheer up! There's some glum faces out there," he called over the heads in the mosh pit to the people standing soberly at the back.

More scenes of mayhem followed as the tour picked up in August, leading the way to the band's anticipated debut at the Reading Festival. Speeding on through The Silhouette in Hull, Academy 2 in Birmingham, Soundhaus in Northampton, Phoenix in Exeter and Zodiac in Oxford, the Monkeys made their first trip across water to play their debut Irish dates at The Limelight in Belfast on August 20 and Whelan's in Dublin on the 21st.

Back in southern England, they played Chinnery's in Southend, The Komedia in Brighton and, the last pre-Reading gig, The Soul Tree in Cambridge on August 26. The next day the band pulled into Reading for their debut festival appearance. It was here that the full scale of Arctic Monkeys' online community became electrifyingly evident, even to the most cynical doubters.

By rights this should have been a run-of-the-mill festival debut, wit-nessed by a few die-hard fans and a handful of journalists checking out the hype. The band had been booked to play The Carling Tent, an arena usually reserved for unsigned up-and-coming bands. It was neither an auspicious arena nor an advantageous time slot.

But the buzz had started passing around the festival as soon as the gates opened, and people began to hold their places at The Carling Tent hours before the band were due onstage. Soon the tent was packed out, with yet more fans turning up to mark their spot even though it was nowhere near the Monkeys' stage time.

The first the band knew about the unfurling scene was when they were chilling backstage before the gig. Suddenly a truckload of extra security was bused past them into the arena. This was soon followed by an extra consignment of crowd barriers being rushed in, followed by yet more security, then more barriers and more security . . .

As the band went on halfway through the afternoon, the arena was packed to capacity with fans bursting out of the sides for as far as anyone could see. Stepping up to the microphone, Alex Turner announced: "Don't believe the hype, Reading – they haven't hyped us enough." As if to vindicate everything that had happened over the last 18 months, the packed festival tent and surrounding multitude burst into song.

Of course, it may have helped that the first song they played was 'Fake Tales Of San Francisco' – the A-side of the only official release so far. But any thoughts that the crowd knew only the Monkeys' recent material were dispelled as the band hurled into 'I Bet You Look Good On The Dancefloor'. The swelling crowd roared their lungs out, word perfect on the unreleased track.

As had become customary, Turner didn't have to sing for most of 'When The Sun Goes Down'. At the front, fans went crowd-surfing crazy, while the band continued to charge through 'Dancing Shoes', 'Mardy Bum' and 'Perhaps Vampires Is A Bit Strong But . . .' with the crowd singing all the way.

Towards the end, Alex asked if everyone who he couldn't see outside the tent was okay. The huge roar of response took everyone by surprise. Not only was it rammed in the tent but there was another festival going on, dancing and singing, unseen beyond the canvas.

Reading definitely needed a bigger tent.

From a whisper to a scream, Arctic Monkeys caught during their rapid rise in 2005. From the left, Matt Helders, Andy Nicholson (on phone), James Cook and Alex Turner. K.TRAGESER/PHOTOSHOT

Alex Turner (with cap) and Matt Helders (third from left) at a school camp. REX FEATURES

Alex Turner as a schoolboy. REX FEATURES

School band: Alex Turner (end of front row on the left), Matt Helders (front row third from left), and Andy Nicholson (far right of the front row) in 1999 Stocksbridge High School photo. REX FEATURES

Buses featured heavily in the young Monkeys lives. In the midst of recording their debut LP, they still found time to hang around bus stops. Pictured at South Thoresby Studios in Lincoln in 2005, from left: Andy, Matt, Jamie and Alex. FABIO DE PAOLA/REX FEATURES

Arctic Monkeys back stage at the Barfly, Liverpool; November 2005. PAT POPE/PHOTOSHOT/GETTY IMAGES

Andy Nicholson donning his trademark dour expression at the Monkeys sold out show at Paradise Rock Club in Boston, Thursday, March 23, 2006. AP PHOTO/ROBERT E. KLEIN

Left to right: Alex (lead vocals, guitar), Andy (bass), Matt (drums) and Jamie (guitar) performing in Cologne in early 2006.
CAMERA PRESS /SUKI DHANDA

Andy Nicholson (bass), Alex Turner (vocals, guitar), Matt Helders (drums) and James Cook (guitar) rehearsing in Yellow Arch Studios in 2006. CAMERA PRESS/PEROU

Left to right: Andy, Matt and Alex with the award for Best New Band at the *NME* Awards 2006. DAVE M. BENETT/GETTY IMAGES

Arctic Monkeys arrive dressed as "country Squires", and pretending to be Alumni from the Brit School, at the Brit Awards 2008, Earl's Court, London. ELLIOTT FRANKS/LIVEPIX

Matt Helders and Alex Turner accept the Nationwide Mercury Prize winners' award for *Whatever People Say I Am, That's What I'm Not* at the awards ceremony in London, September 5, 2006. DAVE HOGAN/GETTY IMAGES

Alex on stage at the HMV Forum in London, August 24, 2006. GARY CLARK/FILMMAGIC

13

Astoria

AFTER Reading the band took another break from touring to record their debut LP, but by the end of September they were ready to set off again. As with their previous two tours, the final series of dates of 2005 had sold out but they were now moving into more prestigious venues and onto the international stage.

Before setting off, Arctic Monkeys made their first UK television appearance on *Later . . . With Jools Holland*. As it was already in the pipeline as the first Domino single, the band naturally played 'I Bet You Look Good On The Dancefloor'. For the first time the nation could see what the fuss was about from the comfort of their living rooms. It made refreshing viewing: the band's unpolished but finely structured power pop exploded out of the TV set, as Alex's spitfire rhythms crashed into a ringing crescendo that lingered well into Holland's following link.

Their sound was matched by their unpretentious attire. There was no sense of London irony here: Arctic Monkeys arrived for TV wearing jumpers and jeans, sporting undisguised late-teen acne with unkempt hair to match their blemished skin. For all the column inches of hype they'd been generating, it was hard for anyone not to appreciate this was the real, electrifying deal.

Their debut international tour began in Liverpool on October 2, 2005. With a marked symbolism, the band were booked to open the tour at The Cavern, the venue that had launched The Beatles on the road to stardom. Although supposedly a secret warm-up gig, word had leaked out and it had sold out before nme.com had had time to announce it.

Adding to the party atmosphere, fellow Sheffield act Milburn were booked as the Monkeys' support band for most of the tour. Milburn had been there from the start of the Arctic Monkeys story, and, although they were destined to split up in 2008, even after Milburn's demise the two bands' paths would remain connected.

The tour got underway with scenes that were by now customary adjuncts to an Arctic Monkeys performance. Each gig sold out in advance, with tickets exchanging hands for sums that made a mockery of their printed value. Fans and journalists had to fight their way into venues through columns of touts. As more than one commentator would observe, all this was happening when the two bands onstage had released only three singles between them.

After Liverpool, the tour officially started at The Waterfront in Norwich on October 5, 2005. But it would be the following night's gig, at London's Astoria, that lingered in the public memory.

By any normal measure, Arctic Monkeys shouldn't even have been playing The Astoria yet – let alone selling it out and leaving a legion of disappointed fans gasping for tickets outside. According to rumours, the gig had already been upgraded twice, originally rescheduled from a smaller venue to The Marquee, from where it had been moved again to The Astoria.

As it turned out, the 1,200-capacity Astoria was still too small to cater for the number of fans trying to get in – which only served to increase the tension building around the venue. With kids fighting over tickets selling for over 10 times their face value, the night was tense both inside and outside the venue. The wait for the Monkeys was peppered with clashes among the audience and those trying to gain admission.

Collisions in the middle of what would soon become the mosh pit spilled over into verbal exchanges. With fists and feet threatening to fly and the risk of confrontation spreading through the crowd, Arctic Monkeys appeared onstage with spot-on timing. Bursting onto the stage with their customary nonchalance, they channelled the edgy energy into an explosion of guitars and drum rolls.

The Astoria's stage had hosted gigs by, amongst others, Prince, The Rolling Stones, Nirvana, Radiohead, U2, Eminem, Blur, Oasis, Amy Winehouse, Red Hot Chili Peppers and David Bowie. In 1994, Manic Street Preachers made their last appearance with guitarist Richey Edwards there before he disappeared. The venue's boards were steeped in legend and another was about to be added to the canon.

Still in their late teens, part of Arctic Monkeys' charm was the huge contrast between their modest appearance and their enormous stage presence. As they entered the vaulted music hall of The Astoria that night, Alex Turner, a slight and elegant youth, capable of making a guitar look outsized, seemed at risk of being swamped.

Instead, the band and their frontman instantly brought the focus of the entire audience onto themselves and projected a charisma that instantly filled the venue. The ecstatic roar that greeted Arctic Monkeys at the Astoria that night is as legendary as the rest of the gig. As if challenged by the amplified assault of the band's opening salvo of chords, the audience turned as one and yelled with every decibel available to their bodies.

The effect was electrifying and unifying. People who had been sparring for a fight were suddenly transformed into hugging chimps, careering arm in arm through the crowd and into the frothing surf of the mosh pit.

"The first riff cranks up and nothing else matters. Scrap? What scrap? The same guys who wanted to rip out each other's eyeballs have now got their arms around each other," recorded Tim Jonze in *NME*.

Kicking in with 'I Bet You Look Good On The Dancefloor', now a little over a week away from its release, and 'Fake Tales Of San Francisco', the response in the packed Astoria was more engulfing than anyone expected. The entire packed dancefloor joined in an uninterrupted pogo wave that seemed to extend from the stage to the back of the hall, sweeping over the bars and crashing up the stairs onto the balcony. Three songs in, the pressure seemed to literally snap Andy Nicholson's synapses as the bass player was forced to scuttle off to stem a nosebleed.

While he was gone, despite the enormous venue the band reverted to pub-gig banter, with Alex fending off a barrage of heckling from members of the crowd about Andy's nosebleed. The rest of the set spun through the entire track list of the recently recorded LP: 'Still Take You Home' was followed by 'View From The Afternoon', 'Ritz To The Rubble', 'You Probably Couldn't See', 'Vampires Is A Bit Strong But . . .', 'Dancing Shoes' and 'Red Light Indicates . . .'. The only song not played live that night was the freshly rearranged 'Riot Van'.

As the gig drew to a close, the band turned up the energy with 'Mardy Bum', 'When The Sun Goes Down' and 'A Certain Romance', ensuring the packed venue rose to the bait, unfalteringly and deliriously singing each verse and chorus back to the band.

For anyone who had not yet seen or experienced the Monkeys, the Astoria gig was a clarion call. For Arctic Monkeys themselves it was a further step upward, adding another chapter to their media story and powering them into the national psyche. Reviewing the gig for *NME*, Tim Jonze wrote: "Once in a while, there comes along a band who unites a generation – a band who sum up what it is to be young, lost, broke and British. The Smiths, The Stone Roses, Oasis, The Libertines . . . Arctic Monkeys might tremble at the prospect, but they're that kind of band." The Astoria gig had ensured the Monkeys' story had gone well and truly national, just at the moment the Monkeys' debut single was about to land.

On Sunday October 9, the tour moved on to The Corn Exchange in Cardiff. The night coincided with support vocalist Louis Carnell's twentieth birthday and Milburn celebrated by tying balloons to his microphone stand. By now the Arctic Monkeys' effect was rubbing off on Milburn, with the audience singing songs back at both bands.

But it was clear which Sheffield band were in the ascendancy. When Arctic Monkeys eventually mooched on that night, Alex sidled up to the mic and announced: "Apparently we're the next big thing." During the set the band delved into an elongated version of 'Vampires Is A Bit Strong But . . .', breaking down into an extended percussion break and a marathon audience singalong.

With only seven days to go until the debut single's release, the tour continued across the UK at Manor Quay in Sunderland, The Coliseum in Coventry, The Bierkeller in Bristol, the ABC Glasgow, The Plug in Sheffield and The Ritz in Manchester.

On October 17, fans could finally buy an Arctic Monkeys record from a shop for the first time – the band marking the occasion with tour stop at Blank Canvas in the New Yorkshire movement's sister capital of Leeds. Despite it being a Monday, the worst school night of the week, the gig had sold out instantly. Many of the people at Blank Canvas were clearly devoted Monkeys fans, but regulars also noted a new influx of people who'd been sucked in by the hype. Although unwelcome to some, the new fans proved Arctic Monkeys were blossoming into a credible, mainstream band. It was exactly the kind of audience transition they needed to carry their new single up the charts. But for both the band and their original fans, it also signalled the end of an era. The challenge for the band lay in keeping their long-term original fans while welcoming their new, more transient extended fanbase. It also inevitably meant accommodating the type of people Alex had targeted in some of his more waspish lyrics.

The Leeds gig began with the usual football-style Monkeys chants, but, although there was an increase in use of phone cameras, the format followed much the usual pattern. Banter between Alex and the crowd had also become a part of the gig routine: when a semi-jocular stand-off hovered between humour and aggression, it felt normal to start with, but soon it threatened to turn into something more serious as some of the crowd began throwing bottles. Were it not for Alex's disarming charm, it might well have turned into an altogether different gig.

Heading north up the A1(M), the next stop on the tour was The Exchange in Edinburgh, followed by the Wulfrun Hall in Wolverhampton and their second TV appearance, a riotous live event for MTV's *Gonzo Show* in Liverpool, before finally settling in for a homecoming gig at The Plug in Sheffield on Saturday October 22.

They returned to Sheffield at the end of the single's first week of sales, when the chances of their debut topping the charts were high.

The booking of The Plug, Sheffield's newest venue, on the weekend before the band released their debut single and the following week, the day before their single topped the charts, appeared to be part of a brilliant strategy, but in fact was the result of a cock-up.

Adele and Scott Bailey had been building their new venue when Barney Vernon and Geoff Barradale had been looking for somewhere new to play.

"Barney really wanted a venue that nobody had played before," explains Adele Bailey. "So we ended up booking them in for the first Saturday." But the venue was still being built. "We'd believed the capacity was going to be 1,400 people, so we sold out 1,400 tickets – in an hour.

"A month later Health and Safety came around and said this room is going to be 1,200 capacity. We had to ring Barney up and say, 'We're in the shit here; we've oversold.' But Barney said, 'Don't worry, we'll do two dates and do the following Saturday as well.'

"On the second Saturday we already knew they were going to be number one the following day. It was just so lucky how it happened."

Expectations amongst their home crowd had turned tickets into must-have items. Even though they'd played the same venue only a week before, there was an added sense of expectation in the air and tickets were selling for upwards of £80. It didn't matter how many times anyone had recently seen the band, everyone wanted to be there.

Once inside, the venue felt even more packed than it had at the previous Saturday's sell-out gig. From the start, the atmosphere was close to hysterical. As the venue filled up, the familiar football chanting began. But instead of the usual shouts about the Monkeys, tonight the crowd was chanting "Sheffield!" or "Yorkshire!", seizing the day as a celebration of regional pride.

First onstage were the other local boys, Milburn, and their short, fiery set prompted further rounds of regional chanting. Then the long, suspense-filled wait for Arctic Monkeys began.

"I remember looking at the boys, they were only babies then, and thinking, 'It's even bigger than we thought,'" says Adele Bailey. "Everyone was looking at each other in awe of what was going on. I remember looking down the stairs and they were all having a pep talk before going on, and thinking, 'The world is their oyster, it really is their oyster.'"

"It's a surreal time to be living in Sheffield at the moment," wrote John Murphy for respected music blog *OMH*. "For the last few years, the local music scene has known all about Arctic Monkeys – they gigged incessantly in the region's pubs, they gave away free demo versions of songs . . . and slowly but surely built up a reputation as one of the city's best new bands.

"But nobody prepared us for this. It's come from nowhere. Arctic Monkeys have suddenly become big – really, really big. There's been ludicrous claims ('they're the new Libertines' – they're not, they're much better, and 'they'll be bigger than The Beatles' – they won't, but who ever will be), their singles get A-list playlist status on Radio 1, and even the local Top Shop could be heard playing them this afternoon."

Arctic Monkeys were about to go stratospheric, but for a band that had achieved so much in such a short time they remained incredibly rooted and unchanged.

Their stage entrance was, as usual, anything but showy. They sauntered on and burst into their accustomed set openers, 'I Bet You Look Good On The Dancefloor' and 'Fake Tales . . .'. As an opening salvo, it was a bit like starting a cup final with a hat trick; the crowd sang and danced like they were supporting their team at Wembley. When Alex stepped up to the mic to thank "everyone who was there at the beginning", they all knew it wasn't just a theatrical gesture.

The band had effectively been touring for a year and their sound was correspondingly tight. It helped that they were playing Sheffield's newest 1,200-capacity venue, decked out with a new sound system driven.

Unlike at some earlier gigs, there was no let-up in the hysteria that greeted the band – if anything, the excitement levels increased as they got deeper into the set. The band chose the night to debut a brand new track, 'Leave Before The Lights Come On', as a gift to the crowd. Pausing before playing it, Alex asked the audience to let him know what they thought. Their response afterwards was, of course, deafening.

'From The Ritz To The Rubble', the B-side of the first single, saw audience participation heighten and, by the closing three anthems of 'Mardy Bum', 'When The Sun Goes Down' and 'A Certain Romance', the band could barely be heard above the audience. Even more than usual, this gig felt like a veteran supergroup picking its way through a catalogue of classics rather than a band celebrating its debut single.

Dressed in T-shirts and jeans, more interested in powering out their music than striking poses, they appeared in many ways to be the same band that had mooched onto the stage of The Grapes two and a half years earlier. They looked and spoke like the same boys – but everyone knew that they weren't.

In common with every gig of the tour, the band didn't hang around to play an encore at the end. But the final chords of 'A Certain Romance' were still ringing in everyone's ears when radio sets across Sheffield tuned in to Sunday's Top 40 countdown and heard Arctic Monkeys officially declared the UK's number one.

On hearing the news, local blogger Denzil Watson wrote: "The band have just this moment been confirmed at number one in the national singles charts. Their ascent to stardom couldn't have been any more Everest-like in its trajectory . . . Incredibly this quartet of 19/20-year-olds have kept their feet firmly on the ground. With their debut album already in the can for Domino Records and slated for release next February and a looming world tour, world domination looks imminent."

Not surprisingly, many of those who'd left The Plug the previous night felt they'd contributed to another piece of history. But Arctic Monkeys were taking it in their stride. They were looking forward to an afternoon in the pub.

14

I Bet You Look Good On
The Dancefloor

" 'I Bet You Look Good On The Dancefloor' stormed straight to No. 1. The record industry, completely outflanked, was left gasping for breath. Ever since, people have been asking how it happened, and why" – Nick Hasted, *The Independent*, December 2005.

The UK leg of Arctic Monkeys' first international tour had been planned to coincide with their first commercially available single. But even without the tantalising prospect of the band's songs finally being available to buy or download, the buzz by this point had made a sell-out tour inevitable. And there was little doubt the single was going to chart in the Top 10. The week before it was released, *NME* put the Monkeys on the cover for the first time.

'I Bet You Look Good On The Dancefloor' was classic Monkeys. A point-blank shot between the ears, it kicked in on a barrage of trademark Helders drum rolls bolstering Cook and Turner's block-chord riffs. Surprisingly for a pop single, it then twisted into a staccato guitar solo before switching to the verse – and Alex Turner's typically sharp observations on an aspiring nightclub romance. It was, as he would later explain, about eyeing up someone when you were really with someone else.

Although Turner was to downplay the song's merits, the opening verse is as good an early example of his comfortable turn of phrase and emotionally detached observation as you could hope for. Its impact was dynamite. Before getting anywhere near a chorus, the verse had locked the listener in; it already felt like a hit and it hadn't even got to the hook. Then, just in case there was any doubt, the power-driven chorus, with Alex's voice hovering between growling ferocity and cracking fragility, ensured that no one could bypass the song. Like it or not, it jumped out from radios, shop-fronts, bars and TV sets.

It was an obvious yet brilliant choice for a first single, but it offered no compromise. It was number one and still sounded like a guitar anthem. It even started with a guitar solo.

To top the charts, the band had outsold some serious pop competition. The Sugababes and Robbie Williams had both released singles on major labels that week, and both had expected to get to number one. It was a considerable achievement not only for the Monkeys but also for Domino and a series of independent companies: from the record's distributor (Vital) and press agents (Bad Moon) to their online PR (Nile On) and radio plugger (Anglo). It was a true David and Goliath moment.

Seemingly choosing to make their job harder, Arctic Monkeys had chosen not to go on *Top Of The Pops* to promote the single. It was redolent of the punk ethos of bands such as The Clash, but the decision was also consistent with a band that had made their reputation via the internet. Having built their fanbase through new media and live gigs, a dusty medium like *TOTP*, with its mimed performances and top-down programming, seemed irrelevant. Their decision was certainly consistent with their powerful live appearances on TV shows, which they'd already made twice.

James Cook explained their decision to Chris Heath for an *Observer* article in 2006: "It's like, 'Do *Top Of The Pops*,' 'All right, can we play [live]?' 'No,' 'We're not doing it, then,' 'You've got to do it,' 'Why?' 'Because that's what you do,' 'No, we're not doing it.'"

Surprisingly, though, one person didn't really agree with the band's choice of debut single. "It's a bit shit," Alex Turner told *The Guardian*'s Dorian Lynskey during a short break from album recording sessions in late September 2005. "The words are rubbish. I scraped the bottom of the barrel. It could be a big song, like. But I'd hate to be just known for that song because it's a bit . . . crap."

Typically, the band themselves celebrated their first chart success over a pint. "When we went to number one we were all in a local pub called The Packhorse with family, friends, bystanders – everyone were there. An emotional day . . . evening," Matt Helders recalled a few months later.

In fact, not everyone had been there: manager Geoff Barradale was at a wedding in Ireland, so he called the band at The Packhorse when the news came in. Amidst the jubilation there was also a sense of utter disbelief. The band were lucky to have such a solid grounding in High Green, where they could celebrate an abnormal situation in a reassuringly familiar environment. But its very familiarity also underlined the strangeness of it all, the unshakeable sense that this shouldn't be happening – not to the likes of them.

True to form, The Packhorse was a down-to-earth local boozer. Tucked down a side lane, round the corner from a more obvious cluster of pubs in the centre of High Green, it overlooks playing fields and boasts the football team (High Green Villa) that, at the time of the celebration, still had Jamie Cook among its line-up. The no-nonsense environment that allowed the newly established stars to drink unmolested in their local pub would prove a powerful asset during the coming media circus.

"The week after it went to number one everyone had to put a reason on why it happened," Alex told *The Independent* later that year. "We were in *The Economist* and all that sort of thing, about 'What are these four unknowns who've topped the charts? It must be the internet' – there were mad things . . . that we'd told 400 fans to share things on the internet . . . it was absurd, really it's just down to people feeling a certain affinity with the songs and starting to care about it."

In their moment of triumph, the inevitable backlash against Arctic Monkeys was already starting to take shape. There was no doubt that they were by now a national phenomenon, but many of the tastemakers in British music journalism were professionally chained to London. To them, it felt like the band had come from nowhere. To hardened music journalists that always smells suspiciously like a manufactured conspiracy.

It didn't help that the band had only given a limited number of press interviews and relations hadn't always been cordial. In tandem with the positive hype being lavished on them, Arctic Monkeys started getting a reputation for arrogance and hostility among some journalists. In fairness to them, they came from a culture of plain-speaking banter, but it didn't always curry favour with the fourth estate. They were also reacting against being forced to play the music industry game.

Journalist Craig McLean recounted one such occasion in Paris when the band reneged on an entire eight hours' worth of interviews, in *The*

Independent: "The record company had set up a whole day of press and they'd agreed to do it, and literally on the day they said 'No' . . . obviously they'd hacked off an awful lot of people. That was a pan-European press thing and they just blew it out."

"They were great guys, maybe a bit shy, but it was all about the music, not the fame, money and girls," recalls the band's online PR agent, Serena Wilson. "A band that's really into music can be quite detrimental to the interview process – [female electro-pop singer] Robyn was the same – it is sometimes quite difficult to do. They haven't got into it to make money, they're into it for the love of it. And sometimes you'll get journalists who haven't done any research turning up, asking the same stock questions they would have asked Steps. And that's going to annoy anyone.

"At that time their fame was all about the online campaign, but they were there to talk about the music."

"I felt for them because they were young and very bright, funny and together," says music journalist Nick Tesco. "The press went overboard about the internet, so they had that explosion of being the first internet band, when they weren't. They were out there playing gigs in their own area.

"I was particularly impressed by Alex and how he'd said that just because they'd got a Yorkshire accent, people thought they were stupid! He grew up in a house with books. If you've grown up in a house with books your mind is expanded. His parents are teachers, proper intellects, which really tells in the guy's lyrics.

"The first time I saw them being interviewed on Saturday morning TV, I thought they were a bit like The Beatles had been at the very beginning, amused at their own success, and all of them very sharp and intelligent guys, which they sort of buried under the media game. I thought the Arctic Monkeys were a bit like that, only a Yorkshire version. They had the thing of being able to deal with the media in a slightly amused way."

As Tesco also points out, if some sections of the media were turning against the Monkeys, then others couldn't get enough of them. Their relationship with the *NME* was extraordinary, but this privilege usually came with a health warning: over the years the magazine has acquired a reputation for building bands up only to turn against them as soon as they are successful.

Strangely, this backlash has never happened with Arctic Monkeys. Almost uniquely, the *NME* has stayed fighting the little chimps' corner, even when other journals have become less charitable.

"They were embraced because *NME* needed a new guitar band at this point," explains Tesco, "but [*NME*] were lucky because the Arctic Monkeys could deliver. So *NME* were bigging up a band that deserved it."

One beneficial side effect of the 'internet phenomenon' had been the story it had given the traditional media. As a result, the Monkeys' ascent had been trumpeted by the offline media every step of the way – creating its own self-fulfilling prophecy. Their demos had been picked up by Radio 1 in March 2005, before they'd signed to Domino. The *NME* had written about them that May, a month before their first self-released single. The band were on the *NME* cover before even releasing anything on Domino.

By the time the label had sent 'I Bet You Look Good On The Dancefloor' out to radio, the stations were falling over themselves to give it power plays. Between September 2005 and the record's release that October, London alternative station Xfm had played the record 250 times – or, to put it another way, once every three hours for a month.

The coverage Arctic Monkeys were getting from traditional media was all the more astonishing because it appeared to happen without a massive marketing campaign or budget. If it was all down to the internet then it certainly made *The X Factor* look like an expensive and bloated way to launch a pop act.

But their success on radio, TV and in the press had also involved the usual music marketing campaign. Domino had already delivered hits for Franz Ferdinand and employed one of the UK's top independent radio pluggers, Anglo, for that campaign. Naturally, as soon as the label signed Arctic Monkeys, Domino returned to Anglo's Dylan White to ask him to work on their account.

Meanwhile, press agent Anton Brookes, of the Bad Moon PR agency, had been working on their account long before Domino had even heard of the band, having been sent some of the 2Fly demos early in the Monkeys' career. On the back of the demos, Brookes had gone to see some early shows and agreed to take them on.

Having been similarly involved with Ash and Kaiser Chiefs, it wasn't so unusual for Bad Moon to help nurture a band early in their career. As Bad Moon were also experienced online promoters, however, some people made the natural link to Arctic Monkeys' internet campaign, querying whether Bad Moon hadn't in fact manufactured the file-sharing story.

Brookes dismissed the idea. The internet had speeded the process up, he agreed with an *Independent* interviewer, but the same thing would have happened for the band in the past via fanzines, word of mouth and cassettes.

Nonetheless, by 2005 Bad Moon's work for Arctic Monkeys had been recognised by the music industry news service *Record Of The Day*, which awarded them best PR campaign for a breakthrough UK act. But Bad Moon were not the only online promotion company involved with Arctic Monkeys: Nylon, an all-female team of top-rated internet PRs, had been started by Serena Wilson, who cut her teeth at the start of the internet era at EMI, Virgin and the latter's subsidiary label Source. She would also be sent to the *Record Of The Day* awards ceremony by Anton Brookes, to collect on Bad Moon's behalf.

In the meantime, Arctic Monkeys were honoured for the first time at the Muso Awards, voted on "by musicians, for musicians". The ceremony was held in November 2005 at Koko in Camden Town, but Arctic Monkeys, like most of that year's winners, didn't attend to receive their trophy.

With the success of the single ringing in everyone's ears, Arctic Monkeys returned to their tour for their first gig in Amsterdam. The Netherlands had already got wind of the Monkeys by this point, but what they didn't know was that Matt had sworn he'd play in his boxer shorts if the band got to number one. Being a man of his word, he duly played the Dutch date in his underwear.

Arctic Monkeys' debut international tour date was at Amsterdam's Paradiso venue on Tuesday November 1. The band would return to the club several times over the next eight years, eventually filling the 2,000-capacity main hall several times over.

For the first gig they played the venue's smaller upstairs room. They also altered their set list to start with the explosive drums and descending block chords of 'View From The Afternoon'. Moving south to Belgium, they stopped to play the Botanique in Brussels before joining the trend-setting music magazine *Les Inrockuptibles* as their hosts for a series of French dates in Lille, Nantes, Paris and Bordeaux.

Their first outing to Berlin was next, at The Mud Club on November 10, followed by The Underground in Cologne. The Atomic Cafe in Munich brought their whirlwind European tour to a close. It had been short and sharp but it had broken the ice.

Two days later they landed in Canada for their first gig in Toronto at Lee's, which was promptly followed by the band's first visit to New York City – the place that Alex would be calling home within two years.

After playing a debut warm-up gig at The Mercury on November 15, they prepared themselves for their first show at The Bowery Ballroom the following night. Despite not yet having an LP available, the Monkeys had started generating interest in New York, largely through the popularity of the British music press. The problem was that Americans had become cynical about over-hyped British bands, so the first test for the Monkeys wasn't going to be 'Are they any good?' but 'Are they worth the British media's hype?'

Their audience at The Bowery was made up of tastemakers, bloggers and a number of expat Brits. Luckily for the Monkeys, the blogs and chat rooms were for the most part impressed – as apparently was David Bowie, who turned up in person to verify the buzz.

By all accounts the British contingent seemed to have led the audience into the mosh pit, which one blogger claimed was 95 per cent British. But the Monkeys left New York with a bedrock of native supporters. Even when Alex Turner dropped his guitar, the band hadn't missed a beat.

Their next appointment was at The Space Land Troubadour in Los Angeles on November 18. Turner had picked up an infection on the flight and struggled with a hacking cough throughout most of the set. It wasn't helped by some insistent heckling that a healthier Alex might have dealt with more easily. Nonetheless, the LA crowd had entered into the spirit of a Monkeys gig.

Popscene in San Francisco on November 19 was followed by the band's first flight to Japan to play Unit in Tokyo on November 23. The tour had been planned to finish there, but a further date at Razzmatazz in Barcelona on December 3 was bookended by gigs at The Garage in Oslo and

Stockholm Arena on December 8. The band's first international tour finished in Copenhagen on December 9.

The band took a rare month-long break from their relentless touring schedule in the run-up to Christmas. By the New Year, everyone from hipster magazines through to the tabloid press was repeating the same prediction. In the words of bestselling tabloid paper *The Sun*, it was going to be impossible to avoid Arctic Monkeys in 2006.

The LP was scheduled to drop at the end of January and the press had already started running the few interviews the Monkeys had granted. The band's second single, 'When The Sun Goes Down' (previously titled 'Scummy'), had been scheduled for release on January 16, 2006 – it also went straight to number one on the UK singles chart.

The band had proved they could top the singles chart with ease – twice. Now it remained to be seen if they could replicate the same feat in the albums chart.

15

Whatever People Say I Am,
That's What I'm Not

HAVING come seemingly from nowhere with their first two commercially available singles, the band's next achievement was in many
ways even more extraordinary. With their second single still at the top of
the charts, their label decided to bring the release of their first LP forward
by a week. The prospect of an indie rock band sitting at the top of both
the singles and albums charts was suddenly a possibility.

For their part, the band were focusing on a more modest goal. Sick of
answering questions about their sudden rise to fame, they hoped the
release of the album would put a stop to the 'Are they up to the hype?'
speculation. Arctic Monkeys had originally anticipated releasing the LP in
2005, but in the end the actual date would be decided by Laurence Bell –
practically moments before it was released.

Nobody had wanted to hang about though. Demand was high – as rapid
sales for the first two singles had demonstrated. Fans were growing
impatient and so was the music industry. After 2005's Mercury Prize was
announced, subscribers to *Record Of The Day* were asked to predict the
names of next year's shortlist: Arctic Monkeys' LP came top of the poll,
despite the fact that it hadn't been given a release date yet.

Not surprisingly, the band's label had acted swiftly to get recording
underway. In a thesis written on the LP in 2008 at Leeds University, Justin
Morey noted that there was an unusual level of "pressure on the band,
management and label to get the album released before the intense interest
. . . began to dissipate".

Morey also noted how the LP was unusual in that demos normally act
as a blueprint for bands and producers. But in the case of *Beneath The
Boardwalk*, the audience was now a part of the equation: the LP couldn't

stray too far from the 2Fly originals, and yet the tracks needed to be significantly different to make the re-recorded versions worth buying.

Geoff Barradale revealed to Morey that the album's producer Jim Abbiss had at first only been asked to remix the original recordings for album release until the band intervened, arguing it would be ripping fans off if they were asked to buy a reworking of something they'd already got for free.

Abbis was in fact the second producer invited to work on the album. Laurence Bell had originally introduced the band to producer James Ford, who was dispatched from London to Sheffield to meet the Monkeys.

Bell and Ford had first come across each other when Ford had been working with Test Icicles, a band Domino had recently picked up. Laurence had signed them for an album deal but the band, which had formed as a joke, were less than enthusiastic about the project. Faced with a group of reluctant artists, he enlisted James and sent them all to France to record. It was by no means any easy project for Ford but Bell had obviously been pleased with the results.

After signing the Monkeys, Bell immediately turned to Ford to record them. It was a fortuitous choice, as the two camps fell in with each other immediately. "When I first met them a couple of them didn't even have passports," Ford recalls. "They had only done their demos, so me and the Arctics did some test runs for the first record and they were really raw and punky.

"It was at the time when they were just about to explode. It ended up with some weird political wrangling and the rug got pulled, so they ended up doing the first record with Jim Abbiss. I don't know why. We'd already started recording four tracks with Mike Crossey and they really liked the recording process. It was all really whirlwind and secretive, but I got on really well with them."

Despite being taken off the first LP by Bell, a lasting bond had been forged between the band and the producer. Ford's involvement in the early stages of the band's work would set a pattern – giving him the most consistent production role in the band's ongoing history. "They're one of the best bands you could ever wish to work with as a producer," he explains of his relationship with them. "They're not only very good at what they do, and obviously Alex is a great songwriter, but they're also really easy to work with.

"They're not pretentious or difficult; they just want to push themselves to the best sound they can make. They're not arsey about it. Helders will happily take direction from me even though he's a much better drummer than me."

But for the first LP, the producer brought in to replace Ford at the mixing desk was the fast-rising Abbiss. Although his most glorious production work, including Arctic Monkeys, still lay ahead of him, Jim Abbiss already had a diverse and significant career. Starting out in the early Eighties, he'd been involved with guitar and electronic bands and had been inspired by the DIY approach of post-punk, early hip hop and electro music to the extent that he'd built his own drum machine.

Abbiss secured his first studio job at Spaceward near Cambridge in 1986, where he trained under Owen Morris. After that he moved to the Power Plant studios in London, in 1988, where his credits included the string arrangement for chart artist Sam Brown. It was also here that he first encountered the acid house movement, taking part in countless remix sessions before becoming chief engineer at Maison Rouge.

He hooked up with Steve Hillage, of System 7 and The Orb, and then started working with seminal Bristol sound producer Nellee Hooper, who involved Abbiss in Björk's *Debut* LP and Massive Attack's *Protection*. This in turn led to Abbiss working with James Lavelle on his UNKLE recordings and The Verve on 'Bittersweet Symphony'. By the time he was approached to work with Arctic Monkeys, Abbiss had just finished working with cult electro-pop act Ladytron.

Arctic Monkeys were something of a dream job for Abbiss. His productions tended to treat recording as part of the creative process and he was at his most fulfilled when he could step into a roomful of musicians and help direct their sound. Confronted by the raw energy of the band, Abbiss set about transferring their sound to studio tracks that maintained the edge and punch of their live performances.

"I want to work with artists who I think are amazing, so to get the best out of them I have to raise what I'm doing as well," he told *Sound On Sound*. "The Arctic Monkeys, for instance, are brilliant musicians, and Alex is a great singer. Like a lot of classic British bands, going back to The Beatles, they don't play complicated stuff when the singer is telling a story, but in the gaps in between they do really interesting stuff."

Apart from 'Mardy Bum', the whole of the first album was recorded at Chapel Studios, in South Thoresby, Lincolnshire in just 15 days, with Abbiss assisted by engineer Ewan Davies. Handily located just an hour's drive from Sheffield, Chapel was chosen for its live recording facilities. "It's a great studio for a live band and it has one of the best microphone collections in the country," Abbiss explained.

For Arctic Monkeys, Chapel Studios was something of a step up. The diverse range of previous artists who had used its facilities included Simple Minds, OMD, Black Grape, Wet Wet Wet, Del Amitri, Bad Company, Napalm Death, The Fall, Lindisfarne, Ten Years After and The Streets.

To capture the live interaction and chemistry between the band, Abbiss decided to record the whole group together with James, Andy and Alex around Matt's kit and everyone wearing headphones. The drum kit was miked up and the two guitar amps were put into a separate sound booth, while the bass amp was taken out and set up in the corridor. The band could play live but everything was recorded on separate channels.

Arctic Monkeys had been touring relentlessly and, for the most part, playing live for two years the songs that they were now recording. When they had originally recorded them with Alan Smyth, they had only just got to know many of the songs. Now they could rattle through them at breakneck speed, which is exactly what they did at every gig.

The only problem was that the tracks sounded miles away from the 2Fly versions and Alex's lyrics were delivered so fast that at times they became a blur. "They had done a lot of touring and were playing things very fast, so I generally tried to get them to play a bit slower so you could hear the words," as Abbiss explained to *Mix*.

Apart from 'Riot Van', which had recently undergone several changes and was still being worked on by the band, none of the songs needed much in the way of pre-production. But they did need slowing down.

The original idea had been to play the songs live without any vocals, getting Alex, Matt and James to overdub the vocal parts later. For a while, says Abbiss, this baffled Alex. Singing while playing the songs had become automatic, so naturally he wanted to perform the songs as he did live. In the end, however, they recorded two-thirds of them with Alex's vocals overdubbed.

Abbiss also added some innovations in the way he used the mics. Instead of using EQ controls for the guitars, for example, he recorded using two microphones with radically different tones: the Royer 121 and the SM57. If he wanted to brighten the treble on the guitar sound he'd increase the SM57; if he wanted to give it more warmth he'd use the Royer.

The master was taken to Olympic Studio in London for mixing, where Abbiss insisted on using the studio's vintage 16-channel EMI TG1 desk that it acquired from Abbey Road. The only song on the LP not produced by him was 'Mardy Bum', which Laurence Bell felt needed extra work at the end of Abbiss's session. By this time the Monkeys were already touring Germany and Abbiss had moved onto his next assignment, so Alan Smyth was sent over to Munich to record a new version closer to the one they'd first done together in 2004.

Whatever People Say I Am, That's What I'm Not was filled with distilled versions of Turner's chronicles of life in High Green, the youthful experiences that would (unexpectedly) connect with different cultures across the globe. It featured the band's two number one singles, as well as reworked tracks from the self-released EP and the 2Fly sessions.

The album brimmed with the subtle immediacy of Turner's lyrics and the fluctuating urgency of the band's arrangements. Some songs posed as partying and clubbing anthems, hiding more complex meanings in their deeper layers, while others offered apparently contradictory conclusions on the uneasy compromises of teenage life.

Loaded with tracks made famous by online file sharing, the album spawned songs that became radio classics without ever having had a single release. 'Mardy Bum' appeared on radio playlists throughout the UK in mid-2006; 'A Certain Romance' was ranked at number 90 in *Pitchfork Media*'s Top 100 Tracks of 2006; *NME* also placed 'A Certain Romance' at number 10 in their list of 100 Tracks of the Decade.

With the debut album finished and ready for release, the band now needed a name for it. In the end the title was taken from Alan Sillitoe's novel *Saturday Night & Sunday Morning*, about a young working-class philanderer in Fifties Nottingham.

In 1960 director Karel Reisz had turned the book into a cult film, starring Albert Finney. The producers had given the film the tag line: "Saturday night you have your fling at life . . . and Sunday morning you face up to it!"

Alex Turner had been drawn to it, noting similarities between its depiction of life in late Fifties Nottingham, the main character's fantasies and working-class escapism, and the subjects of his own songs. But it was a line spoken by Finney's character, Arthur, which struck a chord with Alex: "Whatever people say I am, that's what I'm not."

The band were by now surrounded by a hype machine that had started spinning out of control. Journalists were questioning who they really were and how they got to be so famous so quickly. "Whatever people say I am, that's what I'm not" neatly captured the band's current mood. It also flicked two fingers in the direction of their detractors.

Journalist Chris Heath noticed how Alex seemed amused by the defiance in the title. "I suppose we thought that people were talking about us then," he told Heath. He was right; people were talking about him, even doorstepping his granddad – leading to his famous grandfatherly advice: "I think you might have overdone it, sausage."

Shortly before the LP came out, Matt said he hoped the record would put the whole internet question to bed, neutralise the side issues and re-focus everyone onto the music. As early as January 2006, several newspapers (including *The Sun*) had noted how the LP's title reflected the band's attitude to the hype. "It's flattering for people to say we're the next big thing," Matt Helders told the *Liverpool Echo* in early 2006. "It's nice to hear. But you don't want it to go so far that it's not about the music, that it's about people being told to like it. I don't want people to like us for the wrong reasons. But I think people aren't stupid. They can see through it and realise that they do actually like us."

Alex concurred: "For where we're at [the hype] is too much, compared to what stage we're at as a band. We're just starting really. The attention sets the record up to be a disappointment."

In the end, of course, it barely mattered what anyone wrote about the album – with the possible exception of a message from author Alan Sillitoe, who, Matt later revealed, wrote to the band saying he felt privileged that they'd taken their title from his book.

★   ★   ★

The band had celebrated their debut Domino single going to number one by spending one of their rare days off down the pub. Dedicating the LP's cover to a similar all-day drinking session made absolute sense. An afternoon in the pub was as emblematic of Arctic Monkeys as a guitar, a T-shirt and a bottle of White Magic cider. So they asked their mate Chris McClure to do a photo shoot for the album cover. Apart from being a friend, Chris was the frontman for The Violet May and the brother of Jon McClure. He was part of the clan.

Later, McClure was to claim he wasn't paid for the photo shoot, adding he was happy to do it for free as it gave him something to tell the grandchildren. According to the band, they'd given him, one of his cousins and a friend £70 to spend on boozing in Liverpool. In the small hours of the next morning, having fulfilled his task admirably, Chris presented himself, cigarette in hand, for a photo shoot at The Korova Bar on Hope Street.

It was perhaps a sign of the times that, while the heavy drinking that the image conjured up went unremarked upon, the picture became controversial after the head of Scotland's NHS accused it of condoning smoking. Domino Records countered the criticism, saying the image could just as easily have been a warning about the damage caused by smoking. After all, there was no attempt to make Chris look cool or alluring. For his part, McClure reportedly backed up his claim that he hadn't been paid by announcing he'd be giving up smoking due to lack of funds (although there was some uncertainty about whether he followed up on this).

With the Christmas rush of festive releases looming, there had been little point in releasing the album before the New Year. The LP's release was eventually scheduled for Monday, January 30, 2006.

By the time that Laurence Bell had signed the band, the hype around Arctic Monkeys had switched up a gear. The signing had heralded the start of Monkey mania and so, instead of having to take the usual route and start by promoting the band, Domino and their PR team found themselves trying to calm everyone down and exert some control over the media madness. As a result, every blog site and online magazine was desperate for anything they could get.

As online publicist Serena Wilson recalls: "In the end my job became just saying no to everyone. Everyone wanted to get close to them, to post their music, and my job became managing the 'Nos'."

This, along with the fans' history of file sharing, encouraged an understandable jumpiness about the LP leaking onto websites before its release date. Sure enough, by mid-December the entirety of *Whatever People Say I Am, That's What I'm Not* had been leaked onto a file-sharing site. Sensing time might not be on their side, Bell took a unilateral decision and brought the release date forward a week to January 23, 2006, officially because of "high demand" for the LP.

As it turned out, he needn't have worried. If online leaks had diminished demand, there would be little sign of it in the sales figures.

The album's product manager, Jonny Bradshaw, was on holiday at the time and wouldn't return in time for the release. So Bell called Bradshaw to warn him about the revised release date. "I remember going: 'Oh shit!'," Bradshaw told *The Guardian*. But then he realised his absence was immaterial. "Nothing we could do as a label could make a difference to this band. There was no marketing plan. There was no anti-marketing plan. The stock was sitting in our warehouse, and the normal rules didn't apply. This was happening already."

According to the critic-rating aggregator *Metacritic*, the Arctic Monkeys debut received almost universal acclaim from critics – scoring an average 82 points out of a possible 100. The press and radio coverage had been building up a head of steam that was sure to erupt on release day. Even outspoken feminist Germaine Greer was heard praising Matt Helders' ability to "lay down a beat" on BBC 2's *Newsnight Review*.

That said, not everyone joined the Monkeys' media bandwagon. *Pitchfork*'s review of the album, by Scott Plagenhoef, summed it up as "less than life changing", pithily commenting that the "Arctic Monkeys are yet another in a string of buzzsaw guitar bands with northern accents".

LA Weekly's ambiguous review of the LP, published before its US release in February, approved of the album itself but dismissed the internet hype that went with it. "Arctic Monkeys are the most cynical band in the world. Their surge to prominence in the UK (and hipster notoriety in the US) has been guided by an amazingly successful hype campaign . . . Yet in interviews the band are keen to emphasise their down-to-earth northern roots – '*What's a MySpace? What's a hype?*' Note: Arctic Monkeys recently completed a series of sell-out dates in the US on the strength of their MySpace page; and their LP just became the fastest-selling debut album in UK history. Apparently the Monkeys now feel the need to obfuscate, lest the truth damage their rock mythology. That's like pretending you met your girlfriend in the pub rather than online in case people take the piss."

Despite efforts to replicate the 2Fly recordings and create faithfully improved versions of the songs, some critics and fans complained that the official LP had lost the edge of *Beneath The Boardwalk*. Given that longer-term fans had been living with the old material for two years, it was perhaps inevitable that some would prefer the old recordings.

Tim Jonze at the *NME*, on the other hand, declared the album to be the voice of a generation, with more than enough fire in its belly to inspire other teens to pick up a guitar. "Essentially this is a stripped-down, punk rock record with every touchstone of Great British Music covered," eulogised Jonze. "The Britishness of The Kinks, the melodic nous of The Beatles, the sneer of Sex Pistols, the wit of The Smiths, the groove of The Stone Roses, the anthems of Oasis, the clatter of The Libertines . . .

"So you get the tongue-tied tart in 'Dancing Shoes', the bored band-watcher in 'Fake Tales Of San Francisco' and the guy whose girl's got the hump in 'Mardy Bum' – all sung with a voice so authentic it could land the lead role in the Hovis ads."

Website *Music OMH*, which had been following the Monkeys' story with a commendable detachment from early on, joined in the praise, writing that the album would make its listeners "fall in love with music all over again".

And in *The Observer*, Sarah Boden declared that Alex was "one of the most acutely observant men in pop, his lyrics cast a jaundiced eye over a landscape that is urban but steadfastly provincial . . . It strikes a universal sense of recognition in Britain's alienated spotty teens."

16

Monkeys For Sale

IN the months leading up to the LP's release, Paul Scaife, founder of *Record Of The Day*, sounded a note of caution. Speaking to *The Guardian* in September 2005, he said the sudden hysteria and hype may have made the band appear much bigger than they really were.

He was confident that the LP would sell well but pointed out that the buzz around new bands tends to fade quickly and questioned whether their sales would be as staggering as the hype implied. Scaife now jokes with hindsight about not being any kind of expert on Arctic Monkeys. But his note of caution was based on sound observation.

In the months that followed, Arctic Monkeys proved the hype had solid foundations. But the real litmus test would take place with the release of their LP. This was the moment when the buzz had to translate into the hard and fast ker-ching of shop tills. In the end, no one would be disappointed. Probably not even Scaife.

As soon as it was released, *Whatever People Say I Am, That's What I'm Not* began selling at a truly astonishing rate. As the day of release approached, 200 fans were reported to be queuing outside HMV in Sheffield, which had arranged to open its doors to start selling the record at midnight.

As the day went on, HMV reported a predicted 60,000 sales on day one; extended over the week, these figures suggested it might eclipse Oasis's *Definitely Maybe*, at that point the fastest-selling UK rock debut LP. Meanwhile, Amazon were reporting more sales in a single day than in the entire first week of *Franz Ferdinand*. In the end, the LP shifted just under 120,000 copies on its first day of release, selling 82 copies a minute and breaking all records to become the fastest-selling UK LP in history to date.

The figures were hugely impressive and were building towards an equally amazing full week of sales. What made these first-day statistics all the more astounding was that this was happening in January, traditionally a flat period for record sales, and it was happening not only after the Monkeys had allowed early versions of the songs to be shared for free, but also a month after the whole album had been leaked online.

"Versions of most of these songs were, indeed, freely available to anyone who knew their way around the internet," reported Chris Heath in *The Observer.* "And yet, instead of cannibalising sales, this inspired people to buy a physical copy of this music in record-breaking numbers. The lesson seemed to be that if the music is good enough, and people are excited enough about it, then they are still thrilled to be able to own their own, tangible copy of it."

By the end of the first week the album had sold a massive 363,735 copies, more than the rest of the UK Top 20 combined, securing its position as both the fastest-selling debut album in British history to date and the fastest-selling LP by a band ever. It not only surpassed sales of *Definitely Maybe* but, more tellingly, it smashed the record held by Hear'Say, the act created on TV talent show *Popstars*. Compared with the cost and complication of a TV programme, Arctic Monkeys had presented a leaner, more musically focused alternative model.

Having secured a place in history in the UK charts, the album's success began to spread overseas. Its release in the United States on February 21, 2006 saw it become the second fastest-selling debut indie album in US history. It turned over around 34,000 copies in its first week and reached number 24 in the album charts. In time the LP would also earn the band two Grammy Award nominations and go on to sell a total of approximately 300,000 – notably fewer than the album's British sales but enough to secure them a base in the USA.

The album went to number one in Australia and Ireland and to number six in Denmark, number eight in the Netherlands and Finland, number nine in Belgium and Japan, and into the Top 20 in Switzerland, Germany, New Zealand and France. It also went on to gain a series of awards and accolades: it was named as the fifth greatest British album of all time by the *NME* and Album of the Year in the magazine's annual awards; it was also made Album of the Year by *Crossbeat* in Japan, Album of the Year by *Time* in the US, Album of the Year by *Hot Press* and Best International Album at the Meteor Music Awards in Ireland, and Best British Album at the Brit Awards in 2007. Off the back of the album, Arctic Monkeys also won Best New International Artist at Mexico's Oye! awards. *Rolling Stone* would later list it at number 41 in the 100 Best LPs of the Decade.

In 2009, *Whatever People Say I Am, That's What I'm Not* would be voted the ninth greatest album ever by MTV's online fan poll. Meanwhile, sales in the UK went platinum four times while it also achieved platinum sales in Argentina and Australia, and gold in Japan, Canada, Denmark and New Zealand.

★   ★   ★

In the normal routine of a rock band, it is customary to schedule tours around a release. For Arctic Monkeys, with their continuous gigging, it was more or less impossible to organise a release that didn't coincide with a tour. True, there had been the odd week off, but that was usually either because they were in the studio recording or because it was Christmas.

But, by fluke, they had organised their live schedule to celebrate their debut single's release, marking the occasion with two sold-out gigs in Sheffield. And from here on in, the tours began to take shape around increasingly coordinated release and recording schedules. 'When The Sun Goes Down' was timed to coincide with a home gig in Sheffield, although it only just scraped into the schedule, while the start of their next tour would perfectly marry up with the release of the LP – although it felt more like the record fitting into the tour dates than the other way around.

Having taken over a month off from touring, Arctic Monkeys' first live date of 2006 was a warm-up at The Kultkomplex Café in Cologne, Germany, on January 17. Despite their month-long break, the Monkeys strolled back into the live arena every bit as tight and powerful as they had been at the end of 2005. The gig also featured two extra songs in the band's set list: 'You Probably Couldn't See For The Lights But You Were Staring Straight At Me' and 'Bigger Boys And Stolen Sweethearts'.

Returning to the UK for their debut British show of 2006, the show had been timed to coincide with the release of 'When The Sun Goes Down'. For a second time the band would end up celebrating a number one single with a Sheffield gig, this time at The Leadmill.

The excitement had already been enormous in the run-up to the gig, as the *NME* Awards tour was about to kick off in Dublin the following day, with Arctic Monkeys as main support band. The Leadmill was the first home gig of 2006 as well as being a send-off party for the *NME* tour. Adding to this heady brew, the single had been confirmed at number one earlier that evening. It couldn't fail to be a big night.

The Sun's gossip columnists, usually found loitering outside bars and clubs in London's West End, knew they had to be there. More commonly known for revealing Victoria Beckham's new underwear range and barrier-stepping A-listers at film premieres, showbiz page 'Bizarre' glowingly reviewed the gig. In a further indication of the Monkeys' growing success, the write-up not only drooled over the Sheffield lads but also referred to them as superstar chart toppers – even though they had only two singles to their name.

"It had just gone mad. You'd got paparazzi in the city, ringing you, trying to talk to anybody that had any association with them," says Barney Vernon. "They were all outside The Leadmill, trying to get in. It had just gone bonkers."

The Sheffield show sold out the minute tickets went on sale. Once it became apparent that the band would be celebrating their second chart-topping single, everyone in and around the city wanted to go. By the night of the gig, £8 tickets were changing hands for up to £300. Arctic Monkeys had given the whole of Sheffield something to celebrate and now it was the band's chance to say thank you – which Alex duly did during the course of the gig, not only acknowledging the city but also his home suburb, High Green.

The audience was a mixture of long-term fans and new converts. Fans old and new were united in voice, bellowing along to the songs. As the crowd's combined vocal chords stretched and swelled to fill the room and the guitars chimed the introductory notes of 'When The Sun Goes Down', Alex held his index finger aloft – signifying their new singles chart position. But the best was yet to come.

The band had doubtless intended to come back to their home city on January 22 to celebrate: they knew the singles chart would be announced that night and they could bank on at least a Top 10 hit; they had known since autumn 2005 that they would be on the *NME* tour; and they knew the gig would be their live UK debut of 2006.

What they didn't know was that Laurence Bell would be bringing the LP release date forward to January 23, which was a masterstroke of timing. Even as the last chords of 'A Certain Romance' echoed into the gloom of the Sheffield night, fans were queuing to buy the new LP at their local HMV.

More than a celebration of their new number one single, The Leadmill on January 22, 2006 became the *de facto* launch night for the Arctic Monkeys album tour. Bell's decision had ensured that *Whatever People Say I Am, That's What I'm Not* would stay at number one throughout the three weeks of the *NME* Awards tour.

Had the album come out on its scheduled date, January 30, the band would have been playing an *NME* tour date at The Academy in Newcastle. Instead, the album had been launched at a home gig, in a city awash with excited Monkeys fans and media pundits. The newspapers and every other form of media, new and old, were flooded with Arctic Monkeys stories.

Bell and the Domino team had probably anticipated that every fan at The Leadmill that night – plus a further multitude who couldn't get tickets – would rush out to buy a copy of the LP the following morning. But it got better: the local branch of HMV was opening its doors at midnight, allowing fans to go straight from the gig to buy the album, becoming the first people to own legitimate copies of the LP.

As the gig came to a close, Alex prodded his local followers, entreating them to "go and buy the album", adding, "though you've probably got it from the internet already". As it turned out, the fans didn't need any prodding – hordes of them flooded out of the venue and into HMV.

17

Riding The New Musical Express

FOR the first couple of months of 2006, Arctic Monkeys were booked as the main support act on the prestigious *NME* Awards tour, introducing audiences to the best new bands while celebrating established headliners – a showcase for acts the magazine said were hot right now and those they were tipping for the future.

The line-up for 2006 was exceptional: Maximo Park as headliner and Arctic Monkeys, We Are Scientists and Mystery Jets as support. But by the time Arctic Monkeys arrived in Ireland for the first date, it had become abundantly clear which act was the biggest draw, whatever the official running order.

The tour opened at The Ambassadors in Dublin on January 23. The album had been selling by the cargo-load all day. Britain's brightest indie rock hopefuls were playing the opening night as their record was breaking album sales history.

When the *NME*'s website celebrated the concert the following morning, it was by no means obvious if they remembered who headlined the show. After comparing it to Oasis's legendary gig at Dublin's Tivoli Theatre, which marked the release of *Definitely Maybe*, the *NME* acknowledged that Arctic Monkeys were about to eclipse their Mancunian elders with the fastest-selling rock debut of all time.

Every band on the tour received a massive reception that night, but the other bands made an unusual number of references to the Monkeys during their sets. Blaine Harrison of Mystery Jets reminded everyone they'd been met by a few fans of their own at the airport, while We Are Scientists amused themselves by namedropping Arctic Monkeys in their between-song banter, testing how much audience response they got from each mention.

As ever, the Monkeys tried to distance themselves from the media jamboree. Alex's first public comment on the sales came when he arrived onstage that night. "So it's a fuckin' phenomenon then, eh?" he sneered into the mic. The band answered by blazing their way through a by-now familiar pattern of songs, only interrupted by the bizarre array of clothing flung by the crowd – provoking Turner into calling one bra-flinging woman "stupid".

After two sell-out nights at The Ambassadors, the tour moved on to Ulster Hall, Belfast on January 25. Reviewing the gig for *The Observer*, Sarah Boden noted the absurdity of giving Arctic Monkeys second billing sandwiched between We Are Scientists and Maximo Park.

The band were still performing with a cocky but disarming lack of showmanship. Wearing the standard jeans and T-shirts, their casual attire, like their casual attitude, reinforced their connection with the crowd. Even their silence could speak volumes. The most Alex had to say to the crowd in Belfast was a throwaway "Awfully nice to see ya." For most of the rest of the set he dispensed with any niceties, as the band delivered song after song after song. In all, 10 numbers were squeezed into the limited set time the tour allowed them. The effect was ecstatic, however, with total strangers communing in song, merrily roaring their way through renditions of album tracks they now legitimately owned.

On January 27, the Awards tour charged into Glasgow Academy, on the 28th it filled the voluminous Corn Exchange in Edinburgh and on the day after it rolled into The Academy in Newcastle, to round off the Monkeys' first week at number one in the album charts. (They had only narrowly missed simultaneously being on top of *both* singles and albums charts.)

From here they moved on to Rock City in Nottingham on January 31, Leeds University on February 1 and then Liverpool University on February 2, followed by two nights at The Academy in Manchester on February 4 and 5.

With the album still at number one for a second week, the *NME* tour rolled back into Sheffield on February 7, this time to play The Octagon. With Maximo Park's willing consent, Arctic Monkeys were finally given top billing for their home gig.

For Mystery Jets, the running order change made little difference. If they felt any anxiety about fans who started baying for Arctic Monkeys from the moment the venue's doors opened, they could draw solace from the contingent of Jets fans calling for 'Zoo Time' – which the band duly played.

There was no doubting which band people had come to see, but Monkeys fans were in appreciative mood. They screamed and chanted for every act but reserved special applause for Maximo Park, thanking the band for stepping down from the headline spot.

The loudest response was of course saved for last. Communal singing started as soon as Arctic Monkeys opened with 'The View From The Afternoon'. The opening chords of 'I Bet You Look Good On The Dancefloor' sent crowd-surfers scurrying over the mosh pit and fans listened attentively to the new song, 'Leave Before The Lights Come On', before hollering their approval.

There had been mass excitement amongst the Monkeys' home crowd at recent gigs, but this was a total celebration. Even Andy Nicholson, who had built a reputation around his dour stage presence, seemed to be grinning helplessly all the way through. The good mood was infectious and soon the crowd was bouncing up and down, mischievously shouting for the band to play their cover of 'Love Machine' by Girls Aloud – which they had recently performed on BBC Radio 1's *Live Lounge*.

The audience was clearly taking the piss, and Arctic Monkeys took the gesture as intended. Pretending to respond, the band played the opening chords of 'Love Machine' but Alex suddenly cut the track off and spat into the microphone: "Is that all you like us for? A fuckin' Girls Aloud song? Well, you can have 'A Certain Romance' and fuck off."

The day after Sheffield they played The Academy in Birmingham, followed by the University of East Anglia in Norwich on February 9, then back to the Great Hall in Cardiff on February 11, followed by Cambridge Corn Exchange on February 12 and Guildhall Portsmouth on February 15.

On the latter date, Arctic Monkeys had also been invited to the 2006 Brits Awards ceremony, the UK's annual equivalent of the Grammys. They'd been told in advance they'd won Breakthrough Act of the Year, their first ever Brit Award, but they opted to stay and play Portsmouth. "What's the point of cancelling something that you right like, to go and sit in a room full of people that you fucking hate more than anyone? You'd just be sat there in the room going, 'Oh God, I'm going to punch someone . . .'," reasoned Jamie in *The Observer*, reflecting the band's distrust of the Brits and record label executives.

Instead, they videoed an acceptance speech on tour to be shown in their absence – grabbing Keith Murray from We Are Scientists and persuading him to do the speech as if he was in the band. When the video was shown at the Brits and simultaneously on national TV, it showed the four Monkeys sitting in silence while Murray went through the motions of how grateful he was.

From here the tour moved on to The Dome in Brighton on February 16 and, finally, The Brixton Academy on the following night. The 4,272-capacity venue was rammed with a young and excitable crowd. After joining We Are Scientists onstage for 'Cash Cow', Alex orchestrated the largest singalong yet of 'When The Sun Goes Down'.

They had dominated the album chart throughout the *NME* tour, sticking to the number one slot for as long as the tour was on. But as Brixton brought their triumphal Awards tour to an end, Arctic Monkeys' domination of the LP charts came to a close.

Inevitably, by now touring was beginning to have an effect on the band's personal lives. They had managed to have three days off around Valentine's Day, but a life on tour meant they were more often away than at home.

18

A Certain Romance

GIVEN the band's reticence about talking to the press and their disinterest in talking about anything other than their music, it's not surprising the Monkeys managed to keep much of their private lives out of public view. There may have been a promise of romance (or at least sex) in Alex's lyrics, but not in his interviews. Not that the band had much time left for girlfriends, between their hefty touring and recording schedules.

With the tabloid press and its gossip pages now taking an interest in the band, their days of privacy were clearly numbered. But the red-top press was not going to have an easy time digging up salacious gossip. Rare though it was for a teenage rock band, sex and drugs were not at the top of Arctic Monkeys' agenda.

By their own accounts, Matt and Alex had only a few girlfriends by this point – one of them being Lauren Bradwell. According to Lauren, who spoke to the *News Of The World* in 2005, she dated them both when they were in their fourth year at Stocksbridge School; Matt first and then, a few months after they'd split, in time-honoured style she asked her friend to ask if Alex would go out with her.

She recounted how Alex was already writing songs on the back of his schoolbooks in lessons, and recalled an occasion when Andy and Alex came over and drank their way through her dad's booze cupboard. According to Lauren, Alex was shy but popular with the girls at school.

The relationship lasted for four months – which made it seem serious at the time – but she dumped him for an older boy with a Peugeot 405, which, she not unreasonably claims, inspired Alex to write 'Bigger Boys And Stolen Sweethearts', the B-side to 'I Bet You Look Good On The Dancefloor'. At the time, all her female friends were jealous of her car-driving new boyfriend. But with the benefit of hindsight, she admitted she'd probably made the wrong decision.

Matt had started seeing his girlfriend, Amy Hipwell, while they were both studying at Barnsley College for A-levels. She'd been with him from near the start of Arctic Monkeys and, while Matt had been busy beating his way around the UK, had moved on to study interior design in Huddersfield.

Although the papers would eventually track her down, Amy was by all accounts quiet and unassuming. When she did say anything to the press, she admitted to being somewhat overwhelmed by Matt's newfound fame.

"I bought the *NME* the other day and the Arctic Monkeys were all over it," she told a journalist – seemingly surprised that her chart-topping boyfriend had picked up a bit of press attention.

Serena Wilson thinks one of the reasons Arctic Monkeys kept their centred view of life during the meteoric rise was their long-term connections (such as Amy) to their previous lives. "It's not really rock'n'roll, but they were a working band, that whole rock'n'roll thing seemed really old fashioned – and also they were all long-term friends. It keeps you grounded."

In February 2006, Alex had met Johanna Bennett, the first big love of his life and his first rock'n'roll girlfriend. Johanna was an elegant, black-haired 20-year-old student and singer from the Fens, just outside Peterborough. When they met, she was studying for a psychology degree at Goldsmiths University in south-east London. She was also lead singer of a band called Totalizer, and had connections with Dirty Pretty Things guitarist Anthony Rossomando, who was producing Totalizer's demos.

It was through her musical connections that she ended up meeting Alex outside a bar. "We got into this really intense conversation," she later recalled for the *Peterborough Telegraph*, "and then Alex called me the next day, and we started seeing each other.

"I went through a lot of the 'firsts' with Alex and his band's career. It was very exciting at the time."

The relationship, although kept typically off-screen by Alex, could be intense when they got the opportunity to see each other. It was never going to be an easy ride for either of them. His relentless rehearsal, recording and touring schedule meant most of the contact between them had to be over the phone.

116

In one of the few glimpses into their life together, Johanna was overheard talking by the *Daily Mirror*'s '3 a.m. Girls' at the Mercury Music Prize: "It's really hard because I hardly ever see him. It can be three to four weeks at a time that he'll have to go away with the band sometimes. Our relationship is always on the phone. It's like one long text message – and I miss him."

Although they'd been together for longer, the periods of absence were equally hard on Amy and Matt. It didn't help that both Amy and Johanna were students during the period when the band were still on their way up. By the time Alex and Johanna got together they were on the verge of huge success, but it would still be a long time before royalty cheques started flopping onto the doormat.

With the band away touring most of the time, no one had the ready money to visit each other. Johanna and Alex's relationship wasn't destined to last, but on one of their breaks together they co-wrote 'Fluorescent Adolescent'. They started working on the song in a hotel room. "Alex and I were on holiday," Johanna recalled, "and he asked me what I thought of this line he had just written. It went from there, with us trading lyrics backwards and forwards until it became the song."

When they returned from the holiday, Alex finished the track off at home in Sheffield. Depicting the crumpled dreams of an ageing woman stuck in a boring life, it became a stand-out track on the Arctic Monkeys' sophomore LP. It also featured some of Alex's (and Johanna's) most poignant lyric writing.

Perhaps unsurprisingly, given the relationship between its authors, some of the most striking imagery is sexual.

Another musical legacy of their relationship was the equally standout '505', which was said to have been written by Alex on his way to meet Johanna in a hotel in New York. The song aptly deals with the difficulties of being in a relationship and not being able to spend time together.

After they'd spent New Year's Eve together at the end of 2006, the couple split up in January 2007, long before their relationship came anywhere near the "very common crisis" the couple had identified in 'Fluorescent Adolescent'. The problems they faced, so the newspapers speculated, may have had more to do with Alex's relentless tour duties and the band's continuing penniless existence.

Alex was destined for a longer relationship with Alexa Chung and

Johanna would marry Kings Of Leon guitarist Matthew Followill – with whom she'd move to the USA and have a son, Knox, in 2011.

If the relationship had indeed run into difficulties because of Alex's lack of ready cash, then there was something of an irony in one of his parting gifts to her; he insisted on registering her on the songwriting credits of 'Fluorescent Adolescent'. By the time their co-written song came out as a single their relationship was truly over, but the track peaked at number five in the UK singles chart and the royalty payments soon started amassing.

At one stage they were reported to be high enough for Johanna not to have to worry about her own career (although, as she was living with the guitarist of Kings Of Leon, that may have been a given anyway).

One further legacy remained from the relationship with Johanna. While he was on holiday in France in 2007, Alex recorded a set of songs apparently inspired by the break-up, later released as part of a side project called The Last Shadow Puppets.

19

Tales Of San Francisco

AFTER the *NME* Awards tour closed at The Brixton Academy, the band's next appointment was at the awards ceremony itself on February 23, 2006, at Hammersmith Palais, London. Once again they made history, this time by being the first act to be awarded both Best New Band and Best British Band.

But it didn't stop there; the Best Track award for 'I Bet You Look Good On The Dancefloor' gave them a hat trick that's only been matched by Oasis and The Strokes. Unlike the Brits, the band attended the *NME* Awards ceremony and for the first time the world was treated to an Arctic Monkeys acceptance speech.

Mooching onto the stage, looking like something between a wolf pack and a bunch of stoners hunting for a dropped spliff, the four boys wore coats and jackets that gave the appearance they'd either just arrived or were about to leave. Alex's acceptance speech for the Best New Band award started with a well-aimed jab at the assembled audience: "Nobody told us it were fancy dress," he giggled. Having landed the jab, he squared a knee to the groin by adding: "I don't thank you [pointing to the music industry audience], but who voted for it and that – appreciated."

By the time they were awarded Best Track, the boys had de-robed a little and, thanks to the free booze, were a bit more relaxed. With the four of them still hanging around the stage, looking much less wolfish, Andy passed the speech over to Alex – who said he'd already used all his lines up. "Sugababes though," grinned Alex as a cheer came up from the girls' table, "how about that . . . thank you girls."

"Wrong key though," chipped in Andy, bringing the acceptance speech to a standstill.

The party that ambled onto the stage for their third and final prize had clearly been enjoying the complimentary drinks. They'd also been chatting to some of their new best friends, such as Keith Murray, and, loath to interrupt a good conversation, had invited them onstage to join in the acceptance.

"In all honesty," swaggered Alex, in a statement that would wind up the band's detractors as much as it amused their supporters, "who else were going to be Best British Band? You know what I mean – you can't write about something that much and then tell us we're not Best British Band . . ."

With that, and a quick aside about Russell Brand making 'northern' jokes, Alex departed, saying: "This is the last, we'll not win any more, I promise." He was right. There was nothing left to win. Besides which, he'd run out of things to say.

Having scooped up their Brat Awards, the Monkeys returned to their European tour, picking their way through Germany and the Low Countries accompanied by Mystery Jets. First, following a night of *NME* Awards after-parties, the band pitched up in Paris to play La Trabendo on February 24. The previous night's celebrations had taken their toll, leaving the band looking tired and a little bruised.

Monkey mania had been building in France for six months and the tickets sold out within hours of being announced. In a culture that expects its musicians to be melodramatically showy, the Monkeys' deliberately British, deadpan delivery had every opportunity to fall flat. But the crowd, although nothing like the multitudes the band had come to expect in the UK, reacted joyously to the music. Even so, at least one French blogger observed that the band didn't seem too happy to be there – Andy adopting his trademark grimace and refusing to smile, despite Alex's efforts to coax a grin out of him.

Their next dates took in the Mousonturm in Frankfurt and Amsterdam's Melkweg, which they played without Mystery Jets while the father-and-son duo returned for an in-store gig at HMV's flagship in Oxford Street. After Mystery Jets rejoined them in Brussels at the Botanique, they returned to Germany for more sold-out gigs at Grosse Freiheit 36 in Hamburg, a few doors up from where The Beatles played, followed by the Fritzclub in Berlin and the Bürgerhaus Stollwerck in Cologne on March 4.

Having rounded off their short European tour in Germany, Arctic Monkeys were ready to make their first real impact in the USA, playing a couple of dates in San Francisco and Los Angeles before performing at South By South West (SXSW), the North American showcase festival.

SXSW was a recognised industry platform, an entry point for bands trying to break into the US market. The news that Arctic Monkeys were playing had already started to send ripples across the Atlantic.

Domino's US sister label released *Whatever People Say I Am, That's What I'm Not* in North America a month after its UK release, on February 21, 2006. At first the band didn't seem to be in any rush to support its release. In contrast to the UK, where they toured relentlessly throughout the period it was at number one, they were content to let their American cousins learn the album's songs without hearing them live.

But, although it was nothing like Monkey mania at home, Arctic Monkeys had been attracting considerable attention.

Their entire American tour sold out within minutes of being announced – greatly encouraged by the US press carrying stories about the band's successes at home. By the time they arrived in the USA, the American press was clamouring to cover the band.

But despite this initial good favour, they faced an uphill task that was not of their own making. The repeated failure by a long list of British bands to translate to American audiences left the press highly sceptical about groups with a British media buzz behind them.

Veteran US online music pioneer and commentator Tim Quirk describes a long list of UK acts that contributed to this cynicism: "The Smiths were maybe the first band I'd put in this category – hugely important in the UK but commercially underwhelming (no matter how beloved) in the States, with the list after them encompassing Manic Street Preachers, Happy Mondays, Stone Roses, Blur, Pulp, and The Libertines." The existence of this lineage certainly made the Monkeys' job harder.

When the band had finally reappeared on American soil, on March 11, 2006, it was three weeks after the album's release. But they were clearly approaching the US with a different set of tactics to the UK. They largely eschewed TV appearances at home, but they filmed live for TV sketch show *Saturday Night Live* on the day they arrived in the US.

It was a spectacular start. *Saturday Night Live* was highly respected in the

USA, as indicated by Hollywood star Matt Dillon performing as that night's guest host. For a band wanting to get noticed in North America, it was as good an introduction as you could get.

After the show, the band jetted from the New York studio to San Francisco's Great American Hall, the obvious place to open their first proper US tour, which kicked off on March 13. The San Francisco gig started well, with the band in fiery form and the audience visibly warming to them. But halfway through 'Perhaps Vampires Is A Bit Strong But . . .', disaster struck as Andy's bass amp suddenly packed up.

While roadies rushed onstage to replace the faulty equipment, Alex stepped up to the microphone and sang a solo version of his new song, 'Despair In The Departure Lounge'. It was previously unheard and probably under-rehearsed, but the people who'd been pogoing to 'Vampires' seconds before were suddenly standing in silence, stunned by this unscheduled downbeat track.

With the song finished and the bass amp fixed, the full band swung straight back into 'Vampires' exactly where they'd left off and the awe-struck crowd surged back into their energetic mosh. They had handled a potentially catastrophic meltdown in a way that only a tour-hardened band could. It was a sublimely skilful response. When it was followed by 'Fake Tales Of San Francisco', even the most resistant critics' hearts had been melted.

At the start of the set, Alex had delivered a typically knowing introduction, referring to the band as "the Arctic Monkeys, that's us . . . the phenomenon known as . . .", before dryly mocking their own new status as "international superstars".

But by the end of the gig, they'd shown themselves more than worthy of the title. Sadly, however, neither Andy nor his bass amp would return to San Francisco with the Monkeys.

20

South By South West

AFTER San Francisco, the band moved on to the Henry Ford Theater in Los Angeles before heading to Austin, Texas for their first American festival. The South By South West Festival (or SXSW) had started in 1987 as a platform for regional independent music. Based in North America's largest university town, it had grown to become the most important international showcase in the USA. Having initially attracted 700 people to a one-stage event, it had grown by 2006 to feature more than 1,400 bands playing 60-plus stages over five days in a bacchanalian music industry orgy.

The challenge faced by most acts at South By South West was getting noticed amongst the bewildering choice of gigs and venues. But Arctic Monkeys confronted a different order of problem: the issue for them was how to avoid a roadblock outside their venue.

The news about Arctic Monkeys playing SXSW had gone globally viral as soon as it was announced. The organisers had initially decided to hold back information on the Monkeys, keeping the band's name off the line-up until a few days before the festival in an attempt to minimise problems with crowd control.

In the run-up to the gig, US music e-zine *Pitchfork* published a guide for festival-goers. Instead of recommending Arctic Monkeys, it urged attendees to save themselves heartache by accepting in advance that they wouldn't get into the venue, suggesting a list of other bands in venues that would be relatively empty. Even so, *Pitchfork* couldn't help but acknowledge that Arctic Monkeys were the band of SXSW 2006.

In the end, so many people assumed the Monkeys show at La Zona Rosa would be full that early arrivals walked straight into the gig. But those who turned up later weren't so lucky.

Alex arrived onstage wearing a white hoodie and was at first his usual reticent self. As the gig wore on, though, he became more effusive. Before playing 'Leave Before The Lights Come On', he took the opportunity to rebuff critics: "We're gonna play a new song for you now. One that's not on the album. Just to prove that we're here for the long term."

At the start of the gig the band had burst into 'Riot Van', the brooding new version of which they'd added onto the front of their set. With a long list of UK bands at the festival, several of them (including Mystery Jets, Plan B, The Subways and Dirty Pretty Things) made it into the Monkeys' audience. Among the American acts was Keith Murray, from We Are Scientists, who relived the *NME* tour by joining the band onstage – this time adding his guitar to 'Fake Tales Of San Francisco'. By the end of the gig the anticipated roadblock had formed outside the 1,200-capacity venue, with later estimates suggesting 5,000 people were trying to get in.

Andy Langer, writing in *The Austin Chronicle* a few days after the gig, concluded the band was "hard not to love . . . well-rested, well-rehearsed, and ridiculously tight, with rhythms that stopped on dimes and precariously stacked bridges and choruses that constantly seemed on the verge of collapsing onto each other, yet never did . . . how good was the SXSW debut of the Arctic Monkeys? No less powerful than the hype."

The American press, frosty in their response to yet another hyped Brit band, had begun to thaw. It's particularly notable that *The Austin Chronicle* had been somewhat cooler in their album review a week earlier.

Doubts about the hype, followed by affirmation of the band's live ability, soon became a running theme in reviews amassing around the US tour. Time and again, reviewers approached gigs wanting to dislike the band but found it impossible to carry their intentions through.

Amrit Singh summed up expectations neatly, when he wrote in New York blog *Stereogum*: "Half of you wants to see this band panned, the other to hear why this band are the biggest thing in Britain since Oasis, or The Beatles, or Jesus . . ."

On 20 March, the band were invited by Oasis to open their 19,800-capacity show at The Air Canada Centre, Toronto. The Monkeys received a rapturous response – even if Alex felt that, as the support act, they needed to rein themselves in, in deference to their childhood idols.

Still flying high, the following night they played a sold-out show at

Toronto's Phoenix Concert Theatre. In contrast to the vast Air Canada Centre, the Phoenix became a sea of jabbing fingers by the middle of the opening number, with everyone singing along for the remainder of the set. The band blasted through 60 minutes of frantic rock songs, with Turner teasing the adoring crowd, Helders unleashing a thundering barrage of beats and Nicholson barely coming up for air as he mined bass lines into his fret board.

Having torn their way through the opening four songs, Alex paused to rip off his hoodie and Andy to dump his Burberry, before launching into a sneering version of 'Vampires'. 'From The Ritz To The Rubble' sparked a frantic round of crowd-surfing, after which Turner entered into relaxed banter with the audience, suggesting to the front rows that there was a "little blonde girl" at the back who was having difficulty seeing the stage.

After a few more rousing songs, including 'Red Lights Indicate The Doors Are Secured' and 'Still Take You Home', Alex grabbed his water and lobbed it into the crowd, saying, "What's mine is yours," before taking his foot off the gas for 'Leave Before The Lights Come On'. Turner had clearly been buoyed up by opening for Oasis and his Phoenix performance showed it. America was strengthening the band's tightness and boosting their frontman's confidence.

Most reviewers, whether writing about the LP or the live show, couldn't help but agree that there was something special about this band. As blogger Mark Daniell concluded of the Phoenix show: "Showing he has the makings of a future arena rock star . . . [with] *Whatever People Say I Am, That's What I'm Not* poised to make the band a household name everywhere . . . I guess hype is a good thing. And for now, believe it."

Wild crowd reactions continued to follow the Monkeys wherever they were playing. Making one more stop in Canada, at Spectrum de Montréal on March 22, the band incited their fans to mosh, surf and sing their way through a riotous set, before turning south via Boston's Paradise Rock Club on their way back to New York.

Webster Hall on March 23 was their second New York outing. Since their last show, the buzz had increased massively. On arrival it looked like every Brit under 30 had snapped up tickets, along with New York's in-crowd and every available member of the Big Apple's music and lifestyle media. The gig was that week's hot ticket, and, in a pattern familiar to UK fans, $15 tickets were exchanging for $100 each.

If the crowd was bigger, it was also undoubtedly tamer than the more boisterous gathering that greeted their NYC debut at The Bowery a year earlier. Many were sporting voguish black horn-rimmed glasses, which caused Alex to observe, halfway through the set, "There's an awful lot of people with glasses on. There's a lot of glasses in New York," before the band ripped into 'You Probably Couldn't See For The Lights But You Were Staring Straight At Me'.

Despite the gig being rammed to the rafters with New York's arbiters of cool, the Monkeys soon had the audience jumping – eventually causing the mosh pit to explode with a particularly intense version of 'Fake Tales Of San Francisco'. The Webster Hall was soon reverberating to the cry of "Kick me out! Kick me out!"

Despite their successes at SXSW and the remaining North American dates, it had not been a total victory. America was used to its stars being show people and all-round performers. But the Monkeys weren't onstage to show off. With typical understatement, they left their music to do the talking.

A different band might have taken heed and repackaged themselves for the US. But Arctic Monkeys were not a different band. Yet.

Alex remained the aloof, irreverent and slightly self-mocking frontman. Jamie continued chopping into his guitar with a peculiarly violent intensity. Andy burrowed rolling bass lines while remaining buttoned up and on a distant wing. Matt steered the band through violent storms of rhythm patterns into passages of unexpected calm.

The tour had given the band a new level of experience. They emerged from the US battle-hardened and at the top of their form.

21

Who The Fuck Are Arctic Monkeys?

THE US tour was followed by more dates in Japan. The scenes that greeted the band on their return replicated the familiar adulation at their UK gigs. As one Japanese blogger commented, the calmest people at The Zepp Club in Osaka on April 2, 2006 were the band themselves. Somehow, the parochial teenage tales of High Green, Sheffield translated into a universal spirit that chimed with the very different culture and language of their Japanese followers.

The crowd had started singing as soon as the opening bars of the first song, 'The View From The Afternoon', had kicked in. Even more impressively, they kept on singing along to each song throughout the set. By the end they had sung their way through the band's entire repertoire – which wasn't bad, given how Japanese fans were struggling to understand Alex's Sheffield accent.

It was at a gig two nights later at Studio Coast, in Tokyo, that a guy wearing a T-shirt-and-tie combo burst into their dressing room, offering them his business card. A human tour de force called Brian, he had somehow got backstage and, on meeting the Monkeys, regaled them with stories about himself, filling the room with his presence. Despite having just played a string of successful gigs, the band seem to have been stunned into a reverential silence by this new arrival.

"When he left the room, we were a bit in awe," Alex recalled. "So we did a brainstorm for what he was like, drew a little picture and wrote things about him."

"He was right smooth, very LA," remembered Jamie Cook. "He just appeared with like a business card and a round neck T-shirt and a tie loosely around it. I'd never seen that before. It felt like he was trying to get inside your mind. We were checking out his attire; it inspired us."

A year later, Brian's memory would emerge as the single 'Brianstorm'. Alex explained that the song was an attempt to get inside the briefly glimpsed character's head. Although not itself condemnatory, the song would be interpreted to be an attack on him, prompting a friend of his to join a conversation about him on the blog songmeaning.com:

"Brian is my business partner in Japan," said the anonymous post. "Not surprised he hasn't posted a comment. A big AM fan who casually mentioned whilst having a burger in Tokyo that he met the band with his wife and son backstage and passed me the pic with the family and the band. Did laugh with the shirt, tie combo. He is a smooth cat and a great friend. Super song by the way!"

Having completed their tour with more sold-out gigs at Diamond Hall in Nagoya and Studio Coast in Tokyo, the band returned to the UK. They had become, as Alex had self-deprecatingly said on that first San Francisco date of the tour, international stars.

Three weeks after returning to the UK they released their third Domino single, on April 24, 2006. It had been expected that their next release would be 'The View From The Afternoon', from the album, but it ended up as the opening track for an EP of otherwise new songs entitled *Who The Fuck Are Arctic Monkeys?*

Despite touring almost constantly, the Monkeys had somehow managed to find time to write and rehearse new songs, even working on eight tracks for their second album before they'd finished recording the first one. But most of their live set consisted of songs written almost three years before, which they'd become understandably bored of playing. The only song they'd seriously reworked for the LP was 'Riot Van' and, as the limited amount of new material had shown on tour, they were aching to get some more songs out.

For a band whose members would later happily juggle multiple side projects (including writing film scores, setting up festivals and designing fashion lines, all while still recording and touring), relentlessly playing the same set had become stultifying.

Critics suspected the new material was being rush-released to cash in on the hype, but in fact the band had been showing considerable restraint in their output. The songs on *Who The Fuck Are Arctic Monkeys?* included some tracks they'd impatiently slipped into the tour sets: Alex's ballad about missing his girlfriend, Johanna, 'Despair in the Departure Lounge', was played live during the American tour; 'No Buses' had featured in their set in Osaka; 'Cigarette Smoker Fiona' was a reworking of 'Cigarette Smoke' from *Beneath The Boardwalk*.

But the tracks had only limited exposure before the EP was released. Apart from 'The View . . .', which had been recorded during the LP sessions with Jim Abbiss, the remaining tracks had been produced by Mike Crossey at the Motor Museum studio in Liverpool and Ray Davies' Konk Studios in London. Despite the raucousness of 'The View . . .' and 'Cigarette Smoker Fiona', the feel of the EP was more contemplative and forlorn than earlier material, placing greater emphasis on melody and a new, darker tone that replaced the party spirit of their earlier sounds.

The good-time teen memoirs were being replaced by confessional relationship songs and the emotional darkness that invaded after the stage lighting had gone down. The EP, a stepping stone between the first and second albums, was released, on 10-inch vinyl and on CD, but received noticeably less radio play than their previous two singles.

Perhaps that was hardly surprising. By releasing a five-track EP the band had automatically disqualified the release from the singles chart; it was too long to qualify as a single and too short to be an album (although it still made it into several album charts across the globe, including the number two position in Denmark and number five in Ireland).

By including 'fuck' in the title, they'd also made it an unlikely proposition for radio. All of which was hard to reconcile with the idea that the Monkeys were cashing in on their hype. Indeed, they seemed to be trying to engineer a flop.

Once back in the UK, the band wasted no time in getting back on tour, playing 12 dates from April 13 to 27. Advance tickets sold out within an hour of posting on the band's website. General admission tickets were released on February 2 and tickets to all 12 dates sold out within 10 minutes.

The music site *Drowned In Sound* opined that the tour would be the last chance to catch the band in a venue small enough to see them close up – if you could get a ticket, that is. Touts were already buying up any they could get their hands on and reselling at ridiculous multiples of the original price.

The tour kicked off back at Rock City, Nottingham on April 13, where

Alex appeared in his now regular white hoodie, and 'Riot Van' took its place as opening number for much of the tour. The following night the band headed north to Glasgow to play The Academy, where Alex opened up in an unusually effusive mood: "So we meet again, on a Friday night once more. Always the same. I'm not sure Glasgow exists outside of Fridays and Saturdays."

In a bizarre incident that seemed to trigger something in Alex, a fan threw a sock that hit him in the face as the opening chords of 'When The Sun Goes Down' were ringing out. He suddenly switched and led the band into 'Fake Tales Of San Francisco', only to return to 'When The Sun Goes Down' three songs later – starting at exactly the same point where he left off earlier.

On April 15 the Monkeys headed on to Newcastle, followed by Bournemouth two nights later and, in quick succession, The Pavilions in Plymouth, the Civic Centre in Wolverhampton, The Centre in Newport and MAGNA, a cavernous 3,000-capacity space on the Sheffield/ Rotherham border, on April 22.

As the first homecoming gig since the US, MAGNA was a double-edged event for their most devoted fans. There was no way the Monkeys could still play in the intimate venues of their early days, so the band had started looking for alternative spaces.

"They wanted to do something different," explains Barney Vernon, "and it wasn't really a venue – it's a museum, a history of Sheffield steel, so we put a stage and a PA in. It sold out in five seconds or something silly.

"The ticketing system just collapsed because the demand was so massive. They'd wanted tickets at Jack's Records [a now closed independent record shop on Division Street] so I went down with 300 tickets. They'd had to get the town council wardens to cordon it off because there were so many people trying to get tickets and I could not believe the size of the queue – I couldn't see the end of it! I was carrying the tickets and I knew that loads of these people wouldn't get a ticket and I started thinking, 'If they knew what I was carrying . . .'"

For their core fans, whose crowd-surfing and scream-alongs in the mosh pit had made the gigs so powerful, some of the magic was inevitably lost. The MAGNA represented everything that had changed. For the first time a homecoming gig was attended by a higher number of new fans than long-term followers, with the audience at the front of the stage holding mobile phones above their heads instead of crowd-surfers.

For many it wasn't a welcome change. Long-term fans complained that the very people the band were criticising in 'Bigger Boys And Stolen Sweethearts', 'A Certain Romance' and 'Who The Fuck Are Arctic Monkeys?' were now bouncing around the dancefloor.

Alex, who had once sneered at Johnny-come-lately fans (on the track 'Who The Fuck Are Arctic Monkeys?'), was now apparently happy playing to thousands of late arrivals.

Something else had changed. During the transition from northern venues to several thousand-capacity halls nationwide, the band's sound seemed to swell. Apart from the very earliest gigs, they had always been tight; but now they were super-slick, turn-on-a-penny, spray-on skinny-fit tight – as witnessed by their ability to drop a song midway through and return to it later in the set, at the exact point that they'd dropped it.

As the Monkeys completed their tour with dates in Blackpool, Hull, and Cambridge, they were also about to graduate to their first main-stage festival appearance. Immediately after their UK tour, Arctic Monkeys returned to Europe to play dates in France, Germany, the Netherlands, Italy, Portugal and Spain.

But first the last night of the tour saw the band play their first headline show at The Brixton Academy. Noel Gallagher turned up to watch from among the audience, before spending two hours backstage chatting with the band. The show sold out the entire venue, stalls included, and the Monkeys had carried both floors with them.

The first date of the European tour was at the thirtieth Printemps de Bourges Festival in France. As a showcase for introducing new acts to France, it followed the standard festival format of established performers playing the main stage marquee while newer acts took to the numerous smaller stages dotted around the festival site and town.

Arctic Monkeys were given a headline slot in the main arena on Saturday night. The French crowd lapped them up, dancing, singing, jumping and even crowd-surfing in a most un-Gallic fashion. But, as much as the audience shouted and screamed, Alex, apart from the odd 'thank you' and his regular thumbs up, remained his usual laconic self.

For the rest of the tour the venues were resized to a more intimate scale.

From Bourges the tour moved on to the much smaller venue of Trans-bordeur in Lyon and then to the Bataclan music hall in the centre of Paris.

Next it was Germany to play E-Werk in Cologne, and from there to their second gig at Amsterdam's Paradiso, this time downstairs in the 1,900-capacity main room where they also celebrated Matt's twentieth birthday on May 7. The tour then took them back across the German border to the Jovel in Munster, the Alter Schlachthof in Dresden and the Grosse Elser Halle in Munich.

Their debut Italian show at the Vox in Modena followed. The reception was wild, with the north Italians living up to their reputation for partying, a performance that was repeated by another sold-out show in Milan and a last hop into France for a gig at Theatre du Moulin, in Marseilles, on their way over to Barcelona's Razzmatazz club on May 16.

From here the band was scheduled to play Madrid's Sala Heineken on 17 May, before crossing into Portugal for a gig at the Paradise Garage in the hedonistic city of Lisbon. Madrid and Lisbon were like carbon copies of any other Arctic Monkeys gig – crowds bounced, moshed and surfed in all the right places – but what made the last gigs of the European tour truly remarkable was that the band managed to play them at all.

Tour manager Timm Cleasby would later describe it as a very sad time for everyone. Shying away from giving too many details, he informed *Mixed In Sheffield* that Andy Nicholson had been going through a very tough period during the European tour.

The final crisis came in Spain after the Barcelona gig. Andy had appeared to be fine earlier in the day but had suddenly broken down. Cleasby described him suddenly falling to pieces, saying that he couldn't cope and had to go home.

Cleasby could see it was serious and decided to send him back to Sheffield straight away. But the band still had two more dates left and no bass player. With no other option apart from cancelling, sound engineer John Ashton stepped in as bass player at the last minute, while Cleasby momentarily returned to being the front-of-house sound engineer.

For Ashton it marked the beginning of a long-term collaboration with the Monkeys that would see him contributing keyboards, guitar and vocals. But for Andy it was the beginning of the end.

22

Despair In The Departure Lounge

THE news about Andy Nicholson's temporary departure from Arctic Monkeys broke just as the band were getting ready for their second major US tour. At first, it wasn't clear to band or public whether Andy was leaving or just taking time out.

In the week-long gap after the end of the European tour, Nicholson had told the band that he didn't want to tour America. Everyone involved, from band members through to managers and tour manager, had struggled desperately to find a solution. Eventually, Turner, Cook and Helders decided they wanted Nick O'Malley of The Dodgems as a temporary stand-in for Andy.

Nick, a local High Green boy and long-standing friend and jamming mate of the Monkeys, was in many ways the ideal replacement, but a couple of points counted against him: he'd just broken his arm that week and he didn't even have a passport, let alone an American visa and work permit.

While O'Malley practised playing bass with a broken wrist, Timm Cleasby rushed to secure him a passport and a visa in the space of a week. Nick soon reported that he could still play with his injury and hurriedly learned the band's songs. Cleasby overcame immigration bureaucracy to deliver the necessary travel documents.

With their temporary bassist in place, the Monkeys announced that Nicholson would miss the forthcoming US dates, saying he was suffering from "fatigue following an intensive period of touring". The tours had indeed been relentless and it wasn't surprising that they'd taken their toll. Nicholson clearly approved of O'Malley standing in for him, lending him his equipment and helping him rehearse with the band, but rumours were soon circulating that the split was more permanent than the band were letting on.

Whatever their original intentions, during the tour the Monkeys started to change their opinion on what Andy had done, the way he'd handled it and what should be done in the future. As a result of the tour, they started to think of Nick O'Malley as a permanent member of the band. Discussions about the future started to include Nick, as well as Andy.

On June 20, 2006, three days after the end of the tour, the official Monkeys website announced that the split with Andy Nicholson was permanent: "We are sad to tell everyone that Andy is no longer with the band. Nick O'Malley, who stood in for Andy while he was absent from the recent tour of North America, shall carry on playing bass for the remaining shows this summer.

"We have been mates with Andy for a long time and have been through some amazing things together that no one can take away. We all wish Andy the very best."

Andy had intimated to reporters that he didn't like what the band had become and had always been uncomfortable with its meteoric rise; at one stage, *The Independent* reported him complaining: "We're just four blokes playing some music together, but every night there seems to be more and more people out there. It's kind of like there's this storm around us and we're at the eye of it."

But Alex later explained that Andy simply didn't want to be on the road any more and preferred being at home with his girlfriend, walking the dog. Perhaps his sullen presence and determined refusal to smile onstage hadn't been an act.

Alex tried to shed some more light on Andy's departure while talking to Zane Lowe at Oxegen Festival in Ireland: "To start with we were in Lisbon at the end of the European thing and he decided he didn't want to come to America. And that was cool, and then, I don't know, I guess we found ourselves in this situation by the end of the American tour.

"I mean, a lot happens, it's not just like three weeks in a normal thing, it's three weeks with your head all over the place. I mean, it's a difficult thing to explain, I don't think anyone will really understand this except us three and Andy."

He was reportedly given a six-figure settlement but personal relations between the band and him remained good, with all of them meeting up at the Reading Festival later that year.

"There's only so much you get to hear about as PR," recalls Serena Wilson, "but it was interesting because it was just as they were hitting the big time."

"He dropped out because it was too much to take," says music journalist Nick Tesco. "That's what they said at the time and I really think that was the case. But O'Malley maintained Andy's drive and the intensity. It's so developed for a band so young. And it so complements the lyrics."

Throughout Arctic Monkeys' career, critics have acclaimed Alex Turner's incisive lyric writing and Matt Helders' exceptional drumming. But, just as importantly, the Monkeys' sound had sat on Andy Nicholson's heavyweight bass lines. His distinctive rolling grooves could lock on the chord's root note while simultaneously rumbling around the fret board.

Replacing him was no mean task, but in Nick O'Malley they found someone who fitted the bill perfectly. In the spirit of their original decision to form a band, he was also a mate. In an unprecedented moment of foresight, they'd even invited someone to join who could already play his instrument.

Before jetting off on their third US tour, the band squeezed in a secret date for *Vice* magazine at their venue, The Old Blue Last in Shoreditch, London. The gig was so secret that even Domino boss Laurence Bell didn't find out about it until that afternoon. It was the first to feature O'Malley on bass, and had been hurriedly organised to help him bed in at the 120-capacity venue, before US dates where he'd be performing in front of 15,000-plus people.

The return to the United States saw the band booked into significantly larger venues. They still hadn't got everyone on side but the consensus view was the hype had been justified by the energy and tightness of their live shows.

The first date of the tour saw their first outdoor festival appearance at Washington's Sasquatch on May 25. Although rain had dogged the festival the day before, it held off until the very end of the Monkeys' set. The gig had begun with the usual rowdy crowd antics and it was noticeable that, although this was a festival, there was clearly a large contingent of people there specifically for the Monkeys.

For the rest of the tour they had booked their old American friends from the *NME* Awards shows, We Are Scientists. It was business as usual, with fans filling venues to capacity at Roseland, Portland on May 29, The Warfield, San Francisco on May 30, and San Diego on June 2.

On June 3 a crowd member threw a 'Get Well Andy' card onto the stage at The Wiltern in Los Angeles. It could have been an awkward moment but, with Nick still sporting a bandaged hand, the sentiment might have been appropriate for either bass player. Alex picked up the card, exchanged a glance with Nick and then just got on with the gig.

Further dates took them to Tempe, Dallas, Austin, Norfolk, Houston and Atlanta. As they worked their way towards New York, *USA Today* declared their gig at Sonar, Baltimore to be one of the hottest of the season. From here the band moved on to Roseland in New York and Avalon in Boston, before heading north to play Le Medley in Montreal and Kool Haus in Toronto, bringing Nick O'Malley's debut tour with the band to a close on June 17.

Despite his injured hand, O'Malley had acquitted himself admirably. In an amazingly short space of time he'd managed to settle in, but for both bass players there was a lot at stake. As the tour had gone on, the band's concern had shifted from what was going to happen about Andy to whether they were going to stick with Nick.

The uncertainty was answered with a post on the band's website three days after the tour finished. Within hours of returning to the UK, they'd decided on their future line-up.

★　★　★

Having headlined Printemps du Bourges in April and made their outdoor festival debut in the USA, Arctic Monkeys now embarked on their first tour of Europe's burgeoning festival circuit. Kicking off with the twin Hurricane and Southside Festivals in Germany on June 23 and 25, they were billed alongside the band that had originally inspired Cook and Turner to play guitar: The Strokes.

At Eurokéennes in Belfort, France, Arctic Monkeys blasted not only The Strokes but also Daft Punk offstage, almost prompting The Strokes' Julian Casablancas to concede that the Monkeys were perhaps too good an act to follow.

Belgium's Werchter Festival followed, again with the Strokes and Arctic

Monkeys sharing the billing, while both bands played alongside Pink Floyd's Roger Waters, Bob Dylan, Morrissey and Kanye West at Roskilde, Denmark's biggest festival with a 100,000 capacity.

Norway's Quart Festival was followed by Accelerator in Gothenburg and Stockholm, Sweden. The Monkeys and Strokes both played Ireland's Oxegen Festival on July 8 – where the Monkeys literally took the main stage by storm by playing in the middle of a gale. With the closing European date falling on Thursday, July 9, Alex finally got to play Glasgow outside of a weekend at the T In The Park Festival.

After a three-week break the Monkeys headed off for their first Australasian tour. The first gig took place at a sold-out St James Theatre, Auckland, New Zealand on July 28, after which the remaining shows ran according to script: Metro City in Perth, Australia was followed by two nights at The Palace in Melbourne, The Barton in Adelaide and The Arena in Brisbane, bringing the tour to an end on August 9 at the Enmore Theatre, Sydney.

Returning home via Japan, the Monkeys played the Summer Sonic Festival on August 12 in Tokyo and in Osaka on the 13th, before returning to play Sheffield on August 14 in celebration of the release of their third single, 'Leave Before The Lights Come On'.

The song had been trailed live at gigs for months and was backed by two cover versions – the punkish power-pop of 'Put Your Dukes Up, John' by The Little Flames, a young band from Liverpool that featured Miles Kane on guitar, and 'Baby I'm Yours', a close-harmony ballad originally recorded by Barbara Lewis in 1965. A surprise tribute to Sixties R&B, it featured Oisin Leech of The 747s joining Alex on vocals.

The single entered the UK singles charts at number four on August 20, 2006, the first official Monkeys single not to top the chart. It fared well internationally, perhaps benefiting from exposure on the tour, debuting on the Canadian singles chart at number two and falling short of the number one slot by only 15 copies.

'Leave Before The Lights Come On' was about one-night stands and remorse, a theme picked up by promotional video director Jon Hardwick and turned into a short story about a suicidal woman and her would-be saviour. It was also, of course, the first single the band had made with Nick O'Malley playing bass. Although assumed at the time to prefigure the next

LP release, like three-quarters of the songs on *Who The Fuck Are Arctic Monkeys?*, it wasn't intended to be on an album.

For Alex Turner, the release marked the end of an era. Talking to *NME*, he made it apparent why the band decided to release the track as a stand-alone single: "It's the last song that I wrote about that sort of time, going out and that. My life's not really like that any more."

A secret launch was arranged for the single at The Boardwalk on August 14, giving their loyal long-serving fans the chance to see them back in their home environment. The band was by now too big to play any of their original venues as open gigs.

23

Reading Reloaded

FOLLOWING the release of 'Leave Before The Lights Come On', the Monkeys' festival dates resumed with central European shows at Frequency, Pukkelpop, and Lowlands. With their last few European bookings met and after nearly two years on the road, their near-continuous tour schedule came to an end with a return to the Reading and Leeds Festivals at the end of August.

If anyone needed proof of how successful the Monkeys' year had been, then their rise from the Carling Tent in 2005 to headlining the main stage at Reading in 2006 demonstrated how far they'd come. Not only did the Monkeys sound like the voice of their generation, you could hear their generation singing along. Dispensing with 'Riot Van' as an opener, the band went straight for the jugular with 'I Bet You Look Good On The Dancefloor'. The already charged-up audience broke into a field of bouncing bodies.

This was the band's biggest UK show to date. Having just completed the first chorus of their second song, 'Still Take You Home', Alex suddenly brought the song to a halt and, uncharacteristically, almost chuckled: "Well, good evening! Everything all right? Well, fancy seeing you here . . ." he continued, before launching back into the song. At its end he returned to the banter: "You're a bit quieter than I thought you were going to be, to be honest," he commented wryly, before introducing the current single, 'Leave Before The Lights Come On', as the "black sheep of the family, but we love it all the same".

The crowd unanimously sang their hearts out. As the song finished, Alex stood motionless, catching his breath and taking in the scene. Asking for more lighting to be thrown on the front rows, Alex seemed to recognise some of the people from earlier gigs. Despite it being a festival headline slot, he reverted to the one-to-one banter of Sheffield gigs, whistling: "There's some faces on this front row, fucking hell . . ."

'When The Sun Goes Down' returned to the tried-and-tested live formula, but on a magnificent scale. Alex pulled out of singing the first verse to let the entirety of Reading's main field lead the song. Then, as the crowd was rising to a peak, he held everyone in suspended silence before finally releasing the tension and leading the band into an explosive chorus.

After a riotous singalong to 'Mardy Bum', which saw a bed sheet raised aloft with 'I Love your Mardy Bum' daubed on it, Alex asked: "Are you still with us ladies and gentlemen? Have you still got some fight?" The crowd roared back affirmatively. The gig drew to a close with an unusually chatty Alex thanking the audience "from the bottom of our hearts".

The day after Reading, Arctic Monkeys headed north to Leeds where Andy Nicholson rejoined them onstage, in a public demonstration that they were all still mates – even if they were no longer one entity.

On Tuesday September 5, Arctic Monkeys attended the Nationwide Mercury Music Prize awards ceremony for best album of the previous year, where they were up against stiff competition. Despite the band's confident victory at the *NME* Awards, the Mercury judges were known for making surprise decisions and a Monkeys' Mercury Prize seemed unlikely.

Richard Hawley was also on the nominations list with *Coles Corner*, and, in the Monkeys' eyes, would have made a worthy winner. Another thing that counted against them was that they were clear favourites – and, as the band was aware, favourites tended not to win the Mercury. Alex was later to joke that the prize didn't normally go to bands that had sold as many albums as they had.

When Jools Holland announced that Arctic Monkeys had won, there was genuine surprise at the band's table, triggering an initial stunned response followed by Alex's oft-quoted acceptance speech: "Somebody dial 999, Richard Hawley's been robbed . . ."

"When [Holland] started reading it out we were like, 'Hang on a minute, what if it's us, what are we going to say?'" he told *Soccer AM* shortly after the ceremony.

Yet again, the fastest-selling band in British chart history were completely unprepared to give an acceptance speech. Worse was to come.

After returning to the table for a few more celebratory drinks, the band were ushered through to a press conference where, aided by the complimentary booze, their mistrust of the media bubbled to the surface.

Caught in the glare of flashlights, they faced a barrage of uninspired questions. One hapless hack asked how they were feeling. "That's a reet original question," sneered Jamie. "Do you have one of them bum chin microphones?" he asked, referring to the sporting correspondent's preferred style of mic. The inference was clear: it would have been a cliché even in a post-match interview.

Alex and Matt tried to recover the situation, resolving to answer any sensible questions sensibly. But Cookie was having none of it. When asked why they didn't perform at the ceremony, he simply countered with: "Muse didn't perform – ring them up and ask why they didn't fucking perform."

He may have had a point. The possible inference might have been that they were unable to play live, though any reporter pursuing that line would have looked pretty foolish. But even so, the reaction was overly defensive.

With the tension getting higher, Matt tried to take on a peacemaker role and crack a few jokes. The whole process was clearly winding Jamie up, though; frustrated by the interviewers' relentless questions, he asked them if they'd been taking drugs.

Seizing the moment, another reporter asked Alex if he realised there had been conjecture about the band because they didn't give interviews; his response was that they'd given plenty. It was an invitation for a follow-up: "Why have you stepped away from the media?"

"[Because] you all ask questions like this," rejoined Jamie, still not amused.

"We're doing a social experiment to see if we have to do [interviews] or not," added Matt, again trying to lighten the mood.

Turning up for the after-party, the band were refused entry for being underage. It turned out that the venue had an over-21s door policy, but, luckily, the band had got around exactly this same restriction in the US, where the sale of alcohol is prohibited to under-21s, by using the old dodge of fake ID cards. Flashing their BRITISH IDENTITY CARD at the London bouncer, they were whisked into the club.

It had been an unexpectedly victorious night, but its aftermath was less successful. The entire dispute at the press conference had been filmed and, naturally enough, ended up online – where it engendered a running debate.

The band's personalities remained something of an enigma to the media. Alex was, of course, correct in saying that the band had given plenty of interviews, but it was also true that, for a band in their position, they were surprisingly underexposed. As the Mercury press conference had illustrated, their distance from the mainstream media was beginning to ferment mistrust, fuelling speculation that they had something to hide.

On September 9, 2006, Arctic Monkeys unveiled another surprise. Amazingly for a band that had topped both the albums and singles charts, they gave a rare live TV interview. The lucky recipient was Sky TV's Saturday morning show, *Soccer AM*.

It was good-natured and spirited, though there were signs that the hosts had been warned the band could be lively. As it turned out, if they'd expected a bunch of surly teenagers then they must have been pleasantly surprised. The Monkeys were dream guests, answering questions with amused but respectful banter, joking with their hosts and, at one point, pulling out the fake ID card they used at the Mercury after-party.

Alex said the funniest thing the media had made up about him so far was that Kate Moss had rung his mum, who told her to stay away from her son. "I've never met Kate Moss," testified Alex.

"Well, you're the only rock star who hasn't," quipped co-presenter Tim Lovejoy.

The interviewers tripped through the Arctic Monkeys story with the band remaining amiable throughout. Explaining how they started, Alex said they'd just wanted to play gigs for their mates and that it digressed from there. "It got a bit serious," chimed in Matt with comic timing as on-point as his drumming.

Asked what he'd be doing if he wasn't in the band now, new boy Nick at first seemed a little fazed, before somewhat surreally conjecturing, "I'd probably be a butcher," prompting squeals of laughter from behind the camera. Far from presenting a challenging interview, the band even had the studio technicians in stitches. By the end, the whole studio had been won over.

The band's next media appointment was at the *Q* Awards on October 30, 2006, where they won Best Album. Take That had been presented with the *Q* Idol award for that year, and as Turner approached the podium there was a glint in his eye, while the way Matt was circling the microphone implied some naughtiness was afoot.

Launching into his acceptance speech in his usual offbeat casual style, Turner said: "I'm not old enough to know a lot . . . but even I know that Take That were bollocks!" After pausing to laugh, he added, "but thanks for this one, means a lot to us . . ."

★　★　★

Andy Nicholson may have left the band, but that didn't mean he'd retired from music. Once back in Sheffield he hooked up with old friends and set about redefining himself as an artist. At first he changed his role from bass player to DJ, making a name for himself as a resident at the Threads vs Filthy Few club night.

Long-term Monkeys collaborator Jon McClure of Reverend & The Makers, having lured Alex and Matt into Judan Suki, was also able to bring Nicholson into the orbit of his many projects, some of which had already involved the Monkeys in some way or another. It was as a DJ that Andy started his initial collaboration with McClure as part of spin-off event The Reverend Soundsystem – a monthly club night where Nicholson took on the DJ handle AndyGun.

The two of them also started Sheffield supergroup Mongrel, which featured Matt Helders, Drew McConnell of Babyshambles, Joe Moskow from Reverend & The Makers and producer-performer Jagz Kooner amongst its line-up. Alongside Mongrel, McClure had also started to involve Andy in Reverend, which he officially joined in 2009. Andy also had a stint playing bass for The Lords Of Flatbush, an electro outfit he formed with Louis Carnall, formerly of fellow New Yorkshire band Milburn. (Another former Milburn member, Tom Rowley, also joined Reverend & The Makers, while Milburn's Joe Carnall set up The Book Club.)

24

Favourite Worst Nightmare

THE band had started penning songs for the second LP back in 2005, and recorded them throughout 2006. Rehearsals finally began in earnest from September 8, after the Leeds Festival, and the final recording sessions began on September 16, taking place at Moloco, Eastcote and Konk Studios in London, and Motor Museum in Liverpool.

This time the band called James Ford in to produce the album, while Mike Crossey was to assist as engineer, and also produce a few of the tracks. Ford had originally re-recorded tracks from the 2Fly sessions before Laurence Bell brought Jim Abbiss in to produce the first LP and slow the whole set down. But the Monkeys had continued working with Ford, with whom they developed 'Perhaps Vampires Is A Bit Strong But . . .' While Abbiss had been presented with a set of completed songs, the relationship with Ford was more creatively intertwined. It was this that led music publication *Sound On Sound* to dub him "the fifth Monkey".

"They were on this weird roller coaster thing, so we didn't have a lot of contact," Ford recalls of the period leading up to recording the sophomore LP. "But Laurence had come back to me and floated the idea [of producing the second LP]. It had come from the band, as they were keen to carry on where we'd left off.

"I went up to a rehearsal room in Sheffield and they played me 'Brianstorm' and a couple of others and they were like being punched in the face. I was like, 'I definitely want to try and help you do this' – even though the second album is always the hardest one, as it's under the weight of your own expectations, as well as everyone else's.

"Their thing seemed to be to just get on with it and get it out of the way as they knew it was going to be hard."

Whereas the content of the debut LP had been determined by *Beneath*

Nick O'Malley on stage. ROSS HALFIN

Alex Turner, Nick O'Malley, Matt Helders and Jamie Cook being interviewed on the *Soccer AM* TV show, London, September 9, 2006
REX FEATURES

Left to right: Matt Helder, James Cook, Nick O'Malley and Alex Turner, backstage after their gig at the Great Hall, Exeter University, April 10, 2007. ROSS HALFIN

Arctic Monkeys, dressed as characters from *Wizard Of Oz*, accepting Best British Group prize via video message at The BRIT Awards, London, February 14, 2007. Cookie showed off his footballer legs by dressing as Dorothy. DAVE HOGAN/GETTY IMAGES

Alex in his white hoodie tour uniform, during the Arctic Monkeys performance at the mobbed La Zona Rosa nightclub during South by Southwest, in Austin, Texas, March 17, 2005. TIM MOSENFELDER/GETTY IMAGES

James Cook, Alex Turner, Mathew Helders (holding phone) and Nick O'Malley in a relaxed photo shoot in Barnsley, December 1, 200
SAM JONES/RETNA UK

Still mates. Former Monkeys bassist, Andy Nicholson (fourth from left), hanging out with Alex Turner and Matt Helders and members of The Rascals and friends, backstage at The Rascals gig at Club Fandango, in Manchester, England, October 21, 2007.
SHIRLAINE FORREST/WIREIMAGE

Alex Turner on stage with Greg Mighall, of the Rascals, at the O2 Wireless Festival, Hyde Park, London, July 4, 2008.
P.G. BRUNELLI/LIVEPIX

James Cook at the Wells Fargo Center, Philadelphia, March 10th, 2012. REX FEATURES

Josh Homme, producer of *Humbug*, and Alex Turner in full pout at the Arctic Monkey's Hollywood Bowl gig, September 2011.
ROSS HALFIN

Left to right: Matt Helders, Nick O'Malley, Shirley Bassey, Alex Turner and Paul McCartney at the *Q* Awards, Grosvenor House Hotel, London, October 8, 2007. RICHARD YOUNG/REX FEATURES

Jamie Cook. PAUL STUART/CAMERAPRESS

The Boardwalk, Arctic Monkeys now had a blank canvas for their second album. It made Ford the natural creative partner. They started working on five songs in the rehearsal studio and recorded them at Eastcote, after which they moved back into the rehearsal studio and worked on the next songs, before taking these into Eastcote. This process continued as they moved through a series of different studios. Eventually, when they were ready, most of the tracks were recorded at Moloco's vintage studio, The Garden, which had been used by acts such as Echo & The Bunnymen and Depeche Mode. A final phase of recording was then carried out in Liverpool, at Crossey's Motor Museum studio.

In terms of style and sound, the band wanted the new LP to be heavier and avoid obviously straightforward song structures. They wanted more textures, softer patches and harder ones, with more sonic emphasis to create a more 'produced' album than their debut.

Matt's drumming style had also changed; after he'd seen Joey Castillo from Queens Of The Stone Age playing at the Sasquatch Festival, he'd decided he needed to start hitting harder. And of course it would be the first album with Nick O'Malley, who'd learned Andy's bass parts well but now added a fresh, more driving perspective when interpreting Alex's songs.

Alex also signalled a change in direction when he revealed there would be some dance music influences on the LP to online music magazine *365*: "It may sound a bit strange to our audience, but using bits of electronica on our next album is in fact quite logical," said Turner. "I used to listen to pretty much dance music only, until I discovered The Strokes."

Turner had been writing consistently since the first LP. But the first track they'd written specifically for the new LP was 'Brianstorm', which was one of the first six new songs rehearsed at soundchecks. These were recorded in a three-week session. For the next stint they mixed recording with a break from touring by checking out east London's clubs.

Considering the band had been touring constantly and had already recorded an EP of new songs, as well as a new single and two B-side tracks, it was fairly astounding that they were able to complete their sophomore LP a little over a year after their debut. They were also moving forward musically at an equally rapid pace, developing their techniques, broadening their influences and experimenting with their sound.

"They've got systems that work," James Ford recalled of their song-writing technique. "There isn't any ego animosity between them – that thing of someone not getting their way. They appreciate what a good writer Alex is and the rest of the band are really good at what they do too. So they just do their bit. And it all fits together. It's different to some bands, where you have people vying for attention."

The debut record was soon starting to sound dated next to the more complex but still exhilaratingly powerful sophomore offering. Individually, band members were starting to progress too. For Nick it was a matter of integrating his sound into the recording and writing process to find his niche. Matt had started to take drum lessons to help develop his technique on some of the faster tracks, such as 'Brianstorm', his efforts rewarded when *The Guardian* reviewed the LP and concluded that if everything was taken away apart from the drumming, it would have still been a riveting listen.

Meanwhile, Alex had started looking to different places for inspiration. Instead of tales from his youth, more subtly introspective subjects began to emerge. His relationship with Johanna was already struggling while the new LP was being recorded, and the melancholy that pervaded some passages already felt like a soliloquy to lost love. By the time the LP was released, some reviewers had woven the couple's break-up into the album's back story, even though it was recorded while they were still together – just.

Whatever People Say I Am, That's What I'm Not was the summation of their teenage years, the embodiment of their frustrations and an escape route for their hopes and dreams. The second album would not attempt to repeat any of that but there were recurring themes and attitudes, and Turner was still writing from experience – even if the life he was chronicling had changed dramatically.

The involvement of James Ford at this juncture was perfectly timed for a group ready to start pushing their boundaries. Ford was a restless soul whose musical ventures had crossed into electronic music, indie rock and beyond. He describes the joint approach to production and composition as an open process: "It's different things at different times. Alex has played me songs in embryonic form and I've pointed out structures, which lyrics work . . . Or [at the other end] it's deciding the overall way of approaching the record."

Although self-deprecating in the extreme, Ford was also an able musician who'd been playing guitar, keyboards and bass since he was a mere 11-year-old. He was able to throw himself into the mix or sit back and guide the experimentation as proceedings demanded. He also ended up playing guitar on the brilliantly melancholic 'Only Ones Who Know'.

The resulting album was a complex affair, sometimes throwing together passages of unrelated music, spiralling through genres and mood changes. Some commentators even spotted more than a hint of prog rock among its song structures.

Arctic Monkeys had moved from being a touring band captured in a studio to a band using the studio to create their sound. The LP was at times deeper and more furious than their debut, at others more delicate and wistful. Its influences, although detectable, were not worn on their sleeve, or perhaps they were just too numerous to pin down – leading critics to make comparisons with The Smiths, Richard Hawley, and punk-funkers ESG, none of which sat entirely comfortably. Ennio Morricone's score for *The Good, The Bad And The Ugly* also popped up as inspiration for the opening of LP closer '505'. (The same track also saw Miles Kane of The Little Flames drafted in to play guitar, originating a musical voyage that would lead to The Last Shadow Puppets.) The LP's title, *Favourite Worst Nightmare*, was plucked from a lyric on the track 'D Is For Dangerous', although the band told reporters they'd considered calling it *Lesbian Wednesdays*, *Gordon Brown* or *Gary Barlow*.

The cover was created out of three derelict houses that Juno, the creative company also responsible for the debut LP's artwork, gutted and repainted. After the cover shots had been taken, some of the external walls were removed to allow filming of the interior for a promotional video.

The album was preceded by the release of 'Brianstorm' as a single. A magical assault of drums and sharp lyrical turnarounds, it was a powerful opening. Noticeably more boisterous and heavier than anything they'd released to date, it loudly pronounced that change was afoot. On the B-side they were joined by another Mercury Prize winner, Dizzee Rascal, for the non-LP track 'Temptation Greets You Like Your Naughty Friend'.

The single was released as a download on April 2, 2007, debuting at number 21 on downloads alone. When it was released in physical formats on April 16, it went straight in at number two – kept off the top spot by Shakira's 'Beautiful Liar' but still becoming the band's highest charting single worldwide to date.

The album followed a week later in the UK, on April 23, coming close to the frenzied sales of their debut release – which had hit the streets exactly 14 months earlier. First-day sales topped 85,000 and outsold the rest of the Top 20 combined. In its first week it sold over 220,000 copies – giving Arctic Monkeys the biggest first-week sales of the year so far. It went straight to number one in the UK album charts, while all 12 tracks entered the Top 200 of the UK singles chart as downloads in their own right – sparking another surge of press activity over yet another Arctic Monkeys online phenomenon. In the USA, *Favourite Worst Nightmare* would fare even better than their debut LP, entering the charts at number seven and selling 44,000 copies in its first week. (The LP has since gone double platinum in the UK.)

Like their debut, *Favourite Worst Nightmare* received universally good reviews. The *Daily Express* described it as "shockingly good"; the *Daily Telegraph* acclaimed it as "totally the equal of its predecessor". *The Observer* singled out Cook's guitar work for praise, while *Pitchfork* noted Alex's "new emotional depth" and *NME* declared "the sequel's better. An unforecasted hurricane."

25

Love Is A Laserquest

DURING the making of *Favourite Worst Nightmare*, the band continually made trips to Liverpool, where Mike Crossey had his studio and where Juno, the creative team that created the band's cover artwork, were based. It was on one of these trips that Jamie Cook met Katie Downes, an attractive glamour model and reputed millionaire, at the end of 2006.

The couple started dating, initially keeping their relationship secret. By the end of March 2007, things had started to get more serious; he'd taken her back to High Green to meet the folks, plus his friends and teammates at The Packhorse. It was the start of a long relationship that would eventually end in a marriage proposal.

But while Jamie's love life was coming together, Alex's was falling apart. Alex and Johanna Bennett had spent a happy New Year's Eve together in High Green but the relationship had been troubled for some while. They split up soon after, in early 2007. Rumours circulated in the tabloid press about arguments over money while the Monkeys waited for their royalty payments to come in, and over other partners.

Alex had typically kept press interference into his private life at arm's length, but the strains that a relationship with an Arctic Monkey entailed were obvious. The band were constantly on tour, recording, rehearsing or picking up awards; Alex also had the additional burden of being the band's songwriter. There was little chance of a private time away from the job. He was kind enough to ensure that Johanna got her share of the royalties from 'Fluorescent Adolescent', but this in itself highlighted a problem: the song had been written while the two of them were away on holiday, occupying one of their rare moments alone together.

Luckily for Alex, when the inevitable split came, he had a packed schedule to keep him busy in the run-up to the album's release. And another stunning girlfriend was on the horizon.

★ ★ ★

Having won Best Breakthrough Act at the 2006 Brit Awards, the band were back in the running at the 2007 ceremony – this time nominated for Best British Act and Best British Album. They also continued to pick up nominations and awards elsewhere, including Best New Artist at the PLUG Independent Music Awards in the US and both Best Album and Best Music DVD at the 2007 *NME* Awards.

On February 14, 2007, the night of the Brits, they faced stiff competition from Amy Winehouse, Lily Allen, Muse and Snow Patrol for Best British Album, while Kasabian, Muse, Razorlight and Snow Patrol also vied for Best British Group. The Monkeys had, of course, snubbed the awards in 2006 by shanghaiing Keith Murray of We Are Scientists into voicing their acceptance speech. But they had been on tour then so there was every excuse.

In 2007 they had just taken their longest break from touring for three years. Even if they were busy rehearsing for their forthcoming promotional tour, there was an expectation that they would attend the ceremony. After all, the Brits were televised for a nationwide audience with performances by the nominated acts.

True to form, Arctic Monkeys declined to attend – let alone to perform. Instead, they sent two acceptance videos. In a marked improvement on the previous year, they actually spoke themselves, but there was something distinctly odd about their appearance. Dressed as members of The Village People, they were joined by a real builder, Chris 'Stussy' Newton - drafted in by Barradale as a stand-in for Nick O'Malley, who of course had not played on the debut album. Matt Helders was sporting a flowing Red Indian headdress, while Cook was playing the part of an extremely stern-looking, handlebar-moustached traffic cop.

Keeping poker-faced, the band members greeted the Brit audience as if dressing as a gay disco outfit from the late Seventies was the most natural thing in the world. Without explanation, they appeared to sincerely and graciously accept their award – but the award itself was cuddled tight by builder 'Stussy' Newton, the one person with no connection to their record. It was a deliciously surreal send-up, made all the more enjoyable by Helders' and Turner's cheesy TV personality delivery.

"Sorry we couldn't be there this year at the Brit Awards!" began Matt, framed by the nonplussed builder on his right and Cook, in his New York traffic cop uniform, on the left. Matt at least looked animated; Cook looked no happier than the builder, his fixed expression only broken by chewing gum. "We hope you're having a wonderful time," continued Helders, gesturing to his colleagues. "As you can see, we are" – cue another round of severe chewing from Cook and blank staring from builder Newton.

"We're thrilled to receive the award for Best British Album," chipped in Alex, dressed in a white sailor's uniform and sounding like the presenter of a game show. Everyone looked anything but thrilled. "Our debut had a lot of recognition, but there is no doubt that THIS is a very special award – and appreciated by us all." At which point Helders and Turner said simultaneously, in a tone that conveyed no emotion whatsoever: "Thank you."

But if The Village People had seemed a little out of character, then the friends of Dorothy who accepted Best British Act were like something from the deepest recesses of Terry Gilliam's mind. For the Best British Group award video, Cook was dressed (fetchingly, it has to be said) as Dorothy from *The Wizard Of Oz* – in a shoulder-length wig and blue gingham dress. Looped over his arm was a basket in which the Brit Award sat. Alex, dressed as the Scarecrow, started the acceptance: "Thank you for presenting us with this most prestigious award," at which point Nick, dressed as the Cowardly Lion but wearing an expression more suited to Eeyore in *Winnie-The-Pooh*, gestured mournfully to the object languishing in Cook's basket.

For all the surreal humour of their acceptance videos, the band had become the first act to win both the Mercury Music Prize and Best Album at the Brits in the same year. And they'd done it in front of a television audience of 5.43 million viewers.

Arctic Monkeys were also gaining recognition for kick-starting a new growth spurt in British music. The BPI, the British recording industry's trade body, had just published new figures showing the best home-grown market share since the Britpop era of the Nineties. As a result, an unprecedented number of new acts had been nominated for that year's Brit Awards.

In Ireland, the band received Best International Album at February's Meteor Music Awards – the Irish equivalent to the Brits. In May, the Ivor Novello Awards for songwriters and composers gained them another Best Album prize. In the US, they were nominated twice in February's Grammy Awards for Best Alternative Music Album and Best Rock Instrumental Performance.

Meanwhile, the 2007 *NME* Awards took place on March 1. Arctic Monkeys were, predictably, presented with the Best Album award for *Whatever People Say I Am* . . . Less predictably, they also received the award for Best DVD for the short film 'Scummy Man'. The promo had been directed and conceived by Paul Fraser and Mark Herbert, released by Domino Records on April 10, 2006. Based on the theme of 'When The Sun Goes Down' – 'Scummy' being the song's original title – it documented a night in the life of a fictional drug addict and prostitute called Nina, and featured the actors from the song's promotional video, Lauren Socha and Stephen Graham. The only band member to appear in the film was Matt Helders, who was offered a blow job by Nina at the beginning of the film – which he excused himself from by saying he'd got band practice.

With awards tumbling in and the music industry falling over itself to praise a blatantly disinterested, cocky and irreverent band, it certainly didn't feel like Arctic Monkeys were about to suffer the much anticipated slings and arrows of an outrageous backlash.

26

On The Road

WHILE recording *Favourite Worst Nightmare*, Arctic Monkeys had given themselves a break from touring that lasted from the Leeds Festival (at the end of August 2006) until the beginning of February 2007. It was their longest break from playing live since 2003. To get them back on the road, they'd booked a series of secret gigs across the north of England, announcing each date in the local area the night before.

The opening gig, at The Leadmill on February 10, demonstrated how the secret tour would work. Details would be leaked on the band's website the day before, with tickets sold locally from a fixed time the following day. Once sold out (usually within an hour), there would be no further ticket sales.

The tour would be the first time they'd played the new LP live. News of the Sheffield gig started circulating rapidly, although many of the people who got in were guests and friends. The general verdict that spread around message boards afterwards was that, though the new tunes were slower and heavier, the band were particularly on form. Naturally enough, live bootleg versions of songs such as 'D Is For Danger' were soon circulating on blogs.

The second secret gig took place at the University of Leicester, where rumours had been circulating since the morning of Tuesday, September 13. By midday over 500 people were queuing outside the student union in the hope of getting tickets. Among the tracks played from the new LP were 'This House Is A Circus', 'Teddy Picker', 'D Is For Dangerous', 'Fluorescent Adolescent', 'Do Me A Favour' and 'Brianstorm', as well as the non-album track 'What If You Were Right The First Time?' (the B-side to 'Brianstorm').

For some fans at the start of the tour, an Arctic Monkeys gig without the audience singing along to every word was a new experience. While songs from the debut album were greeted predictably as old friends, no one knew the new ones well enough to join in. As the tour progressed, this naturally became less of a problem.

The next stop on the secret tour took Morecambe by surprise; the somewhat flattered population ensured The Dome was swiftly sold out, leaving some who found out too late questioning whether it really happened at all. The packed Dome went bananas, even after the power momentarily went down.

News about the secret tour was by now beginning to spread across the internet. It moved on to intimate gigs in Middlesbrough Town Hall on February 27 and finally Parr Hall, Warrington the following day.

With just over a month before 'Brianstorm' was scheduled for release, the band resumed touring in earnest, returning to the European circuit via The Fritz at Postbahnhof in Berlin. Here they debuted the psychedelic-influenced 'Do Me A Favour'. This was followed by Store Vega in Copenhagen and a return visit to the manic crowd at The Melkweg in Amsterdam.

A rapturous reception awaited them at the old-time Elysée Montmartre in Paris, where the fans had somehow managed to sell out the venue before the gig was announced and the new songs were greeted with as much enthusiasm as the familiar ones. Continuing south, they closed the European leg of their pre-release tour with another sold-out gig at The Rolling Stone in Milan on March 19. Milan brought an end to this leg of the Monkeys' European tour, but the band's relentless gigging was about to pay off.

On its release, *Favourite Worst Nightmare* went to number one in the Netherlands, Belgium, Denmark, Ireland and Switzerland, and number two in Spain, Germany, Norway and Australia. It hit the Top Five in New Zealand and Japan, and the Top 10 in the USA, France, Sweden and Austria. In the overall European Top 100 it reached number two, achieving platinum sales in Canada and gold in Germany, France, Italy and Japan. On returning to the UK, the band jumped on a quick long-haul flight to Tokyo to play The Zepp Club on March 29, allowing them to promote the album two weeks before its release.

This time the follow-up UK tour wouldn't be a secret. But the band announced they would be taking measures to control the ridiculous ticket resale prices, "trying hard to fight against touting". The measures they adopted were based on Glastonbury's ticketing system, and were intended to ensure their real fans got tickets at the right price. The system asked people to sign up to the mailing list on the band's official website. Mailing list members would then be entered into a random draw and the fans selected invited to buy a ticket.

The new system was announced on Tuesday March 14, and fans had to register by 7 p.m. that evening. The following Friday a random ballot selected fans from the mailing list and sent them a PIN, which they had to use by the following Monday to buy tickets.

The tour dates took place at Southampton Guildhall on April 9, followed by Exeter University Great Hall, two nights at London Astoria, Liverpool Academy, Newcastle Academy, Dundee Caird Hall, Glasgow Barrowlands, Birmingham Academy, and terminating at Sheffield Leadmill on April 22 – the day before the new album's release.

All of the gigs sold out immediately. Despite all the band's efforts to make tickets directly available to the fans, several hundred appeared on auction websites within minutes of going on sale. One pair of tickets for one of the homecoming concerts at The Leadmill was sold for £266 – the original price was £24 per ticket.

The tour's support band were Liverpool's Little Flames, while old friends Reverend & The Makers also joined them on some dates. After the two opening dates in Southampton and Exeter, the tour rolled into the London Astoria for two sold-out headline gigs in a row. Once again, the attempt to weed out touts had failed and tickets exchanged hands outside the gig for hundreds of pounds.

Despite the expected backlash, most agreed that the new album was at least as good as its predecessor and the band's ability to connect with the crowd was as intense as ever. It was starting to look like the overdue 'build 'em up to knock 'em down' routine just wasn't going to happen.

"Rumours of a disappointing follow-up to *Whatever People Say I Am . . .* have been put to bed by this tour," a fan posted after the Dundee gig on April 18. But then, anyone who'd just witnessed two people jump from a balcony to a speaker stack to get nearer the band was likely to have been impressed.

As one blogger opined on the *Chimpomatic* reviews site, there's "no need for razzamatazz when music can speak for itself. With the audience in the palm of their hand the enthusiasm is sucked up and thrown right back . . . I could go on but I expect you won't believe me."

★   ★   ★

Favourite Worst Nightmare was released in the USA on April 24. The band marked the occasion by returning to the States for a short tour, starting with the Coachella Valley Music and Arts Festival on April 27. The band's development between the two albums was greeted with approval – as well as prompting the odd Darwinian pun about monkeys evolving.

For the rest of the tour, the band hooked up with support act Be Your Own Pet and rolled straight out of Coachella into the Los Angeles Troubadour on April 29, followed by The Warfield in San Francisco, Roseland Theater in Portland, Showbox in Seattle, Commodore Ball-room in Vancouver, First Avenue in Minneapolis, Riviera Theatre in Chicago, Clutch Cargo's in Pontiac, Kool Haus in Toronto, The Olympia in Montreal and Avalon in Boston.

They completed the US tour with headline slots throughout May at The Hammerstein Ballroom, New York City, 9:30 Club in Washington, The Electric Factory in Philadelphia, The Tabernacle in Atlanta and Hard Rock Live in Orlando. With O'Malley fully settled in on bass, more beat-driven influences at play and a harder sound, the band seemed edgier than ever. At least one blogger compared their interplaying guitar and drum patterns with punked-up versions of techno and drum 'n' bass.

The band then turned back to Europe in the run-up to their first appearance at Glastonbury, the UK's flagship festival. Heading back to Holland for a smattering of pre-Glastonbury Festival gigs, they played Tivoli in Utrecht with Eagles Of Death Metal, followed by a main stage show at the Pinkpop Festival at Landgraaf, Holland, alongside Scissor Sisters, Linkin Park and Smashing Pumpkins. From here the tour sped through Luxembourg, playing Den Atelier and on to the Rock Am Ring Festival in Nürburgring on June 1.

In the immediate lead-up to Glastonbury the band performed at Dublin's Malahide Castle. The weather had been going against them, but Alex was in relaxed and comfortable mode, starting the night by tossing chocolate bars into the audience. In a delayed response, someone inflated a slew of condoms and set them adrift over the crowd, while Alex took the chance to rib a fan wearing a day-glo Sheffield United top.

Moving on to play the Cardiff International Arena, they were joined by their old mates Reverend & The Makers and The Rascals on June 19 and 20. The Cardiff nights went down a storm, but a few songs into the second night the start of 'Still Take You Home' discombobulated into silence. For a split second it appeared the band had tumbled into chaos for the first time. You could almost see the shocked gasps ripple through the venue, but then Alex stepped forward: "Look after yourselves. Somebody's hurt!" he warned as a couple of girls were lifted over the barrier.

Later that night, Cardiff became the first audience to be treated to a keyboard added to Arctic Monkeys' backline, followed by the added pleasure of '505' played as a previously unheard-of encore.

★　★　★

Most bands spend years waiting for their first invitation to play the Pyramid Stage at Glastonbury. Arctic Monkeys got there before their second LP had been released, for the major headline slot on the festival's first big day, Friday, June 21, 2007.

To mark the occasion, on June 18 the band released a 1,000-pressing limited edition seven-inch single featuring 'Matador' and 'Da Frame 2R'. The songs had first appeared as bonus tracks on the Japanese version of *Favourite Worst Nightmare*; they were also released as a download single.

The band was scheduled to play at 11.05 p.m., at the end of what had been a long, rain-soaked, mud-spattered day. But it turned out to be fortunate billing. By the end of the festival, Glastonbury had experienced one of its worst mud baths since 1998. The Pyramid Stage was a soggy challenge that Friday, but from the moment the Monkeys took to the stage, the entire field, from the stage front to the very back hedge, was united in movement in a way rarely seen before.

Beginning their set with bravado, 'When The Sun Goes Down' was the perfect choice. It was a spine-tingling moment, only matched as a singalong later in the set when the whole of Glastonbury seemed to join in for 'Mardy Bum'.

Other highlights included James Ford joining them on organ to play a cover of 'Diamonds Are Forever', in honour of Shirley Bassey who was playing the same stage the following night. Adding to the feverish excitement, Dizzee Rascal made a brief appearance to sing on 'Temptation Greets You Like Your Naughty Friend', although the effect was dampened by a faulty microphone.

But in the end it mattered little. Arctic Monkeys, it was generally agreed, had played what would become a legendary Glastonbury set – made all the more memorable by the extraordinary audience participation they inspired.

On June 25 they made a quick pilgrimage back to northern Europe, playing the Sentrum Scene in Oslo before heading off to the Annex in Stockholm. On June 28, the band stopped off to play Hamburg's Stadtpark, followed by Belgium's Rock Werchter Festival. Two French dates – Zénith in Paris and Zénith in Lille on July 3 and 4 – completed the continental tour. The band then returned to the UK for another landmark gig: T In The Park in Scotland on the first Friday.

The weather behaved in traditional British fashion, leaving fans to brave fields of mud to watch the now established set of some 15 to 17 songs from both LPs. Alex was again in chattier form than his younger self had been, checking the crowd were "all right" and, on at least one occasion, taking the unusual step of heckling them for not really being "match fit". (To be fair, they were probably weighed down by the weather.)

Alex also announced that it was Jamie Cook's birthday and led the 60,000-strong crowd in a mass singalong, adding: "Anytime it goes quiet at all this evening, you just start singing 'Happy Birthday'." Miles Kane, who Alex described as both the band's best friend and best dressed friend, was also brought on to play guitar on '505'.

A few days after T In The Park, on July 9, 'Fluorescent Adolescent' was released as the second single from the LP, along with a promotional video by *IT Crowd* cast member and all-round comedy genius Richard Ayoade. The song, written by Alex and Johanna Bennett, describes the lost dreams of an older woman; Ayoade's video features Stephen Graham (who appeared in the video for 'When The Sun Goes Down') dressed in a clown suit, leading a gang of clowns in a fight with a normal gang. Flashbacks reveal the rival gang leaders used to be friends and the video ends with the clown leader blowing up the car his former friend is driving. The single entered the UK singles chart at number five and the indie singles chart at number one.

In the same week the single he'd written with his ex-girlfriend hit the charts, Alex was getting to know the next big love of his life.

27

Baby I'm Yours: When Alexa Met Alex

A COUPLE of years older than Alex, the kookily good-looking Alexa Chung was born on November 5, 1983. A former model, she graduated to become the face of Channel 4's *Popworld*. If Alex had inspired yearnings in the nation's teenage girls, then Alexa had done the same for the country's pre-teen male population.

The youngest of four children born to an English mother and part-Chinese father, she'd followed her eldest brother, respected London DJ Dom Chung, into a music-orientated career. Like Alex, she postponed going to university (she'd been offered two places); after she finished her A-levels, she signed to the Storm modelling agency, which had spotted her at Reading Festival.

Among the high-profile assignments that followed were cover shots for *Elle Girl* and *CosmoGIRL!*, becoming the face of the Antipodium fashion line and advertising campaigns for Sunsilk, Tampax, Sony Ericsson and Urban Outfitters. She also appeared in music promo videos for The Streets, Westlife and Reuben. But her TV career took off when she took over as presenter of *Popworld* after Miquita Oliver and Simon Amstell left in 2006 – having unsuccessfully auditioned for the show when she was 18.

Alexa's next venture, a part in Ben Elton's satirical show *Get A Grip* in 2007, was badly received, but soon afterwards she signed a 'golden hand-cuffs' deal with Channel 4 which was reported to be worth £100,000. As part of the deal, she appeared on *Big Brother's Big Mouth* and numerous T4 shows. Most importantly, she fronted T4's music specials and Channel 4's coverage of V Festival and T In The Park. It was on this last assignment that she started hanging out with Alex in 2007.

Before Alex, Alexa had been in a three-and-a-half-year relationship with David Titlow, who was 20 years older than her and had been the singer in Eighties pop group Blue Mercedes. After Titlow, she was briefly linked to Faris Badwan, the singer from The Horrors, Klaxons keyboardist James Righton and Lostprophets singer Ian Watkins.

She had also met Alex earlier, but after July 2007, when she was seen hanging out with him at T In The Park, with Turner still touring, the news that Chung and Watkins were no longer together was made public. Soon after, her relationship with Turner was also acknowledged. The couple quickly became style, gossip column and celebrity magazine dynamite. But Alex wasn't going to get much time to see his new girlfriend.

The band's next tour would take him on a month-long sprint across the European summer festival circuit, starting with a return to Roskilde in Denmark on July 8, 2007, followed by Columbia Hall in Berlin, Alter Schlachthof in Dresden, and Arena in Vienna. After that, they took a rollercoaster ride up and down Italy with the Traffic Festival in Turin, Piazza Castello in Ferrara and the Musilac Festival in Aix-les-Bains, France. The Coliseum in Lisbon was followed by Auditorio do Parque de Castrelos in Vigo, the Benicàssim Festival in Spain, Les Arènes, the Roman amphitheatre in Nimes, and finally the Paléo Festival in Nyon, Switzerland on July 24.

Having played a string of festivals, Arctic Monkeys' next trick would be to stage one of their own. Returning to England in late July 2007, they organised two massive gigs at the Old Trafford Cricket Ground, the home of Lancashire County Cricket Club.

The event was originally planned for one day only, Saturday July 28, but when all 55,000 tickets sold out in a flash they hurriedly added a second day on Sunday. Tickets for that sold out immediately too.

The band had been playing large festivals for the most of the summer, but this was the first time they'd headlined their own gig to an audience of this size. "At that point after the second album, your career either declines and falls away or you start to fill stadiums," Martin Talbot of the Official Charts Company points out. "That's the crossroads for an act, if you don't do it at this point you aren't going to do it."

The band had decided to book the support acts themselves, a job they later admitted was harder than it looked. The choices they made encompassed a wide range of music, including a Japanese Beatles tribute act called The Parrots, who the band had seen while on tour in Japan, Amy Winehouse, Supergrass and The Coral. In the run-up to the event, the press started comparing Old Trafford to The Stone Roses' Spike Island gig in 1990 and Oasis's record-breaking concert at Knebworth in 1996.

Kate Linderholm of BBC Sheffield recalls an excited posse making its way over from the Monkeys' heartland: "We got the coach over from High Green and they were piling onto the coach with crates of beer. We had to stop a couple of times on the way *there* for people to throw up. It was proper High Green good fun. They'd be like, 'Can we just get off the coach? I'm going to throw up!' Then they'd be sick and immediately start rolling a joint and trying to get a couple of tokes in before getting back on the coach."

The gigs were a storming success, featuring playful Yorkshire-versus-Lancashire chants in the crowd egged on by an ever more confident and chatty Alex. Even a complete sound system failure during 'Balaclava' on the first night failed to faze the band. Breaking completely with tradition, the band that didn't do encores rounded off both gigs with three extra songs: 'Plastic Tramp', '505' and 'A Certain Romance'.

In one widely reported oversight, a lack of facilities eventually led to people urinating in the middle of the arena. Allegations were made that the glasses of liquid hurled over the moshing crowd were no longer filled with cider and beer – a rumour that would grow legs and follow the Monkeys to subsequent gigs.

Nonetheless, Glastonbury and Old Trafford ably demonstrated the Monkeys had grown into global festival and stadium headliners.

28

Splendour In The Grass

A WEEK after Old Trafford, the Monkeys returned to Australia for their second tour. New Zealand and Australia had been impressed by them on their first visit and the feeling was clearly mutual. Jamie Cook once responded to a journalist asking if he was enjoying the band's success by saying of course he was, he'd just been to Australia! Matt had also once told reporters the country was so wonderful that he didn't want to leave.

The tour had been organised around their headline appearance at the Splendour In The Grass Festival in Byron Bay, with tickets for all the shows sold out. The Monkeys' first warm-up show was at the 5,000-capacity Hordern Pavilion on August 3, with Queensland's Operator Please supporting. From here they moved on to The Tivoli in Brisbane, followed by Splendour In The Grass's closing night on Sunday August 5.

Splendour In The Grass was an annual bijou two-day festival holding 17,500 people. Operator Please, who surprised some critics by looking even younger than Arctic Monkeys, opened for the whole festival and brought with them an afternoon of sunshine. They were followed by big names such as Lily Allen, Kaiser Chiefs and The Editors. On Sunday, Hilltop Hoods, Bloc Party and The Shins all graced the stage. Arctic Monkeys had been booked to close the main stage on Sunday night and their arrival heralded a full-on mosh pit – as well as rain.

On August 7, 2007 they moved on to Festival Hall in Melbourne for their second highly anticipated appearance in the city. The show had sold out within minutes of being announced and the fervour they aroused with their previous tour a year earlier showed no sign of abating. The excited crowds that formed outside the venue that evening suggested they could probably have filled the 5,000-capacity venue once over again.

The Monkeys strolled onstage to deafening applause and ripped into an hour-and-a-quarter set, sparking a cacophony of singing, chanting, moshing and surfing – 'Still Take You Home', 'Dancing Shoes' and 'I Bet You Look Good On The Dancefloor' received especially manic responses. Once again Alex revealed a more relaxed side to his character, greeting the crowd, supping his beer and taunting a fan with an Oasis T-shirt, telling them his old idols and current friends were boring. As Matt and Jamie's statements had suggested, the Monkeys felt at home in Australia from the start and formed an intense bond with their audience.

After the three dates in Australia the next stop was Japan, to play the Summer Sonic sister festivals in Osaka and Tokyo. The Osaka Festival is close to Glastonbury in size, featuring over 120 acts on six stages that range from a baseball stadium to a beach. Arctic Monkeys played the stadium, which was plunged into darkness just before they came onstage. The band had chosen the theme from *Thomas The Tank Engine* as their customary tongue-in-cheek entrance tune, although it was soon drowned out by the full-to-capacity crowd.

The gig that followed was as joyfully lapped up by the audience as it was confidently performed by the band. The new songs had a broader degree of universality to them, but the older tunes, set in a young teenager's life in a northern English suburb, still rang true in this vast arena on the other side of the world.

★   ★   ★

Returning from their tour of the East, Arctic Monkeys had been booked to play Ibiza Rocks at Bar M on September 1, 2007. Given the opportunity to chill there, they asked to be booked in for a week's working holiday.

The island had remained very much the preserve of electronic music. At the time there was an increasingly heavy influence from Berlin's club scene, replacing the BBC Radio 1 and MTV dance media machines that had dominated the island in the late Nineties.

It hardly seemed the ideal time for Arctic Monkeys to play there, but the buzz around the band and the spirit and freshness of their sound had always gone down well in sections of the dance music community. Many of the older DJs had originally been into punk and the countercultural origins of much dance music meant that there was an appreciation that transcended musical genres. Arctic Monkeys' beats and song structures made sense to a generation brought up on drum 'n' bass and techno.

"The Arctic Monkeys have something to say and can say it in a great way," explains Ross Allen, radio and club DJ, and a former A&R man for Domino. "It's all about Alex Turner and the energy of the band. He is a real poet and his lyrics connect. Plus, the energy of the first two records is amazing. They are the best guitar band in years."

Bar M, where the Monkeys were playing, was originally owned by Ibiza super-club Manumission, which had started Ibiza Rocks, a summer season of weekly live gigs, in 2005. The bar held a packed capacity of 700 people and, after two years, the event was moved to a bigger venue, making the Arctic Monkeys' gig one of the last to be held at Bar M.

It had reached capacity well in advance. The band had brought their old friends Reverend & The Makers with them as support, and it was their most intimate gig for a long while. The audience was packed in tight, ensuring the mosh pit extended over the whole venue. One fan recalled finally emerging from the gig sweaty, shaken, bruised and minus her shoes, which had been prised from her feet by the crush. Amongst the crowd were members of Kaiser Chiefs and DJ Norman Cook, aka Fatboy Slim, as well as Zane Lowe who was DJing that night.

29

Mercury Revising

RETURNING to London, the Monkeys had been nominated for the Mercury Prize for the second year running. It was unlikely that they could win again, and just being nominated twice was extremely unusual – not least because it was rare for a band to release two records close enough together for two consecutive nominations.

Their producer, James Ford, was up for a different kind of double. Another album he'd produced, The Klaxons' *Myths Of The Near Future*, had also been nominated. As it turned out, Ford would be a winner that year instead of the Monkeys, as The Klaxons walked away with the award and the £20,000 cheque.

In his acceptance speech, The Klaxons' James Righton acknowledged their band had been massively inspired by last year's winners: "A year ago we were in the studio making this album and we were sitting in the studio watching Arctic Monkeys win this. We saw that and thought we have to make a new album."

Immediately after the Mercury Prize, the band began their biggest North American tour to date, enlisting rising Texan band Voxtrot as their support. The band started their fourth US tour in New York, headlining their own sold-out SummerStage gig in Central Park on September 5, 2007.

Fans had started queuing for the evening gig halfway through the afternoon. Despite this adulation, Alex managed to roam unnoticed amongst the crowd before the show, although he seemed to recognise some of the audience members from the stage. The gig that night saw the band play at their breakneck edgiest, ripping into their 80-minute set with current openers 'This House Is A Circus', 'Brianstorm' and 'Still Take You Home'.

As a return to New York it was another triumph. As one blogger, Sheryl Witlen, who had already seen them in smaller arenas, observed: "It is not just that they deliver their songs with unbelievable precision and affection, but by experiencing their live show you realise just how full a sound these four musicians create. They are so young, yet they fill up any space they occupy."

From New York the tour moved north, via Providence on September 6, to the Virgin Festival in Toronto, where Alex and James were cornered for an interview. Asked if they could think of any famous virgins (they couldn't), they were asked if they wanted to experience space travel.

The connection between the questions was that Virgin founder Richard Branson had recently announced a VIP space travel project. Cook and Turner seemed less than enthusiastic about the idea, with Jamie observing it was a lot of hassle just to be able to float about for a bit, while Alex joked that space might be a bit like Ibiza, in that people could go there and never come back. On a more serious note, they were asked which of their two albums they would recycle and which they would keep. Both immediately said they'd dump the first one.

The next stop on the tour was the second Osheaga Music and Arts Festival, the two-day rock festival in Montreal held on September 8 and 9, 2007. Here they played in front of a crowd of 25,000. After Montreal they moved back to the USA and Newport Music Hall in Columbus, Ohio, followed by Chicago's Aragon Ballroom and Kansas City four days later.

On September 15 the tour returned to Texas, for the Austin City Limits (ACL) Music Festival. After Austin, the tour continued through Dallas and Houston, where the band had been booked to support Queens Of The Stone Age. On paper it was a gig of the century, but in practice it turned out to be the wrong city for the two dynamos of the new rock'n'roll. As Josh Homme was to reveal to *NME* before the gig, it was something of a ghost town.

In the end, Arctic Monkeys went on at 8 p.m. to play to approximately 1,000 people in a venue that could hold 2,500. But by the end of the gig everyone who was there, including Homme who was watching from the sidelines, had been won over. It might not have benefited the Monkeys' album sales much, but it hadn't harmed their working relationship with Queens Of The Stone Age.

Moving on to House of Blues in New Orleans, band and audience reverted to the usual packed venue, bouncing and singing along. The pattern resumed in Tempe and Tucson, Arizona, before moving on to the San Diego Street Scene Festival and on through Los Angeles' Hollywood Palladium, The Warfield in San Francisco, the McDonald Theatre in Eugene and closing the US leg of the tour at Paramount in Seattle on 29 September, followed by one final show in Canada.

A week after returning to the UK, the band were nominated for three Q Awards: Best Live Act, Best Album and Best Act in the World Today. This time they all agreed to attend the ceremony on October 8 at Park Lane's Grosvenor House Hotel, where they lost the first two to Amy Winehouse (Best Album for *Back To Black*) and Muse (Best Live Act). But the Monkeys beat stiff competition from The Killers, Foo Fighters, Muse and U2 to claim the Best Act in the World Today award.

The whole band went down to the stage to collect the award, perhaps because it was being handed to them by Dame Shirley Bassey – something that seemed to impress the Monkeys as much as the award itself. Among the other musicians at the lunchtime ceremony was Sir Paul McCartney, who was named Icon of the Year.

Flush from the success of winning Best Act in the World Today, Arctic Monkeys set off to prove themselves worthy of their new status with a Latin American tour. In truth, they'd already earned their wings with relentless UK, European, Eastern and American dates – but Latin America was virgin territory.

The first gig was a packed Luna Park Stadium in Buenos Aires on October 24, 2007. Even for a band used to the slightly unnerving sight of people they didn't know and whose language they didn't speak singing their songs, thousands of people singing Monkeys tunes in a South American country they'd never previously visited must have been exciting.

The same scenes greeted them at the TIM Festival in Rio de Janeiro, where fans had been queuing throughout the day to get the best position in the arena. In the full fury of live excitement the band once again ripped into their set, exploding from one song to another with Alex giving only occasional recognition to the crowd. It was magic Monkeys.

Before playing a new song, 'Nettles', Alex quoted the last lines from a poem he'd written and within a very short space of time, some fans were able to quote the poem from YouTube footage. Even more remarkably, Brazilian fans seemed to recognise the words to 'Nettles' – the short B-side to the next single, 'Teddy Picker'. At the time of the Rio gig, 'Nettles' was still two months away from release, yet Portuguese-speaking fans in Brazil appeared to be singing it already. Audience reaction at the TIM Festival events in Sao Paulo and Curitiba was, if anything, even more hysterical than in Rio.

Arctic Monkeys finished their Latin America tour on the last day of October 2007 and returned to the UK for almost a whole month. At the end of November, in the run-up to the release of 'Teddy Picker', they took off for a short promotional tour of France, Germany, Spain and the Netherlands, with Reverend & The Makers returning to support duties.

While touring France, the band dropped 'Put Me In A Terror Pocket' into the first half of their set. Moving on to La Riviera in Madrid, they played to an excited Spanish audience on November 30 and an equally frenetic Catalan crowd at Espacio Movistar, Barcelona on December 1.

In Cologne, the pulling power of the Monkeys once again came to the fore as the band packed out the Palladium on December 3 – an accomplishment in itself, given that several British bands had recently struggled to fill local venues. The band introduced some new material to their loyal German audience, starting with 'Sandtrap' – a reworking of the instrumental 'Wagon', which they'd first played as a set opener in Latin America.

The new single, 'Teddy Picker', was released that same day in the UK. As it rang out around the Palladium, the Cologne venue turned into a sea of bouncing bodies. It was, as one reviewer would remark, a most un-German event.

30

Teddy Picker And The Death Ramps

'TEDDY Picker' was released in the UK on December 3, 2007 and charted at number 20 – its highest mainstream chart position anywhere, although the single went to number one in the UK indie charts. Issued in several different formats, including a limited vinyl pressing, the way it was released had more in common with 'Five Minutes With The Arctic Monkeys' than a full-on chart release. The song's title came from the slang name for an amusement park game. But the subject matter dealt with cheap celebrity – the pointless, self-serving stardom that the Monkeys had themselves been struggling hard to avoid.

Those with a penchant for analysing lyrics soon noticed the song contained the band's second reference to Eighties New Romantic pop group Duran Duran, with the line, "I don't want your prayers, save it for the morning after" (the first had been, "Your name isn't Rio but I don't care for sand," from 'I Bet You Look Good On The Dancefloor').

The single also introduced Arctic Monkeys' new alter egos, The Death Ramps, who were credited for the single's B-side on a limited edition vinyl single. As the press release explained: "We're not allowed to tell you the true identity of The Death Ramps but needless to say they're a band with A Certain Romance (wink, wink)."

Three B-side tracks were included over two limited vinyl editions (250 copies each), with 'Nettles' and 'Death Ramps' on one and 'Bad Woman', featuring Richard Hawley guesting on vocals, on the other. Created as an alternative outlet and described by Alex as a bit of a holiday for the whole band, The Death Ramps would only make a few more appearances – on the B-side of 'The Hellcat Spangled Shalalala', with Miles Kane, and the B-side of 'Black Treacle', with Richard Hawley. The name for this alter ego had been taken from the hills the Monkeys rode their BMXs on when they were kids.

Arctic Monkeys began their UK tour during the first week of the single's release with a smaller number of dates in much bigger venues, playing two nights at London's Alexandra Palace on December 8 and 9, followed by two nights at The G-Mex in Manchester and two at the Aberdeen Exhibition and Conference Centre (AECC). The London dates were the first UK gigs since the mammoth Old Trafford events and both gigs quickly sold out.

Having road-tested several new songs on the European and Latin American tours, the band were ready to unleash their new material on the British public. They opened with the smouldering, unreleased 'Sandtrap' before launching into the new single. "Are you having a good time or, if you're not, are you prepared to?" Alex quizzed the crowd between the band thundering through the set, stopping later to introduce 'Put Me In A Terror Pocket'.

Other surprises that night included 'Da Frame 2R', the B-side of that summer's limited edition 'Matador' single, while guests included Miles Kane – who joined them on 'Plastic Tramp', the B-side to 'Fluorescent Adolescent' – and Dizzee Rascal, who burst onstage halfway through 'Temptation Greets You Like Your Naughty Friend', this time with a working microphone.

His scream-inducing entrance took everyone by surprise but his exit went further, as he bounced off the front of the stage and walked along the crowd barrier, bumping fists and shaking hands. The Arctic Monkeys chants had morphed into hollers of "Dizzee, Dizzee, Dizzee!"

"That was very sharp," admired Alex.

But not all guests had such an easy ride. Tour support for all six dates came from The Horrors and The Rascals with Miles Kane. Both acts had been chosen personally by the Monkeys, but from the start their fans had been intolerant towards the former band. The confrontation was anticipated; The Horrors had been critical of the Monkeys on numerous occasions, with frontman Faris Badwan at one point posing in front of a picture of the Monkeys holding a note saying 'RIP'. Although the Monkeys had been magnanimous in their response, their fans were in a less generous mood.

Before The Horrors had been given a chance to prove themselves at Alexandra Palace, the fans had unleashed a hail of objects. For much of the set it rained glow sticks, cans, shoes and anything else the audience could find to throw, including coins – which prompted lead singer Faris Badwan to taunt the crowd by collecting the money from the stage floor, asking: "Hasn't anyone got any notes?"

Even as the Monkeys came onstage, the atmosphere was still on the edge. The mood changed dramatically once they started playing, but worse was to follow when the tour moved on to two dates at The G-Mex, Manchester. Here the reception dished out to The Horrors was even more hostile – greeting the band with an assortment of missiles that included bottles.

Turner was unimpressed, calling his own audience "wankers" on the first night. On the marginally better second night, he introduced 'D Is For Dangerous' by saying: "D is for . . . dickheads, for what you did to The Horrors."

The tension had been partially defused by the Monkeys, but the atmosphere was hardly subdued. Throughout the set the crowd sang, cuddled, moshed and threw fountains of beer into the air, along with liberated clothing and crowd-surfers.

Before rounding off the tour in Aberdeen, the band squeezed in a secret gig at the Manchester Apollo to film *Arctic Monkeys Live At The Apollo*, for the DVD of the same name.

Although less extreme than the Manchester reaction, a large fight started to break out at the start of the AECC gig in Aberdeen. As with The G-Mex, the situation was immediately restored once Arctic Monkeys arrived onstage.

With the second night at AECC, on December 15, the tour came to a successful conclusion. Whatever the fans felt about the tension at the gigs, few of them realised how long it would be before they'd get the chance to see Arctic Monkeys again.

31

Brits And Brats

HAVING been almost constantly on tour for most of their collective career, Arctic Monkeys suddenly took their foot off the accelerator in 2008 and began a studio period that, from the outside at least, seemed deceptively quiet. The change in pace was dramatic, but their first public appointment of the year was by now familiar.

The band had taken their two previous Brit Awards victories as an invitation to send the ceremony up. So it was with a bullish optimism that the organisers had invited them back. The awards ceremony took place on February 20 at Earls Court, with Arctic Monkeys nominated for Best Album and Best Group.

The first rows of seats at the arena had been given to bright young hopefuls studying at the Brit School – the celebrity boot camp that had turned out Adele, Leona Lewis, Kate Nash and Amy Winehouse, among others.

In contrast to earlier years, Arctic Monkeys had bothered to turn up in person for the first time. As with the previous year, they had also made the effort to dress up. Posing as comedy country squires in tweeds and flat caps, carrying pipes, they pretended they were also Brit School alumni, generally making a mockery of the awards show and manufactured pop acts.

"We all went to the Brit School, we remember you all!" Turner said, pointing at the front row. "We all had a great time in them years . . . After we graduated we formed the Monkeys and we've had a fantastic time since."

The organisers hurriedly shut down the microphones and ushered the Monkeys backstage, before they became overly insulting. Nonetheless, they walked away with the two top prizes.

The following week it was time for the *NME* Awards ceremony. Arctic Monkeys had been nominated for a staggering six trophies and, on past form, it was quite conceivable that they would walk out of the February 28 ceremony carrying every single one of them.

The nomination for Best Live Band had been more or less expected. Their live achievements in 2007 had been extraordinary: Glastonbury, the two Old Trafford Cricket Ground events, six sell-out arena gigs, not to mention countless international festival appearances. The Best Album nomination was also predictable, but in addition the band received nominations for Best British Band, Best Track (for 'Fluorescent Adolescent'), Best Music Video (for 'Teddy Picker') and a second album nomination for the much praised artwork by Juno.

The Arctic Monkeys won the highest accolade, for Best British Band, and also took the awards home for Best Video and Best Track. But they lost out to The Klaxons for Best Album, to Muse for Best Live Band and to *The Good, The Bad & The Queen* for Best Album Artwork. Nevertheless, for the third year running Arctic Monkeys had been the talk of the *NME* Awards.

★ ★ ★

The band might have decided to take a year off from touring, but they were far from idle. Apart from writing, rehearsing and recording the next LP, the various members also used it as an opportunity to work on their side projects.

Amongst their various offshoots, Matt had started a clothing line in 2007, having once joked he only joined the band as a stepping stone into the fashion industry. It came about through contacts of his father's at a clothing company he'd once worked for. They were already making clothes for DJs and rappers, and so they offered to make some for Matt. The Monkeys were mid-tour and busy recording, but Matt, having little time to spare, had happily agreed anyway.

Matt's decision to go into fashion design was no random accident. Alongside photography and music, his extracurricular activities at college had included printing T-shirts.

The first Helders collection, for the Supremebeing fashion label, started rolling off the production line in May 2007. It included a jacket, a zipped hoodie and three T-shirts, issued in a limited run of 600 each. Some of the profit from Matt's clothing line would be donated to the Arthur Rank

Hospice in Cambridge. After a successful first run, more Helders designs followed via the band's message boards and fashion website asos.com. By 2012, he had launched his new club clothing line at Urban Outfitters shops.

Apart from getting his clothing range off the ground, Matt was also doing remixes, adopting a crunk-laced hip hop style that also showed an influence from the Ed Banger school of French electro. His bass-fuelled remixes of The Hives' 'We Rule The World (T.H.E.H.I.V.E.S.)', We Are Scientists' 'Chick Lit', Roots Manuva's 'Again & Again' and Duran Duran's 'Skin Divers' were all released in 2008, while his remix of Yo Majesty's 'Club Action' followed in 2009.

Matt also created an Arctic Monkeys mix LP, as part of the *Late Night Tales* series. For this he recorded (as is customary) a new cover version. Hooking up with Nesreen Shah, he remade mid-Nineties commercial house track 'Dreamer' by Livin' Joy, as an on-point, acidic electro-hop track. Matt also included Alex's first short story, 'A Choice Of Three', on the compilation, with both the LP and the single version of the track released in 2008.

Helders also hooked up with Andy Nicholson on his new project, Mongrel, playing on the tracks 'Barcode' and 'The Menace'. He also joined fellow Sheffield alumni Toddla T for two tracks, 'Boom DJ From The Steel City' and 'Better'. Yet another side project came in September 2008, when Nicholson and Helders opened a pub, The Bowery, with third co-owner James O'Hara, the main force behind the Tramlines Festival.

Still finding time for yet more extracurricular activity, Matt also played for We Are Scientists during their 2008 UK tour. The two bands were of course close friends, but WAS weren't beyond using Helders for a bit of extra PR spin. Naturally they did it with bags of humour, claiming Matt was always on the lookout for extra cash and that he frequently sent bands unsolicited emails, offering his services at surprisingly reasonable rates.

Matt was not the only Monkey with a side project. News about the first Arctic Monkeys offshoot band, The Last Shadow Puppets, had started to break in late summer 2007, although the group was not officially given a name until February 2008.

The Last Shadow Puppets consisted of Alex Turner, Miles Kane and

James Ford. Alex and Miles Kane had first become friends when Kane's former band, The Little Flames, had supported them in 2005. The two had collaborated on several tracks, not least on '505', 'Plastic Tramp' and 'Bakery', which were also worked on by Ford. Kane had frequently played live as a guest with Arctic Monkeys, including at Glastonbury, where Ford also played keyboards, and Old Trafford.

"We were doing some mixes on the second album and Miles Kane, a good friend of Alex's, was hanging around," recalls Ford. "He did some guitar on one of the tracks ['505'] and Miles and Alex had been writing some tunes. We were always swapping music – and there was lots of stuff they hadn't heard, so they were just ravenous for new music. So I introduced them to things like Scott Walker.

"Miles had that Liverpool thing – where they're into classic Sixties stuff. So they started writing these almost torch song-like, epic, Sixties songs. We got excited about the idea of recording an EP and we went away, just me, Miles and Al, to this place in France [a residential studio called Black Box] for a week's holiday. And we just had an amazing time getting drunk and getting into playing the music.

"From planning to do a few songs, it stretched into an album. I played the drums and most of the bass, and we just had a really great time doing it. It wasn't really meant to be anything, but then we ended up getting some strings on it and going for the full bombast thing.

"There was no expectation, because no one knew we were doing it, so it was really relaxed and easy. Like a weird lads' holiday, one of the most enjoyable experiences I've ever had. Then we ended up going on tour with a full orchestra."

More material was written between August and December, with Owen Pallett invited to arrange strings, brass and percussion for the 22-piece London Metropolitan Orchestra. The band also brought in two documentary makers, Luke Seomore and Joseph Bull, to capture the project as it was being created.

On February 20, 2008 the project's name was announced, along with the title of the forthcoming LP, *The Age Of Understatement*. The title track was subsequently released as the first single on April 14, with a new song, 'Two Hearts In Two Weeks', and covers of Billy Fury's 'Wondrous Place' and David Bowie's 'In The Heat Of The Morning' on the flip side. The album itself was released on April 21 and went straight to number one in the UK chart. The second single, 'Standing Next To Me', followed on July 7, while a third, 'My Mistakes Were Made For You', followed on October 20.

Musically, Turner and Kane had taken inspiration from early Scott Walker and early Bowie, while influences ranging from the late Sixties Beatles to progressive rock (an ongoing interest of James Ford's) were also evident. The album also saw Turner and Ford back at what felt like their annual diary fixture at the Mercury Prize, though their nomination lost to Elbow's *The Seldom Seen Kid*.

The band made their debut live appearance on March 4, with an in-store show at Williamsburg's Sound Fix record store in New York, followed by a second low-key show at the Lower East Side's Cake Shop on March 5. This was followed on April 5 by a two-song mini-set of 'Meeting Place' and 'Stand Next To Me' at The Lock Tavern in London's Camden, at a benefit for MS sufferers organised by singer Remi Nicole. They performed as a full band for the first time on *Later . . . With Jools Holland*, with James Ford on drums, Stephen Fretwell on bass and John Ashton on keyboards.

The band also played a secret set at Glastonbury on June 28, where Matt Helders joined on drums for 'The Age Of Understatement' and Jack White played a guitar solo on 'Wondrous Place'. This was followed by gigs with a 16-piece orchestra at Portsmouth Guildhall and Oxford New Theatre, before playing the Reading and Leeds Festivals.

In October and November 2008 they embarked on a major tour of the UK and USA, which finally brought the project to a close, enabling Turner and Ford to return to Arctic Monkeys for their next LP, *Humbug*. Miles Kane has intimated several times (in 2009, 2010 and, most recently, in January 2012) that he and Turner will reform The Last Shadow Puppets for a second album. But James Ford has said that he thinks a second LP is unlikely – although he's refused to rule it out.

★　★　★

Meanwhile, Matt had been invited to participate in the development of a music festival in Sheffield, entitled Tramlines. The brainchild of James O'Hara and a collection of like-minded Sheffield promoters, DJs, labels and musicians, the idea started coming together in late 2008 and early 2009.

O'Hara was also the lead partner in Matt and Andy's Sheffield bar venture and a number of the city's most influential performers, including Jon McClure and Toddla T, also joined up for the festival project. It was intended to showcase Sheffield's hottest talent as well as featuring cross-genre acts from around the country, acting as a particular focus for music in the north of England.

With the news of Helders' and the Monkeys' involvement came hopes that they could bring international attention to Sheffield, aroused largely by a recently established friendship with P. Diddy. Arctic Monkeys had first met Sean Combs (the man known as P. Diddy – formerly Puff Daddy) at one of his parties in New York, filmed for the Monkeys' website while the band was recording in Brooklyn.

Diddy ended up showing Matt around his mansion, at one point stopping to stir grits, while he explained: "A lot of people don't understand I am the biggest Arctic Monkeys fan and [Matt] is the biggest Puff Daddy fan." Later on he told Matt that they were having a 'bromance' together and insisted that Matt hold all three of his Grammy Awards.

"It were great," Matt later recalled of the visit. "Busta Rhymes were there."

Back in Sheffield, Matt accompanied O'Hara to city council meetings, to meet and greet councillors and smooth the passage of the Tramlines Festival. With the council's backing secured, a press conference was organised in early 2009 at The Bowery. The first event took place between July 24 and 27 of that year, with Helders, McClure and Toddla T helping to pick the acts.

Held in various venues across the city, the entire festival was organised as a free event and some 65,000 people flooded into Sheffield city centre for the opening. Music seeped from every corner and spread goodwill throughout the city – crime rates even fell over the weekend.

A year later the festival had more than doubled in size, and in 2011 and 2012 it grew again, with a total attendance of 155,000 over three days.

32

LIVE At The Apollo!

O N November 3, 2008, the *Arctic Monkeys Live At The Apollo* DVD
was released. The title was an example of the Monkeys' self-
deprecating wordplay, referencing the legion of legendary albums 'recorded
live at Harlem's world famous Apollo Theater'. The Apollo Theatre in the
Monkeys' video was, of course, in Manchester.

A joint release between Warp Films, the Monkeys' own Bang Bang
Films and Domino, it was filmed on super-16mm film in surround sound.
The gig itself was captured at the penultimate stop of their continuous tour
activity up until the end of 2007, catching a band at the height of their
powers.

The film was directed by comic actor/writer/director Richard Ayoade,
photographed by cinematographer Danny Chone (who shot *This Is
England*) and edited by Nick Fenton. The DVD release also featured a
'Multi Angle Camera View' of Matt Helders' drumming that became a
cult item in its own right.

The film would also be broadcast on 4Music on February 19, 2009,
the day before Arctic Monkeys received two Brit Awards. (Their only
major release in 2008, the film won the *NME* Award for Best DVD in
2009.)

The next phase of Ayoade's collaboration with the Monkeys was also
taking shape by this time – which would see Alex Turner contributing to
an Ayoade project.

Side projects aside, the main reason Arctic Monkeys had taken a break
from touring was to record the quantum leap of *Humbug*. Despite the
extracurricular activity, the band had been working constantly on new
material and from late 2008 to early 2009 had recorded 24 songs. They
first recorded 12 songs with Josh Homme as producer at the Rancho de la

Luna studios, in Joshua Tree, California in the early autumn of 2008, before the band's Australasia tour kicked in at the start of 2009.

The Monkeys had shared the bill with Homme when he'd been playing with Queens Of The Stone Age. "We'd met Josh a couple of times from playing with [his band]," Matt told Xfm's John Kennedy. "He listened to the demos and said, let's do this, come to the desert."

"We thought we were going for a knickerbocker glory," interrupted Alex, referring to Josh's pronunciation of desert as 'dessert'.

In late 2008, the band relocated to California to find a harder rock sound for their new LP.

This was followed, in the spring of 2009, by another 12-song session, recorded in New York with James Ford at the controls. By now Arctic Monkeys were almost desperate to develop in new directions. The fans still loved it when they played their old classics but the band were restless for change.

It later became clear that the band had recorded more new songs than they needed. When the LP was finally released, just under half of the new tracks were included.

The record that emerged, *Humbug*, would divide the band's audience but also mark a watershed in their musical development, lifting barriers and shifting to a new paradigm. Helders would later say that after *Humbug* they felt like they could do anything.

Arctic Monkeys had adopted a more complex, deeper, darker sound as their sessions with Homme pushed them into new areas. The band conceded that Homme had exerted an authority over them in the studio, but his reputation as a fiery character seemed unfounded. According to Helders, nothing had been too much trouble for him. Anytime they wanted to go back and re-record a detail, drop in a drum fill, or augment a sound, he'd be happy to keep on until they got it right. Perhaps the Monkeys' dedicated work routine had found a perfect match in Homme's persistent perfectionism.

It helped of course that Matt had been inspired by Queens Of The Stone Age drummer Joey Castillo, and that Homme had produced the Queens' albums himself. It was the embodiment of the sound that the band wanted to move towards.

But this was not the whole story. They were also aiming for more melodic and complex structures, some of which had been expressed in The Last Shadow Puppets. Tellingly perhaps, three of the album's more accessible tracks would be produced by James Ford.

★   ★   ★

Although Arctic Monkeys wouldn't release their LP until late summer, they embarked on the first leg of their worldwide *Humbug* tour in January 2009. Over the year since they'd last played live, the Monkeys had changed physically. Alex Turner's Jam-meets-Oasis post-Mod cut had lengthened into long hair, a look also sported by Cook and O'Malley. Helders, for the moment, was the only Monkey sparing a thought for the barbers of Britain.

The first fans to hear the Monkeys' new sound were in New Zealand, where the band premiered the material at small venues in Wellington and Auckland ahead of their Big Day Out festival appearances. The set list evolved as the tour went on, showcasing new songs and some tracks that hadn't been recorded yet.

On January 13 the band returned to the stage at the Town Hall in Wellington, New Zealand and kicked in with the non-LP track 'Da Frame 2R', followed by 'This House Is A Circus' and a mixed bag from the first two albums plus new tracks, including the debuts of 'Dangerous Animals', 'Pretty Visitors', 'Crying Lightning', 'Potion Approaching' and a cover of Nick Cave's 'Red Right Hand'.

Reactions to the new material were encouraging, with both fans and critics noting the psychedelic feel and rich sound quality. Two days later they moved on to Auckland for a second warm-up gig at The Power-station, before playing the first leg of the Big Day Out.

On the festival stage, the Monkeys established the pattern for the rest of the tour, opening their set with a new song – a format they would follow up until their Reading appearance that August. At Auckland the opening track was 'Pretty Visitors', which began the set with the unusual sight of Alex playing the keyboard while the rest of the band took up positions and powered into the verse.

The song's lyrical complexity may have seemed impenetrable to an audience hearing the track for the first time, but the reaction was un-diminished. The crowd whooped and cheered as the song twisted through a series of structural changes.

The new tune was promptly followed by a solid block of six classics from the first and second LPs, interrupted by 'Dangerous Animals', followed by three more crowd-pleasers and their cover of 'Red Right Hand'. Moving on to the first date in Australia, the Monkeys played the Big Day Out on the Gold Coast on January 18, to a packed audience – despite fears that the deepening world recession would keep people away. Before going into 'Red Right Hand', Alex asked the audience: "This is our version of a Nick Cave song – everyone here knows who Nick Cave is, don't you?" The crowd screamed approvingly.

At Sydney's Hordern Pavilion on January 22, the throng received the new 'Dangerous Animals' well but went predictably crazy to the more familiar tunes. Halfway through new song 'Go Kart', Turner stopped proceedings to say: "Someone just threw 50 pence at me," before correcting himself: "No, it's 20 pence, sorry – that's not cool," and leading the band back into the song where they had left off.

The Sydney leg of the Big Day Out, on January 23, coincided with a 37-degree heatwave, and the concrete bowl at the city's showground acted as a large sun trap. By the time Arctic Monkeys came onstage, the crowd was understandably flagging from the exhausting heat. But the band soon had them on their feet, whooping and singing along.

From Sydney the tour moved to Melbourne and another packed and excitable warm-up gig at the Palais Theatre, before the Melbourne leg of the Big Day Out on January 26. Here temperatures topped 40 degrees centigrade, but the audience braved sunburn and heatstroke to see the Monkeys, who received the biggest reception of the day.

Despite the heat, Alex was in a chatty mood, asking the audience to make sure they'd tied their laces up before dancing – and remarking how dangerous they were looking in the build-up to playing 'Dangerous Animals', 'Pretty Visitors', 'Go Kart', 'Crying Lightning' and 'Red Right Hand'.

The Big Day Out dates continued into Adelaide on January 30, where the band were again the festival's biggest pull, although audience response to the new material was noticeably less dramatic than to their old classics. Finally, the Australian tour came to an end with a set at the Big Day Out in Perth on 1 February 2009.

With the band back on the road and the new songs road-tested, they returned to the UK in time for Alex and Richard Ayoade to collect the

NME Award for Best DVD at the O2 Academy Brixton on February 25. Alex's acceptance speech was characteristically brief, if more confident than his previous ones, saying simply: "Thank you very much. I'd like to pass you to Richard, the director of the film."

With the last Ford-produced tracks of the album being completed in New York and the mixing about to start, the band announced that John Ashton, their erstwhile front-of-house sound engineer, would be joining them on keyboards for the remainder of the tour. Ashton had, of course, performed with the band before, stepping in to replace Andy Nicholson on bass in Spain, and had just finished playing live in The Last Shadow Puppets with Alex. The Australian tour had indicated the Monkeys would need more players to recreate the breadth of sound on the new album live, and Ashton was enough of a member of the family to take on the role.

Meanwhile, Alex's personal life had run into problems in early 2009, when Alexa landed a new job on MTV's American programme *It's On*. It was clear she would have to move to the US, and the press was soon prophesying a split in the relationship. Alex had already relocated to London in order to live with Alexa, prompting rumours that he'd become something of a house husband.

With the rest of the band still located in Sheffield, there had also been speculation that the distance was affecting the band. Alex had, of course, suffered the difficulties of a long-range relationship with Johanna – which may have prompted him to move to London with Ms Chung in the first place. It was unlikely that either of them relished the idea of living apart.

But then Alex had been spending more time in the US anyway, as the Monkeys had been recording and mixing the new LP in New York. Gradually, the couple started being seen together more often in the Big Apple and, by the end of April, *The Sun* (amongst other tabloids) carried a story announcing Alex's relocation there. By the summer the pair had bought an apartment together in Brooklyn.

Later it would be claimed that 'Fire And The Thud', on *Humbug*, had been written about the prospect of Alexa moving to New York.

As the first single release from the album approached, the band resumed its world tour with the Heineken Open'er Festival in Poland on July 2. In the headline slot, the highlights of the Monkeys' gig were 'Crying Lightning' and 'Only Ones Who Know', with a hooded John Ashton joining them behind a gold-draped keyboard to add swelling organ chords.

On July 3 the band played the Rock For People Festival at Hradec Králové in the Czech Republic. They closed with a perfect rendition of 'Secret Door' before returning to the stage to play '505', establishing the number as their most frequent encore.

The next stop was Vienna, where the band unleashed rocking versions of 'Potion Approaching' and 'The View From The Afternoon', followed by a repeat set at Prokurative in Split on July 7. The European tour closed with a headline slot at Serbia's Exit Festival held at Petrovaradin Fortress in Novi Sad, on July 9, 2009.

33

Crying Lightning

THE first single taken from the new LP was released on July 6, 2009. One of the stand-out tracks, 'Crying Lightning' was produced by Josh Homme. Built over a smudged bass line that could have been sampled from a lost Stranglers track, the song had hooks galore, twisting through a series of structural subtleties with endless nooks and crannies to explore.

The track debuted on Zane Lowe's BBC Radio 1 show on the same day it was simultaneously released as both a single and a download – as would soon become common practice across the industry. It debuted at number 12 in the UK singles chart and at number one in the indie chart.

Physical copies of the single didn't become available until August 17, the week before the album was released, with 10-inch vinyl copies only available through Oxfam shops. They were sold with a download code that gave fans a free MP3.

Reviews for the single were mixed, but mostly favourable. *NME* seemed somewhat relieved that the track wasn't as dark as rumours had suggested – though they detected echoes of The Doors. Writing for *The Guardian*, Anna Pickard lamented the loss of the boys next door who'd now been replaced by rock gods, while *Pitchfork* lapped up both Turner's turn of phrase and Homme's production.

Meanwhile the band set off for a pre-album release tour of the USA and Canada, this time condensing their sprawling tour of 2007 into three festival appearances and three venue shows. First in line was All Points West Festival in New Jersey, where, having been welcomed by a packed and noisy arena, they ripped into 'Pretty Visitors' and 'This House Is A Circus'. It was a more than competent start, followed by a more dynamically thunderous gig at the 2009 Osheaga Music and Arts Festival in Montreal.

Back in the US, the band stopped off to play The Highline in New York on August 3. Alex appeared to be at his most relaxed and confident. Wearing a black vest, he told the audience: "I should probably have sleeves for a song like this," before playing a slowed-down version of 'Fluorescent Adolescent'. It was a robust return, as even *The New York Times* agreed.

At Paradise in Boston on August 5, a similarly warm reception awaited. When a member of the audience threw something at the stage, Alex went to inspect it. "It's a sweet," he muttered.

"It's a humbug! It's a humbug!" shouted the audience. They'd clearly done their research, as the sweet is far better known in the UK than America.

A warm-up gig at Metro in Chicago preceded the final show of the US tour at the Lollapalooza Festival, where the band once again drew the largest crowd and were judged to have played the best performance by several critics. Having topped off their most successful US tour to date, they returned triumphant for the second leg of their European sojourn.

It started with Norway's Øya Festival, then Gothenburg's Way Out West Festival on August 14, followed by Beat Day in Copenhagen, Highfield in Erfurt, Germany, and Belgium's Pukkelpop and Lowlands on August 22 and 23.

With the 2009 Reading Festival less than a few days away, it was time to return for the first UK gig in two years. The Brixton Academy show on August 26 sold out in customary fashion. It was more than a warm-up for Reading, however, and in some respects its media importance would overshadow it.

Humbug had been released on August 24. Over the first 48 hours it had sold 40,000 copies per day and would shift over 169,000 copies within a month in the UK alone. Like both of its predecessors, the album went straight to number one.

But reactions to the LP were mixed, with opinion divided between those who 'got it' and those who most definitely did not – sometimes in the same review. *Billboard* welcomed the masterful beginning of a new direction, while others saw it as the first sign that Arctic Monkeys had lost their way.

There were some great and mesmerising tracks, including 'My

Propeller', 'Crying Lightning', 'Secret Door' and the polyrhythmic stumble of 'Dangerous Animals'. But to some it was a journey too far.

"I can see why," Helders would tell the *NME* much later. "We've always wanted to make different records every time, but for us, not for anyone else. I understand why people were surprised by it, but it just had to be done. It was an experience we had to go through. We could do anything after that record."

The Guardian's Alexis Petridis argued that the Monkeys were basically faced with a choice: either make the same music forever and appeal to a very conservative fanbase, or press forward regardless of what their fans wanted. He reasoned that they'd taken the latter course and concluded that their best was yet to come.

The Brixton Academy gig had been announced via the Monkeys' fan site only one week before, with a promise that there would be something extra special happening. By the night of the gig, the secret was out: Josh Homme's long-rumoured supergroup, Them Crooked Vultures, was the support act.

Featuring Homme on lead vocals, Nirvana/Foo Fighters legend Dave Grohl on drums and John Paul Jones of Led Zeppelin on bass and keys, the support act alone made it a contender for gig of the year. So far the only song the band had produced was 'Elephant', but that night they shook Brixton Academy to its foundations with a full set.

The Monkeys were left to take to the stage as the after-hum of the Vultures' stack-shaking set had subsided. Their LP had been out for two days, so it should have been no surprise that half the audience already knew the words to the songs. As the set wore on, however, technical problems became evident. The PA started to dip during 'I Bet You Look Good On The Dancefloor', almost fading to nothing at one point.

Unfixed sound problems kicked back in with a vengeance during 'Pretty Visitors', but the band struggled on. 'Cornerstone' sounded like a future classic and 'Only Ones Who Know', 'Do Me A Favour' and 'Fluorescent Adolescent' proved they could pull the crowd along while taking their foot off the accelerator. But some of the momentum they generated onstage became more subdued as the set went on.

After celebrating with coachloads of friends and family during the Leeds leg of the tour, the band headed south for their return to Reading. Always the focus of speculation, a completely unfounded rumour that Arctic Monkeys had pulled out of the gig started circulating before they took the stage.

The band's performance carried their recent musical transition with professionalism and energy. When they came to play 'Dancefloor', it felt like they were greeting it like an old friend rather than a younger sibling who'd outstayed their welcome at a party. But as they moved into the less accessible material of 'Pretty Visitors', they had the fans cheering along its changes of rhythm.

Whatever the press thought, the band walked away from Reading feeling that they'd just triumphed. When Alex had asked in a beery drawl whether the crowd was still with them, the roar from the mass of people affirmed that view.

But the set, like the album, had divided people. Questioned by *The Shortlist* about the backlash after Reading, Alex was somewhat nonplussed: "Out of all the big festival gigs we've done in the past five years, we probably enjoyed that one most. Walking offstage we were like, 'That was great, I had a great time.' But looking at it now [laughs] we probably shouldn't have started with a Nick Cave cover. But then, you only get one chance to open a gig like that with a Nick Cave cover, so you might as well [laughs]."

One thing that most of the critics did agree upon was that the album's second single, 'Cornerstone', was an anthem in the making. Released on November 16, 2009, once again it was exclusively sold through Oxfam in its physical format. But it failed to replicate the success of earlier Arctic Monkeys singles, reaching a peak position of 94 on the UK singles chart.

The next international tour kicked in a couple of weeks after Reading, with the Monkeys returning to the USA for the start of an intense barrage of dates. Beginning with a packed gig at SOMA, San Diego on September 14, their new material immediately started to gel with the American audience.

Next on the list was the Hollywood Palladium in Los Angeles on August 15, where the band picked up more plaudits from the American press. The tour continued through The Fox Theater, Oakland; The Wonder Ballroom, Portland; The Showbox, Seattle; Malkin Bowl, Vancouver; In The Venue, Salt Lake City; The Ogden Theatre, Denver; First Avenue,

Minneapolis; Newport Music Hall, Columbus; Kool Haus in Toronto; The Electric Factory, Philadelphia; House of Blues, New Orleans and Houston, Austin City Limits; and, finally, the Palladium Ballroom, Dallas, on October 5.

After the intensive American tour, a familiar route took them back via Japan for two gigs at the legendary Liquid Room and the Budokan, Tokyo on October 18 and 19 respectively. The band would return home in time for the 2009 Q Awards. Arctic Monkeys had been nominated in no fewer than four categories – Best Album, Best Act in the World Today, Best Track and Best Live Act – but in the end went home with just the Best Live Act award.

After a couple of weeks' recuperation they were off again, for a series of large arena gigs in Europe. Beginning with the sold-out Lotto Arena in Antwerp on November 3, they moved on to two nights at Zénith in Paris, then on to a packed Berlin Arena – where crowd-surfers, rising above the slower beats of '505', suddenly seemed to take on a balletic grace – and two nights in the Heineken Music Hall in Amsterdam on November 10 and 11. Then the Monkeys returned from the Netherlands to the UK for the band's biggest home-turf tour to date.

The first gig on the schedule, the sold-out 11,000-capacity Echo Arena in Liverpool, was followed by Sheffield Arena and Newcastle's Metro Radio Arena on November 16. A two-date stopover at London's Wembley Arena on November 18 and 19 saw the crowd shifting up a gear, with the singalong to 'Crying Lightning' spreading through to the back of the venue. The MEN Arena in Manchester on the 21st witnessed another triumphant return without any of the problems of the Monkeys' last visit (with The Horrors). The Trent FM Arena was similarly success-ful, bringing the English leg of the tour to a close on November 22.

Next up was the Glasgow SECC on November 24, where some of the aggravation of the last Scottish gig reappeared. Unusually, the pre-gig mood had not been lightened by the Monkeys' arrival onstage. In the end the band were asked to stop playing twice by security, while they tried to calm some overexcited rowdiness.

Any fears that the deeper sounds of the new LP had dampened Glasgow's enthusiasm were unfounded. The fans erupted to material old and new from the first chords of 'Dance Little Liar', with the wildest reception reserved for the reintroduction of the supposedly retired 'Mardy Bum', snuck in as an addition to 'Fluorescent Adolescent' in the encore. Moving on through two sold-out dates in Ireland, the packed crowds at The Odyssey in Belfast and The O2 Dublin, on November 25 and 26, sang along to 'Crying Lightning' as enthusiastically as anything on *Beneath The Boardwalk*.

After a short break they touched down in Chicago on December 6, to play The Riviera Theatre. Their successful performance at Lollapalooza earlier in the year was by now a legend in the American press. The buzz was entirely self-made and they were greeted on their return like local heroes.

The next gig was another sold-out event at Mr Small's Theatre in Pittsburgh on December 7, followed by 9:30 Club in Washington. Two days later they returned to New York for two gigs at Terminal 5, where they opened with 'The Jeweller's Hands' and followed with a starkly contrasting version of 'Brianstorm'. Amusingly, they ended the set with a mop-topped Helders getting up from behind the kit to sing a cover of Wham's 'Last Christmas', sandwiched into the middle of 'Fluorescent Adolescent'.

In the two final two North American dates, at House of Blues in Boston and Métropolis in Montreal on December 13 and 14, Matt repeated his performance of 'Last Christmas'. After which the tour closed for the holidays.

34

My Propeller In The Albert Hall

WITH *The Guardian* naming Arctic Monkeys as their Newcomers of the Decade, the accolades still kept on coming. Amidst the praise was the recognition that the Monkeys had outlived the hype by doing it all their own way. If *Humbug* had divided fans and critical opinion, it had also publicly demonstrated they were in charge of their own musical destiny.

To be sure, many fans had struggled with a live set that (at least in its second half) saw the band suddenly adopt a more downbeat, 'shoe-gazing' style. Their transition from boys next door to long-haired rock stars had lost them some of their cheeky charm. Alex Turner, no longer living in a world of riot vans and local bus journeys, had started writing songs with less immediate universality.

But the band were still selling out massive venues and their albums were still topping the charts. Even the singles were still selling, and *Humbug* had proved the band were here to stay.

As a new year and a new decade began, their thoughts started turning to their next album. But first they had a series of European dates and British awards ceremonies to complete.

The first part of 2010 was taken up by the southern European leg of the Humbug tour, starting at PalaSharp, Milan on January 26, moving over the Alps to a packed reception at Summum in the university town of Grenoble and on to Le Liberté in Rennes. Médoquine, Bordeaux followed with manic scenes of crowd-surfing, as did Zénith in Montpellier. The tour crossed into Portugal for their debut in Porto on February 2 and a return to Lisbon. Spain followed: Palacio Vistalegre in Madrid and the Sant Jordi Cub in Barcelona, on February 5 and 6.

The final leg of the tour took them back to Germany, stopping back at Zenith in Munich, the Stadthalle in Offenbach and the Philipshalle in

Dusseldorf, before flying back to Spain for the closing show in Valencia on February 13.

Back home, the Brit Awards were celebrating their thirtieth anniversary. But, no doubt to the huge relief of the organisers, Arctic Monkeys hadn't received a single nomination – despite having released a number one album.

Nonetheless, 10 days after they returned from tour, the 2010 *NME* Awards ceremony was held at The Brixton Academy on February 24. Here Arctic Monkeys were nominated for seven awards: Best Band, Best Live Band, Best Album, Best Track, Best Video and the Giving It Back fan award, while Alex had been nominated as Hero of the Year.

Although Alex had been nominated personally, neither he nor Jamie Cook attended the ceremony. Instead, Nick O'Malley and a fluffy-haired Matt Helders turned up to collect the Best Live Band award, the only one they would take home that year. Asked at the ceremony about their next moves, Matt said: "We're pretty eager to record."

Meanwhile, the third and final single to be taken from *Humbug* was released on March 22. 'My Propeller', although a stand-out track on the LP, had acquired something of a Marmite (love it or hate it) reputation; some critics, such as *The Guardian*'s Alexis Petridis, were left nonplussed by its uncharacteristically obvious phallic references. The 10-inch version of the single was once again only made available through Oxfam shops and featured three new B-sides: 'Joining The Dots', 'The Afternoon's Hat' and 'Don't Forget Whose Legs You're On'. According to Alex, they had been recorded recently, although some of the lyrics had been lying around for a while. The single was not expected to chart, but it just made it to number 90 and hit number seven in the UK indie chart.

The single was released shortly before the one-off Albert Hall show supporting the Teenage Cancer Trust, on March 27. It was their first gig in a month and they were especially excited to be playing in such an iconic venue. The singalong to 'When The Sun Goes Down' was swelled by the RAH's acoustics, and when Alex left a deliberately long pause at the end of the intro it sounded like the cheers were loud enough to smash through the Hall's glass ceiling.

The following night they played a specially arranged gig at the Shepherd's Bush Empire, with a show to showcase tracks from *Humbug* and

Matt Helders. PAUL COOK/CAMERAPRESS

Alex Turner on the V Stage as the Arctic Monkeys headline day one of the V Festival at Hylands Park, Chelmsford, August 20, 2011. SAMIR HUSSEIN/GETTY IMAGES

Alexa Chung and Alex together at Glastonbury Festival, June 27, 2008. DANNY MARTINDALE/WIREIMAGE

Nick O'Malley and a briefly long-haired Matt Helders, accepting the award for Best Live Band Award in the *NME* Awards Room at the 02 Academy Brixton in London, February 24, 2010. SUZAN/EMPICS ENTERTAINMENT

Mick Jones presents Alex Turner with the Best Album award at the Ivor Novello Awards at the Grosvenor House Hotel, London, May 24, 2007. DAVID FISHER/REX FEATURES

Alex Turner speaking at a Submarine press conference, at the Crosby Street Hotel, New York City, May 23, 2011. NEILSON BARNARD/GETTY IMAGES

Alex (left) and Miles Kane, aka The Last Shadow Puppets, arrive at The *Mojo* Honours List 2008 Award Ceremony at The Brewery, London, June 16, 2008. SAMIR HUSSEIN/GETTY IMAGES

The Last Shadow Puppets live at Hammersmith Apollo, London, October 26, 2008. Miles is on guitar to the left, James Ford on drums in the centre and Alex Turner on vocals on the right. STEVE GILLETT/LIVEPIX

The Artic Monkeys perform the Beatles, 'Come Together' during the Opening Ceremony of the London 2012 Olympic Games at the Olympic Stadium, London, July 27. LAURENCE GRIFFITHS/GETTY IMAGES

Matt Helders prepares to launch during day one of the Coachella Valley Music & Arts Festival at the Empire Polo Field, Indio, California, April 13, 2012. KEVIN WINTER/GETTY IMAGES FOR COACHELLA

Matt (left) and Alex (second right) practice their Presley sneer backstage before headlining I-Day festival in Bologna, September 3, 2011. HENRY RUGGERI/CORBIS

Alex Turner does a scissor kick during Metallica's inaugural Orion Music and More Festival, in Bader Field, Atlantic City, June 23, 2012. Introducing the band, Metallica's Lars Ulrich described Arctic Monkeys as "the coolest of the cool". THEO WARGO/GETTY IMAGES

Matt Helders models his stars and stripes "pants", in a bid to help the band blend into their new Hollywood home.
ROSS HALFIN

recent B-sides. Opening with 'My Propeller', the set stuck resolutely to new material: 'Crying Lightning', 'Dangerous Animals', 'Secret Door', 'Potion Approaching', 'Fire And The Thud', 'Cornerstone', 'Dance Little Liar', 'Pretty Visitors' and 'The Jeweller's Hands', after which something extraordinary happened – the band that used not to do encores performed five extra songs.

In the relatively contained space of The Empire, the effect of the fans singing every word to every song was breathtaking.

★ ★ ★

With their new set at its best yet, Arctic Monkeys resumed their US tour on April 1, opening their first gig, at The Fillmore, Miami Beach, with 'Fire And The Thud'. From Miami they moved to The Ritz in Tampa and Hard Rock Live in Orlando, followed by The 40 Watt Club in Athens, Georgia, the excellently named Disco Rodeo in Raleigh, North Carolina, Rams Head Live! in Baltimore, Madison Theater in Covington, Kentucky, The Pageant in St Louis, Liberty Hall in Lawrence, Kansas, Cain's Ballroom in Tulsa, Oklahoma, The Marquee in Tempe, Arizona, and House of Blues in Las Vegas on April 16.

The last show of the US tour saw an unscheduled reunion with Eagles Of Death Metal. The show was at Pappy and Harriet's Diner in the unincorporated village of Pioneertown, in the Californian desert, on April 18, with Earthlings? in support.

Of all the gigs on the tour, this one probably made the least economic sense but was undoubtedly the one they were most looking forward to. The night's outdoor performance, in the forecourt of the desert eatery, attracted an exclusive audience of some 850 attendees, some of them travelling hundreds of miles to be there. But, at the eleventh hour, a cloud of volcanic ash left Earthlings? singer Pete Stahl stranded in Europe.

Luckily, Earthlings? guitarist Dave Catching's other band, Eagles Of Death Metal, all lived nearby. Another fellow Eagle (although he rarely played live) was Josh Homme. It became clear pretty early on at the soundchecks that this would be a very intimate and extraordinary gig.

The band had two more gigs to play before heading home to start work on the new LP. Both were in Mexico, at Estadio Azteca in Mexico City and Foro Alterno in Guadalajara on April 21 and 22 respectively. While he was in Mexico City, however, Matt contracted food poisoning and worried he'd become ill onstage at Foro Alterno. As a precaution, he took a bucket with him and, sure enough, halfway through 'Red Right Hand', he realised he was going to be sick. In a display of true professionalism, he waited until he got to an appropriate break in the song, grabbed the bucket and hurled high-velocity vomit into it.

Sickness over, he rolled back into the song a few bars from where he'd left off. To members of the audience it had sounded like a deliberate drop. Some of them even started clapping along, as if anticipating Matt's build in the middle of a breakdown.

35

Suck It And See

MEXICO brought the *Humbug* tour to a close. Arctic Monkeys wouldn't be back on the road again until 2011. Returning home to start work on the next LP, Matt and Alex were soon pursuing side projects.

Matt's friendship with P. Diddy had continued after their initial bromance at Diddy's mansion. So when the hip hop icon needed a drummer for his backing band, Diddy-Dirty Money, in mid-2010, Matt happily stepped in, performing on Puff's 'Hello Good Morning' single for Jonathan Ross's TV show.

Matt also used the break to make more music with Andy Nicholson, both of them collaborating as part of charity fundraising Anglo-Brazilian supergroup The Bottletop Band, with whom they recorded three songs: 'Voice', 'Be Together' and 'End Is The Beginning'.

In early 2010, Richard Ayoade approached Alex about recording cover versions of tracks by Belgian *chansonnier* Jacques Brel and Scott Walker, for a film he was making called *Submarine*. As Ayoade secretly hoped, Alex suggested he could write his own song. Once he'd started, the songs just kept coming and, in the end, Turner wrote and performed six tracks for *Submarine*.

Turner turned to his old friend James Ford to record the songs. The two of them set about getting the tracks down in an intimate arrangement with just voice and guitar, trying to reproduce a close-up Rick Rubin or analogue Steve Albini sound.

Submarine was Ayoade's directorial film debut, a coming-of-age story. He was better known as a comic actor, starring as Maurice Moss in hit TV comedy *The IT Crowd* and as Dean Learner in earlier cult comedy series *Garth Marenghi's Darkplace* – as well as making appearances in *Nathan Barley* and *The Mighty Boosh*.

The film debuted in Canada in September 2010, at the thirty-fifth Toronto International Film Festival. Its positive reception led to a US distribution deal and a month later it premiered in the UK, at the fifty-fourth London Film Festival. It eventually went on general release on March 18, 2011, with the soundtrack released simultaneously as an EP. Its six songs were 'Stuck On The Puzzle (Intro)', 'Hiding Tonight', 'Glass In The Park', 'It's Hard To Get Around The Wind', 'Stuck On The Puzzle' and 'Piledriver Waltz'. Ayoade went on to be nominated for a BAFTA at the sixty-fifth British Academy Film Awards.

Alex had continued writing his own material constantly, but after he'd had his songwriting pad stolen in late 2009 he switched up a gear, filling up moleskin notebooks in an attempt to recapture songs that had been lost. The band had started developing embryonic versions of the songs for the album in early 2010, around the time that Matt had been telling journalists they were keen to get on with recording.

Alex had also been talking about working with Josh Homme again for the fourth album, but it'd been suggested that Homme was too busy to take on the commitment. In the meantime they'd carried on working with James Ford, who, even when other producers were mooted, was often involved somewhere in the background. Ford had already taken part in the recording of the first three LPs and had been involved in at least two of the band's side projects.

Sure enough, the Monkeys eventually announced that Ford would be producing their fourth album in January 2011. He had worked closely with Alex on the *Submarine* soundtrack, which would yield two tracks for the forthcoming Monkeys LP, as well as guiding the recording techniques. The last track on *Submarine*, 'Piledriver Waltz,' would be re-recorded with the band, while the other contribution was the single 'Don't Sit Down 'Cause I've Moved Your Chair' – the inspiration for which came while Alex was recording the *Submarine* sessions with James.

"I said it to somebody whose chair I moved, and I didn't want them to hurt themselves," Alex explained to *NME*. "This was while we were in the studio doing the *Submarine* recording and James [Ford] said, 'Oh, that sounds like it could be like a Sixties garage *Nuggets* tune.' So then we thought, 'Well, okay if that's what you can't do, then what sort of ridiculous things can you do that are probably more dangerous than if you just sat down?'"

Ford was glad to return to being behind the desk for their fourth LP, telling *Sound On Sound*: "I'd never force myself on them, but if they ask me to work with them, I'm more than happy. They're such a talented bunch and such a nice band to record and to be around, I'd be daft not to take up the opportunity."

The way the band collectively composed each song had changed. Earlier songs had often developed organically during sessions. An assortment of riffs, beat patterns and melodies would be segued together around Alex's lyrics until they'd constructed a whole track. It was a procedure that could take days to complete, sparking new ideas and different songs in the process. 'I Bet You Look Good On The Dancefloor', for example, had originally been inspired by a drum loop Matt had been playing which Alex created lyrics and a melody around. And '505' had come about through the band experimenting in the studio, Alex describing the process as being like a jigsaw, drawing different elements together until they worked as a whole.

For many of the songs on the new album, Alex had reversed the process. Instead of them emerging from disparate elements he'd start with the song ideas in their purest form, building structures and lyrics, and finding melodies and other parts to go with them.

Alex had also been grappling with how to write lyrics that resonated with his public but were still based on personal experience. The first two albums had been born from a life many could easily relate to, even if they hadn't lived it themselves. But fame had taken Alex further away from the everyday; his experiences were increasingly distant from his former muse.

He'd confessed to being a bit of a romantic on several occasions, complaining that, when faced with fewer real-life subjects for songs, he found himself returning to love as an inspiration. But now he started to fuse more abstract, less personal concepts to themes that were close to his heart, keeping it close enough to feel the emotions and sentiments but also objective enough for him to be detached. He'd also realised in the early stages of writing the LP that not everything had to be explained; it was okay to leave a few blanks.

Alex had begun by writing songs for the fourth LP on his own, in his Brooklyn apartment. After a while he was joined there by Jamie, with just the two of them working on the guitar parts. The four band members then convened at a synagogue in east London in the autumn of 2010, rehearsing and working on the song structures over an intense six-week period. In this final phase of pre-production, James Ford joined the band to help with the arrangements.

"I'll happily get involved wherever they need me. Like, I remember in 'She's Thunderstorms', for instance, just trying to get it to flow and suggesting going to the middle eight early. Those sort of things probably happened on every song. But it's not me dictating that, it's just lots of different suggestions . . . Having someone else around just gives them an extra kind of push in a different direction," James recalled.

One of Ford's specifications was that everything had to be ready to be played, all the lyrics finished and structures worked out before they started recording. So the band rehearsed to a point where the songs were ready to be played live. In the very final stages of pre-production, James brought a portable digital recorder to the synagogue to make a live demo of the tracks. As a result, by Christmas they'd got what he described as a two-mics-in-the-room version of the entire LP to work from.

"We talked about getting all the songs together and doing it in a weekend. We didn't do it in a weekend, but we had a strong foundation," Alex explained to *The Aquarian* online. "A lot of the pre-production was in London. We decided what everybody was going to play, what key we'd do it in. Then in LA, we'd record one song a day and put it to bed."

Suggestions that the LP would lose some of the darker elements of *Humbug* started to circulate in early 2011, with *Q* suggesting the Monkeys were returning to a more accessible sound. It was certainly true that they had been experimenting with old practices, valve hardware and recording to tape – using old techniques to push their own sound forward.

But anyone expecting talk of 'vintage' techniques to mean a return to the first two albums would be disappointed. If *Humbug* had been a necessary passage through a dark patch, then the new album was the light they had been heading to on the other side. When critics would herald the new album as a return to form, they also had to acknowledge that the band was playing in a different landscape.

"One of their strengths is how they perform live and their instinctive reactions between them, so it's [a matter of] trying to get that onto record.

Even quite a few of the vocals were sung at the time. With Alex's vocal, he's a good enough singer to do a whole take from beginning to end and keep it on the record," explains Ford.

"It was very much that we wanted to do it without computers – stemming from the way we'd worked on *Submarine*, where we did it on tape.

"It's got nothing to do with the sound, but just the way you approach recording. You can only fit three takes on the reel, so if you think you can do it better you have to record over one of the takes to do it. So it forces you to make decisions as you go along. It changes things.

"So that's what we did with this last record. We set up live and did a lot of pre-production, just trying to get away from the Pro Tools recording, when it's really hard not to fiddle! If the snare's out of time and the drummer knows you can fix it, then why wouldn't you? It's much easier if you can't change it and you can say, 'That's the way the recording is.' It's easier to get that rough-around-the-edges thing. We have an unreasonable level of perfection these days. There's something inherently wrong about that."

The roots of the unfussy live sound on the new LP were in Alex and James's sessions for *Submarine*. Recorded at One Inch Studios in east London in 2010, most of the six tracks had been performed in one take, deliberately aping the old techniques. Ford describes it as a brilliant but minimal studio, stocked with audiophile vintage recording equipment including a Sixties eight-track and a Fifties half-inch mono recorder.

He wanted to capture the intimacy of sound that modern producers such as Albini still excelled in – where it felt like the singer was sitting in the room with you. A lot of the tracks were just Alex singing and playing guitar, but even when James joined in on piano, drums or bass, or Bill Ryder-Jones (formerly of The Coral) also played guitar, they would just huddle around one mic.

The experience of recording without once turning on a computer had an impact on both Alex and James. It brought a discipline, tension and energy to the performance. None of the studios that the Monkeys had used until now – including Moloco, Eastcote and Konk in London, The Motor Museum in Liverpool and Mission Sound in New York – had been filled with flash contemporary equipment. Their needs were more about finding a space they could feel comfortable in.

The band had already decided they wanted to record the album in California. They initially tried to get into the Shangri-La studios in Malibu, which had been built for Bob Dylan and The Band. It was fully booked, so they tried Sound City Studios in the San Fernando Valley, LA.

The studio was an ideal choice. Renowned for its drum sound, it was used on Nirvana's *Nevermind* and had been owned by the legendary Vox Amplification firm in the Sixties, before being refitted in the early Seventies. Its history was littered with classic recordings, including Neil Young's *After The Gold Rush* and Fleetwood Mac's *Rumours*. Even better, it hadn't been redecorated since the Seventies and, as Ford would later recall, you could tell it had seen some dark days.

The final factor that made it ideal for the album was that it didn't have in-house Pro Tools or any other software system. It also helped that the custom-made Neve 8028 desk and Studer A800, Mark II, 24-track were the godfather of tape systems.

Ford wanted to give space to the drums and the studio was also perfect for that. They provided a specialist drum technician to work alongside him and an old Ludwig kit for Matt with a big, open sound.

The band shipped their own Selmer and Magnatone amps in for the session, to keep the guitar sound as close to the rehearsal sessions as possible. The studio had a range of boutique fuzz pedals for guitar and Ford tried to get as close as possible to the Les Paul neck pickup sound on both lead and rhythm. They also experimented with the Coopersonic valve-slapped pedal on the guitar solos, which had tracks such as 'All My Own Stunts' fizzing with creamy saturation. For Cookie's spacey guitar parts, Ford borrowed a trick from Hendrix and set up a second microphone on the opposite side of the room.

As with the first LP, the band were closely grouped, facing each other in the live room, recreating the synagogue rehearsal room's atmosphere. The amps were either set up in separate booths or sometimes in the live studio with the band.

The band were recorded live with an SM57 microphone for vocals, so that the vocal take could be used if they wanted to keep it. Although most were overdubbed, some of the original live vocal takes, such as on 'Library Pictures', survived onto the finished LP.

Ford avoided complex tinkering with the live takes, even if it meant keeping imperfections on the record, arguing that human frailties connected people with the music. If required, they re-recorded some parts, with guitar solos and percussion overdubbed, but Ford avoided any tape edits at all.

Turner's vocal overdubs were tracked at the end of the day and were generally recorded several times, with the best take selected at the end. If necessary, a bridge or a verse could be spliced together, but once again they avoided complex editing.

The album featured more vocals from Matt than usual, singing harmonies with Alex but also a lead on 'Brick By Brick', where Nick also sang bass vocals – as he did in a few places on the LP. Jamie was the only Monkey who totally avoided singing.

Dispelling the idea of possible rivalry between Ford and Josh Homme, the *Humbug* producer also popped in to add his voice to 'All My Own Stunts' – although Ford admits it felt quite strange to give the big man his critique after the first take. Ironically perhaps, the one track that Ford and Turner had recorded before, 'Piledriver Waltz', gave them the most hassle. They had been living with the song for a while and had a clear aural concept of what it should sound like. But it proved hard to recreate the sound in their heads with a full band; it was only when they were on the verge of dumping it that they managed to pull it back from the abyss.

With the album complete, James Ford brought in Craig Silvers, a mixing engineer the band were familiar with. Silvers, an analogue engineer, knew the studios in the area well and Ford later described how the details he added changed the mixes hugely. They also decided to add an entire new guitar track at mix stage on 'The Hellcat Spangled Shalalala'.

By the end, the process from entering the studio to final mixdown had taken a total of five weeks. The band were now eager to put their music out.

On March 4, 2011, the Monkeys premiered a track featuring a hard rocking bass and guitar break on the internet, a fine example of their fudgy new lead guitar sound. 'Brick By Brick' also had Matt singing lead, alongside a ludicrously low bass vocal by Nick.

The track wasn't intended as a single, but as a teaser for the fourth album. It was perhaps an odd choice for that purpose, but 'Brick By Brick' clearly sounded like a band having fun. If they had intended to show the world that a cloud had lifted, it certainly did the job. The song had been written in a bar in Miami during their US tour, with the band listing actions you might want to perform bit by bit. Alex once described the song to *NME* as "just a fucking laugh", pointing to the fact it had the phrase 'rock'n'roll' in it three times as evidence.

In a sense, the song was taking the piss, building the rudiments of a rock song together so simply that it became a bona fide, if self-knowing, rock anthem – much to the confusion of earnest music critics who could hear its 'knuckle-grazing' swagger but none of its self-mocking references. The online response to the song was phenomenal, with over 1.5 million viewing the video in its first month of posting online.

On March 10, 2011, the band announced the album's title as *Suck It And See*, saying they'd also considered calling it *The Rain-Shaped Shimmer Trap*, *The Thunder-Suckle Fuzz Canyon*, *The Blondo-Sonic Rape Alarm* and *Thriller*. The title they settled for is a reference to graffiti in a scene from Stanley Kubrick's *A Clockwork Orange*, seen as Alex DeLarge waits for a broken elevator in his decrepit apartment building.

The first single from the LP, 'Don't Sit Down 'Cause I've Moved Your Chair', was played for the first time on air on Zane Lowe's BBC Radio 1 show and simultaneously released as a digital single on April 11. Three vinyl versions were released with different B-sides: 'Brick By Brick' (seven-inch); non-LP track 'I.D.S.T' (seven-inch); 'The Blond-O-Sonic Shimmer Trap' and 'I.D.S.T' (10-inch).

"People ask us why we released 'Don't Sit Down . . .' as the first single," explained Alex to *The Shortlist*, "because it's not the poppiest one on there – it's really guitar-heavy. But because we've got that fanbase, and we're one of the guitar bands that have a shot of getting on the radio in the daytime, I almost feel like it's our job to put that sort of tune out."

It was released to a singles chart absolutely dominated by R&B and pop. Arctic Monkeys were in a unique position in that they were able to straddle not only different radio stations – Radio 1, Xfm, 6 Music and commercial radio – but also able to reach into both the singles and the albums market.

"They're very unusual in that they are both a singles act and an album act as well," Martin Talbot of the Official Charts Company confirmed. "They've sold 2.8 million albums in the UK, and 2.1 million singles.

There are very few acts that have as many big singles as the Arctic Monkeys have had, while also selling so many albums. I don't know if there is anyone else like that."

Despite being a supposedly uncommercial choice, released on three different dates in awkward formats, 'Don't Sit Down 'Cause I've Moved Your Chair' went in at number 28 in the UK singles chart and number four in the indie chart. Overseas, it became their highest charting single in Belgium (number five) and second highest in Denmark (number six). In the UK, despite its unconventional formats, it sold 81,000 copies.

The band began the first leg of its tour promoting the LP in Sweden, at the Cirkus, Stockholm on May 5, 2011. The band debuted four songs from the as-yet-unreleased LP, including 'Don't Sit Down . . .', 'The Hellcat Spangled Shalalala', 'Brick By Brick' and, as an encore, 'That's Where You're Wrong'.

It was the first time they played the soaring sonic psychedelia of 'The Hellcat Spangled Shalalala' in public and the song's first outing was preceded by a Swedish fan yelling, "I want to have your babies!" at the front of the stage.

The reaction to the new songs immediately triggered a slew of positive comments on message boards. As one blogger posted, the new material was pulling wavering fans back into the fold: "Restored my faith in *Suck It And See*. Two very solid tracks. I'm officially excited again."

Anticipation of the tour had already seen a flurry of ticket sales, with a majority of the US tour dates having sold out. The first was back at the by now familiar 9:30 Club, in Washington DC, on May 17. Although the band had yet to develop their full-on rocker look, Alex arrived onstage sporting a leather jacket and newly shorn hair. Their US fans seemed delighted by the new look.

Opening with the first live outing of 'She's Thunderstorms', further debuts were made that night by 'Library Pictures' and 'Reckless Serenade'. As yet unreleased, the first of these was greeted with great whoops of delight and audience members screaming "ip-dip dogshit rock'n'roll!" Of all the songs since *Favourite Worst Nightmare*, 'Library Pictures' felt the closest to original Arctic Monkeys in spirit, even if its sonic style belonged firmly to the current album.

Alex and the rest of the band were also in party spirit, with one reviewer incredulously complaining he was too chatty, saying more in the first 15 minutes than in all their other shows combined. Meanwhile, Matt liberally scattered spent drumsticks into the audience while the crowd merrily joined in on 'Don't Sit Down . . .'.

The tour couldn't have started on a better footing. The following night's sold-out gig at The Electric Factory in Philadelphia was more of the same. One reviewer complained he'd got stuck at the back, and hadn't been able to get far enough forward to join in the crowd-surfing.

The successful run carried on to their sold-out return to the 2,300-capacity House of Blues in Boston on May 19, where they moved the explosive 'Library Pictures' to the top of the set. Despite Matt's problems with his snare at the start, the Monkeys turned in a roof-battering performance as the tide of crowd-surfers overwhelmed the front-of-stage security.

On May 21 they headed to Toronto's Kool Haus for a third sold-out date. Alex started by asking, "How you feeling, Canada?", prompting the crowd to break into a chant of "Arctic Monkeys in CAN-A-DA." Satisfied, the band powered through 'Library Pictures', 'Don't Sit Down . . .', 'She's Thunderstorms' and 'The Hellcat Spangled Shalalala' – every one of them jubilantly received.

At Olympia de Montréal the following night, the band added the title track from the new LP to their set, giving the song its first live outing before moving down to New York to play a sold-out open-air gig at Rumsey Playfield on May 24, where the queues had started to form at 11 a.m. that morning. Rumours had been circulating for some time about Alex and Alexa Chung's relationship being in trouble, but for this gig in their home-town, at least, she was firmly at his side.

At the start of the set Alex was having some problems with his guitar, though he later explained his new-look leather jacket had been getting in the way. The sold-out crowd went crazy that night, although some complained the mosh pit got so boisterous that they had to spend the entire gig trying to keep from being trampled.

On May 26 the band had been booked to play Clutch Cargo's in Detroit, but the gig had been quickly moved to The Fillmore in response to the demand. The new venue also quickly sold out. The following day they played The Rave at the Eagles Ballroom in Milwaukee – a gig advertised with a video trailer promising the show would (cue overblown and under-sincere cinema blockbuster voice-over) "be a Good Party! Good Time!"

If the Milwaukee venue didn't quite know how to get the message over, First Avenue in Minneapolis didn't need to. The tickets sold out practically as soon as they'd been announced and the crowd went barmy for every minute of the Monkeys' new set, only dipping momentarily onto the back heel for 'Cornerstone' before surging into a roaring version of 'I Bet You Look Good On The Dancefloor'. The set also included the debut live performance of 'All My Own Stunts', as well as a storming singalong of 'When The Sun Goes Down'.

First Avenue had become one of a number of homes from home for the Monkeys. They'd been selling it out since their first visit to Minneapolis, and, as a mark of respect, devoted one of the songs that night to the staff at the venue. This had gone down well with local fans, who appreciated Arctic Monkeys returning rather than moving on to bigger places.

But elsewhere, one Canadian reviewer was questioning why they were playing the same venue they'd visited on two previous occasions. At the same time, if anything was going to move Arctic Monkeys up to North American stadium status then it looked like *Suck It And See* was the album to do it.

On May 30, a week before the album got its official release, Domino Records streamed the entire LP on the *SoundCloud* music service website. Within a few hours of the public gaining access to the streams, the first two tracks had gained over 10,000 listens each – by the end of the week every track had amassed 10 times that number.

When the band played a sold-out gig at The Ogden Theatre in Denver that night, the audience had officially been able to hear the full LP for the first time. Reviewing for buzzine.com, Andrew Shaw described the band's performance that night as "bare-knuckle loud. Every sinew and every song pounded out like a bomb designed to level the building."

The audience response was little short of rabid, with wave after wave of unfettered enthusiasm breaking against the crowd barriers. "You seem to be in a really good mood, Denver," Alex observed from the stage. The following night the tour rolled into Salt Lake City for another riotous gig, belting out an insanely powerful version of 'Don't Sit Down . . .'.

With days left until the album's release, the band played their penultimate sold-out show at The Fox Theater, Pomona, California on June 2. After one last gig the following night, at the Hollywood Palladium, they were ready to return to the UK for their traditional home-town celebration – which would be by far their biggest yet.

★   ★   ★

Suck It And See was finally released on June 6, 2011 and hailed by most critics as a return to form, although it fell short of universally good reviews. The music press, usually in the vanguard of any backlash, was unanimously impressed. The *NME* was in no doubt about its brilliance, applauding it as a new departure rather than a return to form; *Q* described it as "the sound of a band drawing back the curtains and letting the sunshine in", and *Mojo* rejoiced that it was the band's best LP since their "untouchable" debut.

Although the *Daily Telegraph* heralded a return to melodic form that put the band on a par with The Stone Roses and The Smiths, other broadsheets were less favourable. *The Guardian* gave the album four out of five stars after many caveats, which made its star allotment seem generous. *The Independent On Sunday*'s overall positive review remarked that Arctic Monkeys had finally released something partially worth listening to, at a point when no one cared any more. *The Observer* was even less impressed, giving it three stars out of five.

Some pundits doubted whether the band had maintained enough of a fanbase. "After ['Don't Sit Down 'Cause I've Moved Your Chair'] stiffed at No. 28 in the charts," wrote *The Independent*'s Simon Price, "it's debatable whether *Suck It And See*, the Sheffield band's fourth album, will even make it out of the sweet-wrapper."

In fact the correlation between the singles and albums charts was pretty loose by this point, with LP chart toppers not necessarily even entering the singles charts. But the Monkeys' single had been dribbled out on different dates and in different formats, making its chart position misleading anyway.

On its release, *Suck It And See* went straight to number one in the UK album charts, proving that the Monkeys' core fanbase had not been anything like as negatively affected by *Humbug* as some journalists had predicted. Arctic Monkeys had once again entered the records of chart history, becoming only the second band to debut four albums in a row at the top of the charts – the only act to equal them being Keane.

They also had to knock pop queen Lady Gaga's worldwide bestseller album, *Born This Way*, off the top spot. No mean feat in an era when commercial pop acts had nearly annihilated guitar bands in the singles charts. As Noel Gallagher had observed, it wasn't a good period for guitar music.

Meanwhile, the US media seemed ready to assess Arctic Monkeys in their own right. *Pitchfork* described the album as a coming of age, bristling with easily overlooked details that made it the band's most rewarding listen to date. The much respected American indie publication *Spin* claimed "four albums in, and the [Monkeys have] hit a remarkable mid-career groove that most bands their age will never see"; *Rolling Stone* agreed, hailing it as the band's best LP since their debut.

Internationally, the album had charted better than any of its predecessors: Australia (number four); Austria (12); Belgium (one); Canada (three); Denmark (two); France (seven); Germany and Greece (four); Ireland (three); Italy (seven); Japan (12); Norway (four); Portugal (seven); Spain (three); Switzerland (eight); US *Billboard* (14); US Top Independent Albums (four); US Alternative (five); US Rock Albums (six).

In the midst of a 12-month tour, Arctic Monkeys had at last got rid of the hype. It hadn't been burst by a backlash, as many had expected, but had simply floated away. With *Suck It And See*, they had also produced their most internationally successful LP yet.

36

Got Their Mojo Workin'

WITH the band back in the UK, the next stop on the tour was two mini-festival shows in the Don Valley Bowl, Sheffield. The shows had been timed to coincide with the album's first-week chart placing. At the time of organising the gig it had been a gamble; there were no guarantees that the album would sell at anything like the same rate as its predecessors and the band could no longer count on a tailwind of media hype. Despite a loyal live following, they were now a long way from being the newest kids on the block.

The two 10,000-capacity homecoming shows were held in a huge festival marquee on June 10 and 11, 2011. By the time the gigs were being staged, it looked likely that they would take the number one slot from Lady Gaga.

On the opening night, new Sheffield band and Monkey mates Dead Sons were given the opening slot, with rapidly rising London band The Vaccines, who had been the main support on the last US tour, appearing mid-evening. Regular collaborator and band ally Miles Kane was given top support billing. On the following night, Mabel Love, another up-and-coming local band, were moved into first support slot while Anna Calvi took the middle and Kane returned as main support. On both nights, Miles reappeared onstage on a motorbike to join the Monkeys on '505', the track he helped write for the second LP.

Alexa Chung was seen with Alex at the gig, despite the rumours surrounding their relationship. It was also reported that Alex's rarely seen father, David Turner, was present, as was his old friend and housemate Jon McClure.

Ticket sales for the gig entailed an innovation to outsmart the touts: ticket holders had to show the banking card they'd used to buy tickets to gain entry to the arena. At last, the system proved difficult for the touts to crack. Inside the arena the event was spacious enough to feel like a festival, with fans hanging outside on the grass around the large festival tent.

To commemorate the gigs, the Monkeys had produced a T-shirt bearing the Sheffield coat of arms, with the band's name written where 'Sheffield' should have been. Alex wore it for the first night.

On both nights the band chose Hot Chocolate's 'You Sexy Thing' as the track they walked on to. The song had become indelibly connected to Sheffield after film director Peter Cattaneo used it in the dole-office scene of his iconic Sheffield-based comedy, *The Full Monty*. Some critics failed to see the connection between an indie rock band and a late Seventies disco pop tune, but many local fans got the joke instantly, singing and dancing along before the band took to the stage.

Alex had recently told the press that Arctic Monkeys had stopped playing a lot of their older material because they no longer felt like the same band. But they made an exception for Don Valley, where classic songs from the debut LP crept back into the set. As soon as they were onstage, Alex announced: "Let's start from the beginning, shall we?" and the band launched into 'The View From The Afternoon'. The crowd response was instant and euphoric: plastic beakers of beer and cider flew through the air.

Other early songs followed: 'Still Take You Home', and 'Mardy Bum', which was brought out of retirement for its first live performance since 2007. Turner introduced it by saying he would need some help singing the next track, leading the band into a simplified guitar and vocal version. Within two strokes of the stripped-down chords the crowd realised what it was, singing the whole song for him. It was the best example of crowd participation all night, but far from the only one. The crowd sang along to every song regardless, whether it was from the newly released album or any of the previous three.

The encore included 'When The Sun Goes Down' and 'A Certain Romance' – another track that hadn't been heard live since 2007. The event was literally 10 times the size of those first early gigs just up the road, but the audience connection felt as strong. The Monkeys had been around the world and had come home to Sheffield, taking their crowd all the way with them.

★　★　★

In mid-June the tour kicked back in again. On June 16 they rolled into Paris for a secret concert at La Cigale. The gig had been announced a few days before and had sold out immediately, with the black market pushing the resold tickets up to ludicrous prices. The set had returned to the more evenly balanced US tour version, with songs selected from all four LPs and more emphasis on the last three – much to the delight of the young Parisian crowd.

From here they set out on the festival circuit, starting with the massive Southside Festival in Neuhausen Ob Eck, Germany, set on a former military airfield. Then it was on to the Hurricane Festival, where they headlined alongside Germany's veteran industrial metal band Rammstein and Queens Of The Stone Age. At Berlin they played the sold-out 2,000-capacity Admiralspalast on June 20, with Miles Kane as support act. It was here that Alex threw the crowd by singing 'Don't Sit Down . . .' in German. Everyone loved it. But the irony was that the German crowd, word-perfect on every song so far, had learned the song in English and didn't know the lyrics in their own language.

Moving on to E-Werk in Cologne, the band reintroduced 'When The Sun Goes Down' into the set. On June 23 they returned to Paradiso in the Netherlands for a sold-out gig, before making an impromptu decision to drive the tour bus over to Glastonbury, where Alexa was hanging out with a group of friends.

According to the *NME*, Arctic Monkeys' bus rolled into the Glastonbury festival site on June 24. Faced with the unexpected arrival of one of the country's most legendary live acts, the festival hurriedly reallocated pop singer Example's space to the Monkeys. Example was understandably furious, claiming he had to commission a festival buggy every time he needed to change his underpants. But there was no question of the Monkeys' bus being moved.

Why they were there when they barely had a gap in their European tour dates, remained a mystery. They made it clear they were not there to play any secret gigs, and if they had rolled halfway across Europe to try and patch up Alex and Alexa's relationship, their noble efforts appeared to have been wasted. Alexa spent most of her time watching bands with her friends, such as Pixie Lott and Fifi Brown, while Alex and Alexa were hardly seen together in public.

After their brief visit to Glastonbury, the band travelled to Roeser in Luxembourg for the Rock A Field Festival on June 26, followed by Le Bikini in Toulouse and Le Zénith in Nantes on the 29th. From here they rejoined the festival trail, headlining at the Belgian Rock Werchter Festival on July 1 and the third day of Denmark's major Roskilde Festival, before a final appearance at Eurockéennes in Belfort, France closed the European tour.

Returning to the UK, the band were booked to play the iTunes Festival at The Roundhouse in Chalk Farm, Camden on July 6. If the capital's journalists still harboured doubts about the Monkeys' dwindling fanbase, the gig was a heartfelt rejoinder as fans bounced around rowdily to old and new material alike.

By now the band were attracting majority audiences of new fans who hadn't been there during the file-sharing phenomenon of the early years. You didn't need to be a maths teacher to work out that kids leaving school to queue at Rumsey Playfield in New York, or the iTunes Live show at The Roundhouse, were not the same bunch who'd been sharing MP3s in 2004. While some of the new fans joined in the mosh pits at the front, older veterans were sedately pulling on their raincoats at the back, hoping to enjoy the gig without enduring a cold, beer-drenched tube journey home.

When Turner and friends led the Roundhouse crowd through old-school favourites 'Brianstorm', 'I Bet You Look Good On The Dancefloor', 'The View From The Afternoon' and a rousing singalong to 'When The Sun Goes Down', it wasn't only the old fans who were singing along. Many from both contingents left The Roundhouse drenched in beer, cider and sweat. Two days after the gig, six of the songs recorded at the concert were made available as a special *iTunes Live* EP: 'Brianstorm', 'Don't Sit Down 'Cause I've Moved Your Chair', 'Crying Lightning', 'The Hellcat Spangled Shalalala', 'I Bet You Look Good On The Dancefloor' and '505'. The collection captured the band's live energy, including a raw 'Crying Lightning' that exposed the song's primal strength.

The Roundhouse gig also aroused another wave of speculation about the health of Alex and Alexa's relationship. They were seen together onstage at the iTunes Festival, but once again hadn't been glimpsed as a couple offstage. Although officially still together, word was spreading that they were no longer an item.

According to 'official' accounts of their understandably private relationship, the couple had first started seeing each other at T In The Park. It was here that Alex and the band now moved on to, playing the headline slot on Friday night – but without Alexa in tow.

With Beyoncé headlining on Saturday, Jarvis Cocker and Pulp on the bill and Tom Jones warming up the afternoon before Arctic Monkeys, it was a remarkable year for the festival. Rain had been predicted by the bucketload, and had indeed ensured a muddy field. But the day turned out to be unexpectedly sunny. Jarvis memorably remarked on the passing of the *News Of The World* newspaper, closed as the result of a phone-hacking scandal, by pretending to wipe his bum with the final edition.

Glasgow had played a long and special part in the Monkeys' history. Perhaps for this reason, the band unwrapped the Don Valley version of 'Mardy Bum' for the fans. Everyone sang along at the top of their voices and, by the end, Alex had to conclude: "Scotland, that was beautiful." The Monkeys delivered a commanding performance that night, which had fans ferociously tweeting about it into the next morning.

From here they moved on to headline the Oxegen Festival in Ireland, followed by Les Nuits de Fourvière in Lyon and further headline slots at Super Bock Super Rock in Portugal and Benicàssim in Spain, alongside The Strokes and Arcade Fire, and immediately before Primal Scream – although the *NME* declared the Monkeys' set to be the de facto headline slot.

With one last stop at the scenic Gurtenfestival in Bern, Switzerland on July 17, the band headed off for a flying visit to the Far East, playing Fuji Rock Festival in Japan and Jisan Valley Rock Festival in Seoul on July 29 and 30.

There was another US tour on the horizon, but before that Arctic Monkeys had one more award to collect. This time it would be their first from *Mojo* magazine, the respectable, grown-up face of British rock journalism.

When the Monkeys had been nominated for Best Album at the *Mojo* Awards in July, the *Daily Telegraph* observed that they had probably enjoyed the longest period of critical favour of any British band in the history of rock. The awards were held at The Brewery, in London, on July 22, 2011 and all the Monkeys, bar Jamie Cook turned out for it.

Alex's friend Richard Ayoade had been selected to present the award – which he assured the audience didn't mean it was "entirely without merit". In making the award, the magazine's editor, Phil Alexander, described the winners as incredibly special performers: "I think it's because they fit in a long line of truly great British artists. You can draw a line between the lyricism of Ray Davies and Alex Turner, stopping at John Cooper Clarke along the way."

In their acceptance of the award, a mature and relaxed Alex took command of the acceptance speech, making sure the people in the team behind their success were given recognition. "It's great for us to be in this room with so many fantastic people," he announced with a rare humility. "Thank you Ian [McAndrew] and Geoff [Barradale] and Laurence Bell and I hope you all have a wonderful evening."

The band had finally got their *Mojo* gong.

37

The Hellcat Spangled In The London Riots

A S the band headed back towards the nation Alex and Alexa had adopted as home, the news finally broke that the couple had split up. They had been conspicuously private in their relationship, so sightings of them together had been rare even at its height. But information had been leaked to red-top UK tabloid the *Daily Mirror*, via an unidentified source who claimed to know them both. On July 31, 2011, the newspaper confirmed rumours that had been circulating after a number of sightings at industry events where both had been present, but were not seen together.

At Glastonbury, it was claimed the couple had hardly spoken to each other. Reports said they had tried to salvage the relationship but things had turned sour between them again. It would turn out that there was an enduring apprehensiveness between the two of them, with Alexa choosing to avoid a confrontation. But no real reason emerged for the break–up, the accepted wisdom being that, after a clearly intense start to the relationship, they simply became more distant as their work schedules kicked in. The *Daily Mirror* quoted an unidentified source as saying: "Things haven't been going well and they haven't seemed like a couple for the past few weeks.

"They want to stay friends so it's best to split now. They've been through a lot together and all their friends are sad they've called time as a couple."

"Alexa is concentrating on getting her American TV career back on track." Alexa's spokesperson, Liz Matthews, confirmed, telling the paper: "It's completely amicable – but yes it's true. They have split."

Alexa, now 27, had been invited by American film mogul Harvey

Weinstein to present a new fashion TV show called *24 Hour Catwalk*, at the very moment the Monkeys were stepping into a world tour that would last at least until January 2012. By August 2011, it seems that Alexa had already moved out of the apartment where the couple had been living in Williamsburg. It must have been some relief to Alex that the next US tour wouldn't be starting in New York.

The tour kicked off with the news that US supermarkets were stickering over the LP's title, despite assurances that 'suck it and see' was a totally innocent expression in the UK.

The opening gig was held at The Palladium Ballroom in Dallas on August 1. The band had been touring the US for five years now and, although they returned regularly to the same haunts, the age demographic of the crowd was widening. Their catalogue was starting to pull in new young fans – as demonstrated by the parents dropping them off at The Palladium Ballroom. But the new tracks, with their broader influences and greater depth, were also keeping the older generation loyal.

Dallas was followed by a return to Stubb's in Austin, where the band put on an outdoor show on a sweat-drenched Texan summer evening. The night was already humid enough for people to be sweating before the band emerged onstage. Before long, the staff at Stubb's were handing out bottled water to fans rooted to their positions at the front.

The night also held a visually stylistic significance. Jamie had already been sporting a shorter-haired, rock'n'roll look in place of his previous long-haired stoner image and, somewhere between Dallas and Austin, Alex had entirely ditched his Sixties mop and emerged as an updated Fifties rocker. The fans at Austin didn't know it, but they had been the first to witness the new, sharp-looking Arctic Monkeys.

Next stop was House of Blues, in Houston and Chicago, for warm-up gigs before returning to Lollapalooza Festival, at Grant Park, Chicago on Sunday, August 7, 2011. The festival had a record 90,000 in attendance on Sunday, but two flash storms had turned the park into instant mud soup. The second half-hour storm had just started to abate when the Monkeys took the stage for an abbreviated set, in an attempt to get the festival back on schedule. They naturally kept 'She's Thunderstorms' in the set, with Alex dedicating it to "Mother Nature".

The tour wound its way back through The Showbox in Seattle, Crystal

Ballroom in Portland and a packed warm-up gig at The Independent in San Francisco on August 12, before playing the city's Outside Lands Music and Arts Festival the following day. The band went down like a storm, winning over yet more American fans to the Monkeys' cause. Introducing 'Brick By Brick', Turner took the chance to highlight the song's repetitive tongue-in-cheek lyrics, joking: "If you don't know the words, I think you can figure it out." Via a cumulative process, the Monkeys were starting to click with a mass US audience. Their next single, however, was about to run into unexpected trouble at home.

★   ★   ★

Arctic Monkeys released 'The Hellcat Spangled Shalalala', the second single from *Suck It And See*, on August 15. In mid-July, Domino unveiled the video for the single, signalling the start of its promotional campaign. Created by Focus Creeps, it was the first of a series of videos the duo would create for the singles from *Suck It And See*, featuring model Scarlett Kapella alongside live footage of the band and fans.

The band were finishing the last dates of their US tour and preparing to head home for a festival date in Holland and both legs of the V Festival in the UK, all timed to coincide with the week of the single's release. But on Saturday, August 6, 2011, as they were warming up for Lollapalooza in Chicago, parts of London erupted into rioting.

The disturbances had been sparked by the London Metropolitan Police shooting dead an armed suspect named Mark Duggan, in Tottenham, north-east London. A protest and vigil planned for the following weekend had turned violent and, as police vehicles were set alight, along with a London bus and targeted buildings such as a magistrates' court, the lawlessness began to spread.

Duggan's family distanced themselves from the subsequent action as the protests transformed into a looting spree, at first centred on Tottenham Hale Retail Park and shops in Wood Green, followed by further acts of arson. Over the weekend and the following days, the violence spread through other parts of London: Hackney, Brixton, Walthamstow, Camden, Peckham, Battersea, Croydon, Ealing, the West End, East Ham and Enfield all witnessed looting and rioting, while outbreaks of lawlessness spread to other cities across the UK. The consequences included five deaths, numerous injuries and an estimated £200 million worth of property damage.

Among the buildings destroyed was the Sony CD manufacturing warehouse in Enfield. Although Sony was a major label, its CD pressing business held the UK's largest stockpile of independent label records. When the warehouse went up in flames, millions of independent records were destroyed – including almost the entire stock of 'The Hellcat Spangled Shalalala'. The single had gone up in smoke days before its release.

The band was forced to cancel the full release, but on August 14 the remaining stock was retailed as (very) limited edition seven-inch vinyl direct from the band's website. Not surprisingly, the song only managed to chart in the Top 200.

A new Death Ramps track was released on the B-side. Called 'Little Illusion Machine (Wirral Riddler)', it had been co-written by Miles Kane and recorded with another stalwart Sheffield musician and producer, Ross Orton.

Five days after the limited single release, the band made a quick stop-off at the Lowlands Festival in the Netherlands, before returning for their much anticipated headline appearance at the V Festival's twin sites on August 20 and 21.

During the tour, Arctic Monkeys' long-haired stoner image from the *Humbug* era had been mutating into a sharper style. At first this was personified by Alex, Matt and Jamie's return to shorter hair, followed by Alex's adoption of a leather jacket and tight black T-shirt. By the end of the US tour an altogether more rock'n'roll image had emerged, with Alex now sporting a jet-black quiff.

Gossip columnists postulated whether this was Alex shaking off Alexa by adopting a new persona, but the transformation had passed through the whole band. Arctic Monkeys had taken on a look that would come to define their *Suck It And See* era.

Their headline slot on day one at V Chelmsford was a potentially difficult gig. As the most commercial of the UK's festivals, it could have easily been one pop crowd too far for the Monkeys. The day had been mired in rain and most of the festival-goers were there to hear the current Radio 1 playlist and hand-me-down pop.

V had begun in the mid-Nineties, at the height of the Britpop era. Back then it had been dominated by guitar bands. By 2011, however, Arctic Monkeys were a rarity on the festival main stage, playing indie rock in a sea of mainstream music, listened to by an audience hungry for recognisable tunes. As *The Sun* noted, Dizzee Rascal, who was playing the Channel 4 stage at the same time the Monkeys were on, had a much easier task. Armed with a set full of radio-playlisted urban hits, Dizzee was a natural fit for the pop-friendly festival. It was a telling barometer of the times.

And yet the fans stayed, sang and cheered throughout a Monkeys set that contained the usual mix of songs from all four albums. When Alex asked if they were "familiar with a song called 'Mardy Bum'", they were delighted to shout it back at the band.

Moving on to Weston Park the following day, the challenge was as big but the audience response was bigger. As a drownedinsound.com reviewer said, their closing set had finished the V Festival "in idyllic fashion".

After V, the band returned to Europe; before playing Munich's Energy In The Park, to close this leg of the tour on August 28, they stopped first in France for the Rock en Seine Festival. The album had been going down well with the French, but the excitement around *Suck It And See* was soon to be surpassed by Alex's new haircut; comparisons were drawn with James Dean and Elvis – although no one seemed to hold it up to the great Johnny Hallyday himself.

In truth, leather-clad Alex's quiff probably had more in common with the Hamburg-era Beatles.

38

Back In The USA

THE day after the Munich gig, a short video compilation from Don Valley was released online. As the rumour mill kicked in, news of a DVD release started circulating, gradually transforming from possibility to confirmed certainty. The teaser had been called *Don Valley Bowl Trailer*, which at least implied there would be more to come. But no further details were given.

Soon, fan sites were filled with messages pleading for more information and one US site (arcticmonkeysus.com) took the unusual step of consoling fans by second-guessing that the band wouldn't release anything until the end of the tour, which meant nothing would happen until spring 2012.

It was a good guess, but wrong.

Just to make things more confusing, a chunkier clip from Don Valley was posted online on December 20, 2011. This time it was a well-edited 10-minute compilation of three songs from the festival: 'Don't Sit Down 'Cause I've Moved Your Chair', '505' and 'Mardy Bum'. Some people read it as a longer teaser, put out to keep fans ticking over until the full DVD was ready.

But when the Monkeys were directly questioned about a DVD release, they flatly dismissed the whole thing as a rumour. The video clips were, it seemed, only intended as short online excerpts from the gig and nothing more. A year later, there was no sign that anything more substantial might be released.

By mid-September, news had also started filtering through that Alexa was now dating Theo Hutchcraft, the singer from Hurts. In a bitter twist to the chronology of their former relationship, it was reported that the new couple had met at Coachella, where Alex and Alexa apparently met for the first time some four years before.

There would be other little pieces of press speculation to irritate the ex-couple. Alexa would be linked to several more people over the coming months, while Alex's new love would eventually emerge at an airport in 2012.

★   ★   ★

In the run-up to their late September US tour, the band announced their next single and made a one-stop trip to Italy. They had originally been lined up to play Italia Wave in July, but had rescheduled to appear at the I-Day Festival in Bologna on September 3, 2011, before releasing the video for their next single, the title track 'Suck It And See', scheduled for release on October 31.

In late September, they embarked on a three-date US tour with TV On The Radio. The New York-based indie art rock band had suffered the premature death of bass and keyboard player Gerard Smith earlier that year but were currently touring their new LP, *Nine Types Of Light*. The tour had originally been announced in early June as a one-off double header at The Hollywood Bowl, the venue that had played such a significant role in the story of The Beatles in America. The two bands had assembled a strong indie roster that included Noah Lennox's Panda Bear, Warpaint and Smith Westerns.

Buoyed by the interest the first gig had aroused, the two bands announced plans to extend the gig into a short co-headline tour, kicking off with the Las Vegas Cosmopolitan on September 23, followed by San Diego's Open Air Theatre and finally The Hollywood Bowl on the 25th. The Monkeys went on first, which may have been appropriate as they were the younger band by a long distance. But then the playing order barely mattered; the sound and attitude of both bands complemented each other, and fans of one could just as easily appreciate the other.

The set was a variant of the *Suck It And See* tour playlist, from their arrival onstage to 'You Sexy Thing' through to the set closer, on this occasion 'When The Sun Goes Down'. Notable moments included Alex paying homage to his new hair by saying "thankyouverymuch", Elvis style, and Matt wearing stars and stripes trousers.

After The Hollywood Bowl the two headliners went their separate ways, the Monkeys heading north with Smith Westerns to play to their ever-loyal Canadian following at The Orpheum, Vancouver. This was followed by an extensive North American tour, taking in MacEwan Hall Ballroom in Calgary, The Odeon in Saskatoon, Burton Cummings in Winnipeg, The Egyptian Room in Indianapolis, two dates at The Pageant in St Louis, the War Memorial Auditorium in Nashville, Hard Rock Live in Orlando, Revolution Live in Fort Lauderdale, The Tabernacle in Atlanta, House of Blues in Atlantic City and Rams Head Live! in Baltimore.

For the last three gigs of the 2011 US tour, the band moved on to the LC Pavilion in Columbus, Stage AE in Pittsburgh and finally to a special gig for website-registered fans at the 500-capacity Music Hall of Williamsburg in Brooklyn. The tour had finally brought Alex back to the boho manor he and Alexa had called home.

But this time, after New York, the band were heading home to the UK. "It's been really good," Alex told *NME*, "America has really started to like us."

39

Lost New Year

THE video for 'Suck It And See' had been released online before the band's North American autumn tour. It starred Matt Helders in an erotically charged rock'n'roll fiction – a five-minute remake of *Badlands* crossed with *Almost Famous*. The video was inspired by the rock'n'roll mythology of lost weekends in the Californian desert, imagining what would happen if a rock'n'roller went off on one and never came back.

"It's a strange thing to do, isn't it?" Matt said to the *NME*. "Was I worried that people might not get the joke? I wasn't really that bothered. As long as people see that we don't take ourselves too seriously." In the run-up to the single's October 31, 2011 release, the band released another video to YouTube, this time for the as-yet unannounced B-side, 'Evil Twin'. The raunchy promo continued the lost weekend/outlaw theme.

During the single's week of release, the Monkeys made a rare TV appearance and agreed to perform it live for Graham Norton's TV show on October 29. The band had always refused to do pre-recorded British television, but, despite being mainstream, Norton's show was credible and allowed acts to perform live. They rose to the occasion in typically laid-back fashion, delivering a flawless TV version of the single that finished in time for the credits to roll.

'Suck It And See' was released as a download and on seven-inch vinyl. The A-side had, of course, already been available on its namesake album, and soon the digital B-side was selling faster, but neither made it inside the Top 100.

With the single launched, the band's full *Suck It And See* UK tour finally kicked in with a schedule including 10 arena shows in the autumn. It was their most ambitious tour of the UK yet, the next logical step up the rock'n'roll ladder. It kicked off at Nottingham's Capital FM Arena on

October 28, with recent tour companions The Vaccines as the natural choice of support band.

'Evil Twin', which had debuted in St Louis on October 4, had now become a regular part of the set list, but once again it was the reappearance of the stripped-down 'Mardy Bum' that inspired the biggest singalong. With everyone roaring "you got the face on", it seemed like the Monkeys had finally got over the fear of sounding like a covers band playing their own older songs. It might have helped that they didn't really have to sing; they had their faithful audience on hand to do that.

The O2 Arena had originally been booked for October 29, but demand for the 20,000 tickets was so high that an extra night was added. On the first night, Alex breezed onstage greeting the crowd with his own form of corporate rebranding: "Hello, Millennium Dome," he smirked, before opening with 'Don't Sit Down 'Cause I've Moved Your Chair'. The band then moved on to 'Teddy Picker', picking up the pace and carrying the crowd with them. Soon the whole filled-to-capacity arena seemed to be singing along, arm in arm.

By now 'Brick By Brick' had settled into being the anthem that was inherently jocular in its DNA. The audience burst into full voice, merrily joining Matt in declaring their desire to "rock'n'roll". Having adopted the classic garb and the hair, Turner now started adopting classic stadium rock postures – standing on the monitors and kick drum, dropping to his knees, pointing into the sky and at the audience.

Leaving 40,000 happy fans in their wake, the tour moved on to the Cardiff Motorpoint Arena, where the 7,500-capacity crowd could barely contain their pre-gig excitement. The loyal Welsh fans sang through the set, naturally reserving their wildest fever-pitch response for up-tempo numbers such as 'Brianstorm' and 'I Bet You Look Good On The Dancefloor'. The night came to a close with spontaneous outbursts of Monkeys songs heard across Cardiff, as fans drifted home, wringing the last notes of the mosh pit from their sweat-soaked shirts.

On November 2 the tour took over the MEN Arena in Manchester. The city had played host to some of the band's earliest gigs, as well as some of its more recent and troublesome. It was also home to some of the band's longest-serving fans. But others were newer faces, too young to have been there on that tense night with The Horrors, let alone the Night & Day and

Jabez Clegg gigs. Both new and long-term fans lapped up the first salvo of more recent songs, including 'Don't Sit Down . . .', 'Teddy Picker' and 'Crying Lightning'. The biggest cheers still went to the vintage songs from the first LP, while Alex playfully introduced 'Brick By Brick' with a cryptic message: "Love it or hate it – you're wrong."

Way back in 2006, at their first victorious Mercury Prize ceremony, Alex had answered a volley of press questions by asking them why they were all being so serious. 'Brick By Brick' was another way of asking the same question. Delving further into fun and frolics, Alex staged a shout-off between the left- and right-hand sides of the stadium, before blasting into 'Dancefloor'.

Next it was the Midlands' turn to sing, laugh, hug and get covered in beer and cider. If the 15,000-plus crowd gathered in Birmingham's LG Arena was anything to go by, the Arctic Monkeys audience had by now distilled into an enviable cross-section of the record-buying public, a robust mixture of discerning adults and nonconformist youth. Reflecting the crowd's diversity, the band mixed up its repertoire but, unlike the *Humbug* tour, kept energy levels high throughout the set.

At the Metro Radio Arena in Newcastle, Arctic Monkeys dived nose-first into three songs before Alex paused to acknowledge the riotous crowd. Moving over the Scottish border, they returned to Aberdeen. The last time they'd played there the locals complained about the rowdiness of Glaswegian fans. This time the Monkeys booked a second gig, two nights later, in Glasgow. Both sold out.

After a final gig at Liverpool's Echo Arena on November 9, the band signed off their Facebook page: "Thanks to everyone who came out to see us on the UK tour, hope you enjoyed yourselves and see you again soon. Thanks to The Vaccines for supporting." Apart from announcing the release of 'Black Treacle' as a single, it was their last posting in 2011.

Throughout the tour the Monkeys had powered into their sets, blasting their audience with three introductory belters before taking a relative breather and then starting up again at full charge. Perhaps they'd learned from Reading, when they'd been accused of arrogance for starting with little-known mid-tempo songs. But they also seemed the most relaxed they'd ever been.

"I've done things onstage recently that I never thought I would have done," Alex reflected. "That didn't come naturally to me at all, like singing, it's something that has built up over time. But now I'm doing stupid crowd participation things like shouting, 'just this side sing'. That was a gag that we used to have in the practice room, but I actually went through with it the other night."

The band had settled into playing stadiums – something they'd previously dismissed but now made sense as their next big career move; especially in America.

"I used to think that we'd never be able to play arenas," Alex admitted to *The Shortlist.* "I used to think . . . it was too frantic and it wouldn't really work in a big open space. You do require a few bells and whistles these days, but it can be done tastefully – it doesn't have to be tons of lasers and everything . . . [though] pyrotechnics are exciting . . . that is tempting . . ."

"We should just go over the top with it," an enthusiastic Helders jumped in. "Like when you go to Disneyland and they do a bit in the Animal Kingdom where they pretend the bridge has fallen down . . . We could do something like that, as if something's gone wrong. Like a stunt. The light falls on me . . ."

"Sets the drum kit on fire . . ." chipped in Alex.

". . . and everyone's screaming," continued Helders, "then I come back on and do 'Brick By Brick'!" At which point their plans for a stadium tour collapsed into laughter – but not for long.

★   ★   ★

The Monkeys announced they would return to the US in early 2012, to play their first stadium tour as a support act for The Black Keys. Having sold out sizeable venues in the UK, USA and Canada under their own power, and played headline slots at large festivals, they still weren't quite ready to reinvent stadium rock on their own.

Before heading back to the States, they broke their long absence from Australia to play New Year gigs at The Falls Music and Arts Festival in Tasmania and Victoria, on December 30 and 31 respectively. It had been up to three years since their last visit and the Monkeys' return to Tasmania brought the 1,600-capacity crowd to their feet – pogoing, punching the air, hugging each other and singing.

The following night the Monkeys had been given the New Year

headline slot, designed to climax as the clock struck midnight. Punters had been crawling along the Lorne foreshore in a slow-moving 10-kilometre jam to get onsite but, despite the delays, the band had taken to the stage on time. After playing for just over an hour, the Monkeys brought their set to a finish with perfect punctuality, leaving the stage before the stroke of midnight.

It was a moment of precision that might have led into the most spectacular New Year countdown and firework display ever. Instead, the festival fell silent.

It soon transpired that Arctic Monkeys had been intended to perform the 10-second countdown to welcome the New Year in. Unfortunately, no one had told the band.

As confused fans started popping bottles and counting down themselves, the promoters hurriedly explained the situation backstage and Alex rushed back to the microphone. "Sorry, we thought someone else had organised a countdown," he spluttered. "Let's do one now then, shall we?"

The amused crowd was more than happy to celebrate the New Year twice and Alex soon warmed to his compère role, introducing the next act, Crystal Castles, before leaving the stage with the party back in full swing.

For entertainment news desks across the world, the Arctic cock-up started the New Year with a smile. *The Huffington Post* pleaded in vain for someone to send through a video clip of the countdown, but, amazingly for a Monkeys gig, the incident seemed to have evaded the cameras.

The Australian tour continued on January 3, 2012 with a sold-out concert at the 5,000-capacity Festival Hall in Melbourne, followed by Belvoir Amphitheatre in Perth and the Southbound Festival in Western Australia. The 2,500 devotees who packed into Adelaide's Entertainment Centre Theatre on January 10 had been waiting since 2009 for the Monkeys to return. Tickets had become rarities soon after they were announced.

The Monkeys had at one stage been thought of in much the same way as Oasis and their 'lads' following. But the audience packing gigs in Australia demonstrated a different demographic. In Adelaide, as elsewhere, a mostly female audience filled the arena – presenting the testosterone-friendly local support act, Violent Soho, with an unexpected challenge.

Miles Kane, fulfilling his regular role as the Monkeys' main support act, proved a more natural fit with the 'ladies'. The whole crowd whooped and hollered and sang in their best Oz Sheffield accents through the Monkeys' entire set.

Taking to the stage in his rocker-style leather jacket, Alex stripped down to his sleeveless tour vest emblazoned with a crowd-pleasing Australian flag. Kane came back onstage to join in on 'Little Illusion Machine' and, later on, returned to play guitar on '505'.

The band moved on to two more sold-out shows in Sydney, starting with the 5,500-capacity Hordern Pavilion, where they were greeted by a seething mass of appreciative fans. Sydney, like Adelaide, had been waiting expectantly for the Monkeys to return and tickets had sold out so quickly that a second show, at the 1,600-capacity Enmore Theatre, had been hurriedly booked. It too sold out in a flash, becoming the tour's closing date on January 13, 2012.

40

Black Treacle

THE fourth single to be taken from *Suck It And See* was 'Black Treacle', a low-slung rock ballad wrought from the ashes of Turner and Chung's relationship and riddled with the imagery of shattered hope. The promotional video was uploaded onto YouTube on January 5, 2012, while the band were still touring Australia. It continued the theme developed in the promo films for 'Suck It And See' and 'Evil Twin', both of which had also been filmed in California, featuring Matt as an escaped convict brandishing a knife, an abandoned woman stranded in the desert in a wedding dress and Alex sporting a sharp-looking hairstyle.

The single was released after the band's return to the UK on January 23, on seven-inch vinyl and download. It was limited to only 1,500 copies and backed with a new Death Ramps track, 'You And I', a scuzzy, fuzzbox-guitar fuelled rock track featuring long-term Monkeys favourite Richard Hawley on guest lead vocal.

The B-side had been recorded as part of an ongoing session with Sheffield-based producer Ross Orton, one-time drummer for cult synth act Add N To (X), a third of dance act Fat Truckers and half of Caveman with Pulp guitarist Steve Mackey. His work with the Monkeys had been greeted by some critics as the closest they'd yet come to hard rock and as a signpost to where they were heading next.

Speculation on the band's rock trajectory gained ground in subsequent interviews. Alex told Radio 1's Zane Lowe that the band were considering a straighter rock LP while the press reported that a new track they'd recorded, 'R U Mine?', contained the blueprint for a heavier, more anthemic sound well suited to stadium-sized venues. Reports circulated that the band were continuing to work with Ross Orton, taking him out to the Californian desert to record in their preferred studio setting.

With rumours abounding about their fifth studio LP, the band headed off for another eight-date European tour promoting *Suck It And See*. They played to a massive 15,000-capacity crowd, packed into Madrid's Palacio de Deportes, before moving on to Barcelona's slightly bigger Palau Sant Jordi. From here it was on to the much smaller (2,000-capacity) Casino de Paris on January 31, a quick trip to the Zénith in Lille and back for two more packed Parisian gigs at Olympia and Zénith. From here the tour moved to Toulouse, Caen and finally Les Arènas in Metz on February 8.

Returning to the UK, the Monkeys performed a cover of Katy B's 'On A Mission' for BBC Radio 1's *Live Lounge*. During the subsequent interview the band announced they were going to release a brand new single in a few weeks, while Turner confirmed they wouldn't be playing any more European festivals in 2012. News about the new single was confirmed in another BBC Radio 1 interview on February 16, when Turner also announced the Monkeys would be returning to the studio in the summer to record more material, although he stopped short of saying it was for the fifth album.

When the 2012 *NME* Awards were held on February 29 at the O2 Academy in Brixton, Arctic Monkeys were nominated for Best Band, Best Track, Best Album, Best Video, Best Artwork and Most Dedicated Fanbase. "We're up for all the big ones," Matt Helders said, "we're very happy. We had a lot of fun making *Suck It And See* and it's great to be up for Best Live Band. That's all we do – record or play live – so it's good to be recognised!"

Alex had also been nominated as Hero of the Year, but in the end Arctic Monkeys walked away with only one prize, Best Live Band. In a break with recent tradition, they accepted the award by video – albeit without the surreal spoofing of their earlier Brit Award acceptance videos.

★   ★   ★

When the new single was announced, questions also surfaced about which label would release both it and the next album. Rumours about Arctic Monkeys leaving Domino Records had been circulating since the summer of 2011, when *The Sun* ran a story on bids from several unnamed rival labels.

Arctic Monkeys had signed a four-album deal with Domino and were bound to the label for the duration of their promotional duties for *Suck*

It And See. Despite press speculation, the band were characteristically sanguine; Ian McAndrews told *NME* they'd received enquiries from other labels, but were happy with Domino.

The band themselves were deeply entrenched in planning their next phase of stadium activity in the USA, and were probably in no mood for back-room discussions about labels. The video for a brand new song, 'R U Mine?', suddenly appeared on the Arctic Monkeys YouTube channel on February 26, 2012. Shot in long sequences, the video featured Matt and Alex up close in a car driving around California, preening and miming to the song. It felt both surreal and uncannily intimate. With a special release designed to coincide with Record Store Day, an annual celebration of vinyl records, 'R U Mine?' was the first single since *Suck It And See* that hadn't been taken from the album.

As it was one of Alex's most accomplished recent songs, Arctic Monkeys were under pressure to get 'R U Mine?' out. They were about to embark on their next US stadium tour, as junior headline partners to the newly ascendant Black Keys.

With no sign of a new deal being struck – with either Domino or another label – some news stories concluded that the band would return to their roots and release their next single on their own label. It certainly looked that way. The digital single was released on February 27, 2009, followed by a white label seven-inch vinyl on April 24, Record Store Day. But, apart from the presentation, it appeared to be business as usual between the band and the recording company.

'R U Mine?' received a hugely positive response, with *NME* saying it sounded "like a band in love with the sonic possibilities of their guitars again". It was put onto BBC Radio 1's 'A' list and debuted at number 23 on the UK Singles Chart.

Even though the Monkeys had played some of their largest dates yet on their last US tour, there was a sense that they'd become entrenched in mid-capacity venues. They had frequently filled festival main stages, for sure, but the time had come to move towards larger arenas.

Playing a stadium tour presented challenges. It wasn't as if the bands who were their peers regularly filled stadiums in the USA. To help make the leap, Arctic Monkeys had to look for partners who shared some musical common ground and were capable of drawing a stadium crowd.

Although The Black Keys had been on the scene for almost exactly as long as the Monkeys, they were a very different proposition. In contrast to the Sheffield band, who'd seen their early hard slog rewarded by a meteoric rise, The Black Keys had spent eight years constantly gigging and recording to gradually build their fanbase.

Mainstream success eluded them until May 2010, when they released their sixth album, *Brothers*. The LP spawned an unexpected slow-burning radio hit, 'Tighten Up', which spent 10 weeks at number one in *Billboard*'s Alternative Singles Chart. The LP entered the charts at number three in the *Billboard* 200, selling 1.5 million copies worldwide, while a phenomenal turnover of deals made them Warner Brothers' most licensed band of 2010.

In celebration of this extraordinary turnaround, The Black Keys were awarded Best Alternative Music Album and Best Rock Performance by a Duo or a Group at the Grammy Awards in February 2011. At the time when they were most in demand as a live band, in early 2011, the band suddenly cancelled all their shows and retreated to the studio with producer Danger Mouse (the man behind Gnarls Barkley's hit 'Crazy') to record their seventh LP, *El Camino*, which debuted at number two on the *Billboard* 200 and sold 206,000 copies in its first week.

With their new album released, The Black Keys were ready to support the album with the first headline arena tour of their career. They approached Arctic Monkeys to be their main support act at precisely the right time.

"We've been looking for a tour like this since we started because we've never done a support tour, not in England, not anywhere," Matt Helders explained to the San Francisco *Examiner*. "It's a massive tour, and I think we've done as much as we could on our own without doing something like this."

The partnership between Arctic Monkeys and The Black Keys presented a perfect solution for both bands, allowing them to move up the live acts' league table. But there were also problems, as fan blog *The Steam Engine* pointed out:

"The Black Keys will be playing the big arenas, Madison Square Garden, United Center, etc. . . . with the Arctic Monkeys opening for them. Everything about that sounds fantastic other than the whole arena thing. Good for them, bad for us."

As a logical progression in the band's careers, the stadium tour probably made more sense for Arctic Monkeys, a British band looking to increase its standing in the US, than for The Black Keys – who had just secured their status as a leading alternative US act. But if a backlash against stadium rock was in the air, it wasn't strong enough to deter ticket sales.

Despite previously toying with the idea of pyrotechnics, Arctic Monkeys opted for a simple stage set-up. In contrast with The Black Keys' immersive video screens, disco balls and other high-tech props, the most complex part of the Monkeys' stage show was a strobe light.

The first show of the tour took place in Cincinnati, Ohio on March 2, 2012 and immediately highlighted a recurring problem for the Monkeys, as a significant number of fans arrived during their set. The song list contained the usual mixture of tracks from the LPs, but the following night the band added 'R U Mine?' to their set at Detroit's Joe Louis Arena. Detroit was clearly primed for the Monkeys, with fans turning up early to catch them.

After playing 'Suck It And See' and 'Library Pictures', Alex brought the crowd's attention to Matt's drumming by saying: "We know you love drummers, Detroit." Helders took his cue, emerging from behind the kick drum to reveal his Stars and Stripes leggings. It was the perfect moment to introduce the crowd to the new single, which was, along with every song that followed it, greeted with a rapturous response. By this point the few stragglers who had missed the start of the set had arrived, and for the rest of the show the Monkeys played to a full house.

Following Detroit, the tour moved to The Schottenstein Center in Colombus and on to a packed Cumberland County Civic Center in Portland, Maine on March 6. It was the band's first time in Portland but their rapid-fire set was pumped with energy, garnering an ecstatically wild response to 'R U Mine?'.

Next the tour bus rolled into the 20,000-strong sold-out TD Garden in Boston, followed by The Verizon Center in Washington, DC and The Wells Fargo Center in Philadelphia on March 10. As the set came to a crescendo, Turner left the stage after uttering a chirpy "Thanks for 'avin' us, Philly, and enjoy The Black Keys!", leaving some members of the crowd wondering why such a big act had been given such a short support slot. One Black Keys fan later blogged that they'd have been happy to pay the ticket price for the Arctic Monkeys' performance alone.

On March 12 the tour made its first scheduled stop at a sold-out Madison Square Gardens, before heading over the border for The Bell Centre in Montreal. The following night the Monkeys returned to play a sold-out show at The Air Canada Centre in Toronto, where they first supported Oasis during their North American tour in 2006.

Moving back south to the USA, they played the Bankers Life Fieldhouse in Indianapolis and the Van Andel Arena at Grand Rapids, followed by the United Center in Chicago. Here Alex picked up on an abbreviated name for the windy city, taking time to thank "Chi Town" between practically every song. He was in playful mood, introducing Helders with "Matt is our drummer. He's who your girlfriend is thinking about." The arena had again been half full when the band had taken to the stage at 7.30 p.m., but by the end they'd won over the full crowd.

The Quicken Loans Arena in Cleveland followed on March 20, before the tour made its second stop at Madison Square Gardens and The Constant Convocation Center in Norfolk, Virginia, where the *Daily Press* noted how the concert reasserted loud guitar music as a vital art form. Once again the band faced the daunting prospect of playing an opening set to an audience still arriving; once again they won them over. The *Daily Press* especially praised Turner's voice: "Rich and expressive, cocky and nicely abrasive – it was spot on throughout."

The sold-out Bojangles' Coliseum in Charlotte proved to be one of the more energetic dates on the tour, after which Arctic Monkeys broke away from The Black Keys to make a four-date stop-off in Central and South America, in the run-up to Coachella. Kicking off with the Sports Palace in Mexico City on March 28, they moved onto the Lollapalooza sister festival in Santiago, Chile, Quilmes Rock Festival in Buenos Aires, Argentina and Lollapalooza in Sao Paulo, Brazil on April 8.

Returning to the USA for Coachella weekend one, the Monkeys played a packed 800-capacity warm-up gig at The Glass House in Pomona on April 11. Two days later, Alex performed an afternoon acoustic set for KROQ Radio live at Coachella. The three-song broadcast featured acoustic versions of 'Reckless Serenade', 'Love Is A Laserquest' and 'Suck It And See'.

Their set at weekend one of the Coachella Festival, on April 13, was described by the *Pure Volume* website as "47 minutes of Brit-rock heaven".

KROQ's website observed how Arctic Monkeys had brought their own crowd to the festival: "Dip-dye coiffed baby hipsters bounced and shimmied. Jordan Lawlor, the young curly haired multi-instrumentalist from M83, danced with his cute girlfriend. But Arctic Monkeys didn't seem to care. They were all business with their post-punk, Britpop swagger, angsty and unruly, with guttural guitars and slurred words. Frontman Alex Turner seemed unfazed by the cheers of dancing hipsters around him, announcing songs with a sardonic tone in his voice albeit with a sort of charm."

With weekend two of Coachella in Indio, California on April 20 earning similar plaudits, the band headed on for well-received shows at Edgefest in Frisco, Texas and Cynthia Woods Mitchell Pavilion in Houston on April 24. Here the band pulled in a predominantly female audience while their rockier sound continued to translate well to their American fans.

More packed dates followed at The Frank Erwin Center in Austin and Chaifetz Arena in St Louis. From here the tour twisted its way through The BOK Center in Tulsa, two nights at 1st Bank Center in Broomfield, The Maverik Center in West Valley City and Oracle Arena in Oakland. The Power Balance Pavilion in Sacramento, California saw the band deliver more crowd-pleasing sets, followed by The Rose Garden Arena in Portland, Oregon, KeyArena in Seattle, Rogers Arena in Vancouver, The Scotiabank Saddledome in Calgary, Rexall Place in Edmonton and The MTS Centre in Winnipeg. The Target Center in Minneapolis, on May 15, should have seen a loyal crowd turn out for the Monkeys, but once again they were just filtering into the venue during the first half of their set.

With Turner playing up to his role as both showman and comedian, the band fired through 'Brianstorm', 'This House Is A Circus', 'Still Take You Home', 'The View From The Afternoon', and 'Dancefloor'. When Alex finally announced the end of their set, the full arena started booing and calling for more. "Grow up," Alex quipped, before closing the set with 'R U Mine?', by which point the crowd was definitely his. The Bradley Center in Milwaukee was followed by Merriweather Post Pavilion in Columbia on May 18, bringing the US arena tour to a close.

One final date remained, Metallica's inaugural Orion Music + More

Festival at Bader Field, Atlantic City, New Jersey on June 23. Here Arctic Monkeys had been given the headline slot on the second stage, timed to fill the run-up to Metallica's closing performance on the main stage. For a band contemplating a rockier sound, the compliment could hardly have been more apt. On the night, Lars Ulrich took it upon himself to introduce the Monkeys as "the coolest of the cool", a title they did their best to live up to with the roaring set that followed.

Arctic Monkeys and The Black Keys had successfully packed out a tour of dauntingly large venues, with the Monkeys accounting for a significant proportion of the crowd. Often the audience members were fans of both bands, but the Monkeys frequently won over new recruits. Nonetheless, rather than gaining higher status from the gigs, the Monkeys sometimes struggled to get more than a passing mention as the support and were often entirely overlooked by local reporters. Even harder to overcome, the timing of their slot meant they often performed as the audience arrived. For the band's existing fanbase, this seemed well below the band's station.

Even in the face of these obstacles, Arctic Monkeys had come out of the tour well, with Alex in particular taking on the role of support act with relish. Both bands had attracted positive reviews, but in truth the Monkeys had already played venues as big as this under their own steam. They would do so again before too long.

41

Olympic Monkeys

IN mid-July 2012, Jamie Cook's romance with Page Three model Katie Downes, whom he'd met while recording in Liverpool in 2006, came back into the media's glare. *The Sun* reported that Jamie had proposed to Katie – and she had immediately accepted. The proposal to the 28-year-old model had come at the end of the band's US tour.

At the same time, Alex had been spotted in LA with his new girlfriend, the actress Arielle Vandenberg, who Turner had been dating since soon after his split from Alexa Chung. Meanwhile, a series of intimate photos posted on the web appeared to confirm that Helders had also found new love with model and actress Breana McDow. Breana had starred alongside Matt in the series of lost weekend videos made for *Suck It And See*.

In the meantime, the band were taking a short break before a rather prestigious date.

★   ★   ★

Despite the involvement of thousands of volunteer performers and its promise of being one of the most spectacular events in British history, the secrecy surrounding the £27 million opening ceremony of the 2012 Olympic Games in London was almost total. Created by celebrated British filmmaker Danny Boyle, who had, among many other credits, directed the cult film version of Irvine Welsh's *Trainspotting*, it was acknowledged only that the ceremony would involve a celebration of Britain's success in popular music.

Boyle had made stars of Nineties dance act Underworld, when he used their song 'Born Slippy' for *Trainspotting*. When he turned to them to oversee the music for the project, their appointment intimated that electronic music would feature in the ceremony. It was also known that there would be an appearance by at least one rock music great, drawn from a long list of British stars of the Sixties and Seventies.

Some other snippets of information were drip-fed out to the eager media, but as the ceremony drew close, little else was known. In June, Boyle unveiled a number of further elements underlining a strong musical connection, including 'mosh pits' at both ends of the east London arena and, in a nod to the Glastonbury Festival, a model of Glastonbury Tor.

Then, with the opening of the Olympic Games just days away, Juan Martin Rinaldi, an Argentinean journalist, managed to obtain a photograph that appeared to show Alex Turner rehearsing for the show. Rinaldi posted the photo on his Twitter account and soon the web and offline media were abuzz with speculation about Arctic Monkeys playing the ceremony.

Throughout most of the four-hour opening event, there was no sign of either the Monkeys or a platform on which they could appear. Suddenly, near the climax of a spectacular show, the opening bars of The Beatles' 'Come Together' rolled out and Arctic Monkeys confidently panned into view. Their live rendition of the classic was both faithful and fresh, turned into a moment of stunning beauty by a stream of winged and floating cyclists flowing out from under the stage and into the air.

Arctic Monkeys' live appearance at the Olympics was broadcast to 27.3 million people around the world. More significantly, Boyle had chosen the band for perhaps the most important slot in the whole ceremony, before Sir Paul McCartney took to the stage to represent The Beatles, the greatest band in British history. Boyle was celebrating the history of British rock and he'd put The Beatles and Arctic Monkeys at either end of the bookcase.

Fittingly, as the ceremony came to a close, the Monkeys' version of 'Come Together' became an online sales sensation. Several of the tracks included in the ceremony had been earmarked for inclusion in a Universal Music compilation called *Isles Of Wonder*, which had been released minutes after the ceremony closed on Friday, July 27, 2012. Within days the Monkeys' cover of The Beatles' track had started racing up the UK charts, climbing to 14 on the iTunes singles chart and 16 in the UK singles chart.

Meanwhile, the second song the band played that night, 2005's 'I Bet

You Look Good On The Dancefloor', also slipped back into the UK charts, entering the Top 100 at number 78. In less than two days after its release, the opening ceremony compilation, which included tracks from such greats as David Bowie, had reached number five in the British album chart. By the end of the weekend it also topped the iTunes album chart in the UK, France, Belgium and Spain, and reached number five in the United States.

The Olympic organisers explained, soon after the games, that the leading artists had all received a token contractual fee of £1 for playing at the ceremony. But the slot Arctic Monkeys had played was priceless.

Even though he hadn't taken part himself, The Beatles' Ringo Starr tweeted the following message immediately after the show: "Well done Danny Boyle, great show all, Arctic Monkeys' 'Come Together' – send me a copy and well done Paul, great show all around."

42

The Secret Door

IN the late summer of 2012, Arctic Monkeys took part in *NME*'s sixtieth birthday celebrations, featuring on one of eight special edition covers of the magazine, while the *NME* also re-ran the first article they had ever written about the band.

As Alex Turner had announced earlier in the year that the band had no plans to play any festivals in 2012, after their appearance at the Olympics the Monkeys suddenly went off-radar. The understandable assumption was that the band were busy recording their new LP; information that started to leak out suggested they'd returned to the desert to record.

It was believed that the Monkeys were back at Rancho de la Luna with Josh Homme, although rumours in Sheffield also suggested they were recording in the desert with Ross Orton. Turner, Helders and O'Malley had all agreed in various interviews that the band were interested in pursuing a heavier sound, with Alex telling *Artrocker* magazine that the band felt the heavier tunes on *Suck It And See* were them at their strongest. He also suggested they wouldn't be revisiting their early sound:

"I think we're going to go the direction of those heavier tunes. We did 'R U Mine?', and I think that's where it's going to be at for us for the next record."

Turner also said he was looking forward to writing songs with his bandmates: "[Usually] it's just the four of us hashing it out in a rehearsal space, but those kind of songs were in the minority on the last record due to circumstance really."

As summer turned into early autumn, a message from Matt's mum, Jill Helders, tried to settle online speculation, tweeting: "I don't know if it helps to clear things up but lads are in the desert!", adding "and now we start on 5th album titles!"

Apart from Jill's contribution, much of the other information about the band's recording activity came from the fan site arcticmonkeysus.com. It was they who had widely circulated the news that the Monkeys were back at Joshua Tree: "Info' comes from the top. I won't lose sleep if u don't believe it but you can't speak to my credibility. When have I been wrong?"

The fans had got fully behind the rumours and #ArcticMonkeys-5thAlbum was trending heavily on Twitter. By the end of September, a further message from an anonymous poster (calling themselves Twit Face) said: "the desert mission is accomplished Arctic Monkeys have recorded their demos for album 5."

It was also clear the band hadn't been recording with James Ford, something he confirmed himself in November 2012: "I know they're currently writing towards the next record. I have worked a lot with them now and I think it's probably time for someone else to work with them for the next record. Sometimes a fresh perspective is needed."

It had been suspected for a while that the band had not only decided on LA as their preferred recording location, but also as a more permanent home. If the demo stage of the desert mission had been accomplished, there was still little sign that Arctic Monkeys were on their way home to Sheffield. Indeed, successive reports all seemed to imply they had no intention of leaving California in a hurry.

On October 8, there was a rare sighting of the Turner family together as Alex was spotted with his parents, David and Penny, at a hotel in Santa Monica. Two weeks later, he was again seen hanging out in LA when he turned up to watch rising Californian guitar pop trio, Haim, perform a homecoming gig at The Fonda Theatre in Hollywood.

A month later, *Artrocker* reported on November 16 that the band had started to build a new rehearsal facility in Hollywood, again signalling a more permanent move to LA. It transpired that the rehearsal space was kitted out in advance of recording the fifth LP, and was going to be used as a practice and compositional space for bringing the new songs up to performance level for recording. By March Alex had told *Another Man* magazine that the band had finished rehearsing and would be recording the LP in the spring.

There was no doubt the band had taken to America's West Coast for personal reasons, not least that Alex had found new love there. But there were also strong career currents pulling them towards the hotbed of American music and media. Speaking in November 2012, James Ford confirmed that the band were currently based in LA; the band themselves made no attempt to hide their ambition to finally crack America. Following the last LP and single, and The Black Keys tour, everything was pointing in the right direction.

But, for the swathes of Americans who had yet to succumb to the lads' Sheffield charm, the biggest boost had been their slot in the Olympics' opening ceremony – even though American TV coverage had cut to a commercial break during the Monkeys' second song.

There was a real sense that the time was ripe for Arctic Monkeys to become a major success in the USA. But this did not mean the UK and Europe had slipped entirely off their map. The band had taken the unusual decision of dedicating the entire second half of 2012 to their fifth LP and hadn't gigged after their appearance at the Olympics. But in late November, as the first details about the Arctic Monkeys' next tour began to emerge, they were all European dates. As spring 2013 approached, a host of US dates also started to emerge, alongside the news that the band would be headlining Glastonbury with the Rolling Stones.

Whatever 2013 would herald in the studio, it was clear the band would also be back on the live circuit.

43

When The Sun Goes Down

PREDICTING the future for Arctic Monkeys is a perilous practice. For example, in an interview with *The Sun* in late 2011, Alex Turner said the band would be taking a break from recording until 2013 and keeping their heads down for the rest of 2012. But before a month had passed, he told Australian radio station Triple J that the Monkeys would be recording a new EP in Sheffield "in a few weeks".

A couple of months later the new single had been released, accompanied by an ongoing dialogue with the press about the next LP – which was going to be at least partially recorded in 2012. Following that, the band popped up at the opening ceremony of the Olympics.

So much for keeping their heads down.

But as the band approached the tenth anniversary of their debut performance, they'd more than delivered on their early promise, producing four albums that had stood up to critical scrutiny. Every one of them had gone to number one in the UK and sold well around the world: an impressive catalogue by any standard.

"On the whole, bands have one good album in them," music journalist Nick Tesco has pointed out. "They've made four albums, of which three are REALLY good and stand the tests of time. So they're already ahead of the curve." He also pointed out that the other LP had some good tracks on it – although he refused to go so far as naming the 'less good' album.

In many respects Arctic Monkeys are the same group of mates who climbed onstage at The Grapes in 2003. Of course, success has also changed them: by November 2012, Turner alone was reported, in *Heat* magazine's annual Under 30 Rich List, to be worth over £9.8 million. But the band remains a family affair. Even the Monkeys' line-up change involved people from within the band's circle of friends in High Green.

And despite Andy Nicholson's early departure, they have managed to navigate their passage to world fame with surprisingly few personal traumas.

In an interview with *The Shortlist*, Alex had pointed to the band's High Green background as one of the things that helps keep them together: "We grew up together pretty much on the same street. So we'd hung around with each other a long time before we were a band . . . You're bound to argue, but I think we get around a lot of that stuff. It's maybe something about where we're from. We're all pretty laid back."

Despite the group's settled membership, the constant presence of Miles Kane on their recent tours has prompted journalists to ask whether he was being considered for a more permanent position. There's little doubt Kane is popular with the band. In 2012, Nick told an Australian website that he thought Kane was "on fire at the minute. He's got a great sort of show-manship ability . . . And he's a good mate."

Asked whether Kane might join the band, Cook and Turner both said they would probably let him in if he asked. Given that Kane and the Monkeys already share managers, any more long-term collaboration between them would have been easy to initiate.

But creating a permanent position for Kane in the band is perhaps unnecessarily complicated. A more likely window for a future collabora-tion would be a sophomore Last Shadow Puppets LP – although the chances of any side projects reviving before the fifth LP and tour are remote indeed.

Looking forward, it's possible the band will choose to wind down their relentless touring activity – as indicated by their taking the second half of 2012 off. They had already told *The Shortlist*, in late 2011, that they were missing people at home and getting to an age where they were starting to miss out on mates' stag nights and weddings. As time goes on, however, the opportunity to slip into larger-scale tours may seem like an attractive option – although the band will undoubtedly find other creative ways to fill any extra time.

The band's management company, Wildlife, split up in 2008, but the team looking after Arctic Monkeys remains in place, with Ian McAndrews and Geoff Barradale managing the band as they have from the start. It's also notable that other acts Barradale and McAndrews have represented at various stages – such as Miles Kane and Reverend & The Makers – have also been integrally involved in the Monkeys' story.

Doubters and detractors continue to question the band's musical ability. At times the Monkeys have played into this reaction by not giving interviews, or initially staying away from TV and radio, fuelling speculation that they might have something to hide – or that they were aloof and over-cocky.

But allegations, such as Alex's lyrics are written by a secret Svengali, seem driven more by a dubious desire to discredit the band, rather than by any hard evidence. It's of course possible that he inadvertently contributed to these rumours, as he's often described the band's songwriting process in the plural ('we'), as well as talking about how Helders' drum patterns have suggested songs to him or how he and Cookie locked themselves away in his Brooklyn apartment, working on guitar lines.

In the run-up to recording their fifth LP, Alex complained that writing the fourth album had been a lonely project, conducted in his New York apartment – whereas their earlier LPs had all been written with the band together in the rehearsal studio.

James Ford has described how the band usually work together in rehearsing and arranging Alex's songs, and has talked about his own contributions to the Monkeys' material. The influences of Josh Homme and Ross Orton have also been audible in the band's recordings, but none of this implies that Alex isn't the author of his own material.

Arctic Monkeys arrived amidst a blaze of music press claims that they'd changed the music industry forever. While some of the grander notions, such as the promise of a new 'do it yourself' era, have failed to materialise, they certainly prefigured methods of working that have now become standard practice, such as artists going to labels with a ready-made fanbase.

They were early exponents of aspects of the digital market which are now commonplace, not least in their frequent early use of download singles – as well as their combination of digital and other formats, such as vinyl and radio. In many ways the digital phenomenon they were best known for is only a small part of their more innovative practices.

As the *NME* has often pointed out, the very existence of Arctic Monkeys has inspired many a bedroom full of new young rock'n'roll wannabes. Artistically, Alex's songwriting and vocal delivery have informed a new crop of British singer-songwriters. The lyrical content of his songs at first reflected the small-town confines of his schooldays, but his vocal delivery has also drawn from hip hop. These were accidents of Alex's personal journey but they were repeated by a new wave of British performers such as Ed Sheeran, often with very different social and musical backgrounds. But, mirroring the parallels between Sheeran's half-rapped vocals and Alex's delivery, there were also occasional similarities in their subject matter.

At the end of 2012, the *NME*, the band's loyal media champion, confidently announced that Arctic Monkeys were on the verge of conquering America. At the same time, their semi-regular producer, James Ford, summed up his thoughts on them: "In my eyes they're just one of the best British bands.

"They are super, super talented. I think they'll just keep developing and keep moving forward."

By the summer of 2013, Arctic Monkeys had been a touring band for 10 years. But they were still young, with much of their career ahead of them. There was every reason to suspect that, as good as the first 10 years had been, the best was yet to come.

In the end, it will always come back to their songs: that familiar otherness of Alex's compositions and the wisps of beauty that penetrate even their rowdiest anthems. It's hard to see why they should ever stop.

Discography

Albums

WHATEVER PEOPLE SAY I AM, THAT'S WHAT I'M NOT

UK release: January 23, 2006
Tracks:
1 The View From The Afternoon
2 I Bet You Look Good On The Dancefloor
3 Fake Tales Of San Francisco
4 Dancing Shoes
5 You Probably Couldn't See For The Lights But You Were Staring Straight At Me
6 Still Take You Home
7 Riot Van
8 Red Light Indicates Doors Are Secured
9 Mardy Bum
10 Perhaps Vampires Is A Bit Strong But…
11 When The Sun Goes Down
12 From The Ritz To The Rubble
13 A Certain Romance
Formats: Vinyl, CD
Label: Domino
Highest chart positions: UK Number 1, Australia Number 1, Ireland Number 1, New Zealand Number 5
Sales: UK 4 x Platinum, Australia 2 x Platinum, Canada Gold, Japan Gold

FAVOURITE WORST NIGHTMARE

UK release: April 23, 2007
Tracks:
1 Brianstorm
2 Teddy Picker
3 D Is For Dangerous
4 Balaclava
5 Fluorescent Adolescent
6 Only Ones Who Know
7 Do Me A Favour
8 This House Is A Circus
9 If You Were There, Beware
10 The Bad Thing
11 Old Yellow Bricks
12 505

13 Da Frame 2R
14 Matador
Formats: Vinyl, CD
Label: Domino
Highest chart positions: UK Number 1, Australia Number 2, Belgium Number 1,
    Canada Number 4, Denmark Number 1, Spain Number 2, Germany Number 2,
    Japan Number 4, Ireland Number 1, Netherlands Number 1, Norway Number 2,
    New Zealand Number 4
Sales: UK 2 x Platinum, Australia Gold, Canada Gold, Japan Gold

HUMBUG

UK release: August 24, 2009
Tracks:
  1 My Propeller
  2 Crying Lightning
  3 Dangerous Animals
  4 Secret Door
  5 Potion Approaching
  6 Fire And The Thud
  7 Cornerstone
  8 Dance Little Liar
  9 Pretty Visitors
  10 The Jeweller's Hands
  11 I Haven't Got My Strange
  12 Sketchhead
Formats: Vinyl, CD, Download
Label: Domino
Highest chart positions: UK Number 1, Australia Number 2, Belgium Number 1,
    Denmark Number 4, Spain Number 5, France Number 1, Germany Number 4,
    Japan Number 4, Ireland Number 1, Netherlands Number 2, Norway Number 2,
    New Zealand Number 3
Sales: UK Gold

SUCK IT AND SEE

UK release: June 6, 2011
Tracks:
  1 She's Thunderstorms
  2 Black Treacle
  3 Brick By Brick
  4 The Hellcat Spangled Shalalala
  5 Don't Sit Down 'Cause I've Moved Your Chair
  6 Library Pictures
  7 All My Own Stunts
  8 Reckless Serenade
  9 Piledriver Waltz
  10 Love Is A Laserquest

11 Suck It And See
12 That's Where You're Wrong
Formats: Vinyl, CD, Download
Label: Domino
Highest chart positions: UK Number 1, Australia Number 4, Belgium Number 1,
  Canada Number 3, Denmark Number 2, Spain Number 3, Germany Number 4,
  Ireland Number 3, Netherlands Number 2, Norway Number 4, New Zealand
  Number 1
Sales: UK Gold

Singles

FIVE MINUTES WITH ARCTIC MONKEYS

UK release: May 30, 2005
Tracks:
1 Fake Tales Of San Francisco
2 From The Ritz To The Rubble
Label: Bang Bang
Album: Whatever People Say I Am, That's What I'm Not
Format: 7″ Vinyl

I BET YOU LOOK GOOD ON THE DANCEFLOOR

UK release: October 14, 2005
Tracks:
1 I Bet You Look Good On The Dancefloor
2 Bigger Boys And Stolen Sweethearts
3 Chun Li's Spinning Bird Kick
Label: Domino
Album: Whatever People Say I Am, That's What I'm Not
Formats: Vinyl, CD
Highest UK chart position: Number 1

WHEN THE SUN GOES DOWN

UK release: January 16, 2006
Tracks:
1 When The Sun Goes Down
2 Stickin' To The Floor (CD only)
3 Settle For A Draw (CD only)
4 7 (7″ Vinyl only)
Label: Domino
Album: Whatever People Say I Am, That's What I'm Not
Formats: 7″ Vinyl, CD
Highest UK chart position: Number 1

LEAVE BEFORE THE LIGHTS COME ON

UK release: August 14, 2006
Tracks:
1 Leave Before The Lights Come On
2 Put Your Dukes Up John
3 Baby I'm Yours
Label: Domino
Album: n/a
Formats: CD
Highest UK chart position: Number 4

BRIANSTORM

UK release: April 16, 2007
Tracks:
1 If You Found This It's Probably Too Late
2 Brianstorm
3 Temptation Greets You Like Your Naughty Friend
4 What If You Were Right The First Time?
Label: Domino
Album: Favourite Worst Nightmare
Formats: 7″ Vinyl, CD
Highest UK chart position: Number 2

MATADOR

UK release: June 18, 2007
Tracks:
1 Matador
2 Da Frame 2R
Label: Domino
Album: n/a
Formats: 7″ Vinyl
Highest UK chart position: Non-chart release

FLUORESCENT ADOLESCENT

UK release: July 9, 2007
Tracks:
1 Fluorescent Adolescent
2 The Bakery
3 Plastic Tramp (CD/10″ Vinyl only)
4 Too Much To Ask (CD/10″ Vinyl only)
Label: Domino
Album: Favourite Worst Nightmare
Formats: 7″ Vinyl, 10″ Vinyl, CD, Download
Highest UK chart position: Number 5

TEDDY PICKER

UK release: December 3, 2007
Tracks:
1 Teddy Picker
2 Bad Woman
3 The Death Ramps (CD/10″ Vinyl only)
4 Nettles (CD/10″ Vinyl only)
Label: Domino
Album: Favourite Worst Nightmare
Formats: 7″ Vinyl, 10″ Vinyl, CD, Download
Highest UK chart position: Number 20

DEATH RAMPS

UK release: December 3, 2007
Tracks:
1 The Death Ramps
2 Nettles
Label: Domino
Album: n/a
Formats: 7″ Vinyl
Highest UK chart position: Non-chart release

CRYING LIGHTNING

UK release: August 17, 2009
Tracks:
1 Crying Lightning
2 Red Right Hand
3 I Haven't Got My Strange
Label: Domino
Album: Humbug
Formats: 7″ Vinyl, 10″ Vinyl, Download
Highest UK chart position: Number 12

CORNERSTONE

UK release: November 16, 2009
1 Cornerstone
2 Catapult
3 Sketchhead
4 Fright Lined Dining Room
Label: Domino
Album: Humbug
Formats: 7″ Vinyl, 10″ Vinyl
Highest UK chart position: Number 94

MY PROPELLER

UK release: March 22, 2010
Tracks:
1 My Propeller
2 Joining The Dots
3 The Afternoon's Hat (10″ Vinyl only)
4 Don't Forget Whose Legs You're On (10″ Vinyl only)
Label: Domino
Album: Humbug
Formats: 7″ Vinyl, 10″ Vinyl
Highest UK chart position: Number 90

DON'T SIT DOWN 'CAUSE I'VE MOVED YOUR CHAIR

UK release: May 30, 2011
Tracks:
1 Don't Sit Down 'Cause I've Moved Your Chair
2 The Blond-O-Sonic Shimmer Trap (10″ Vinyl only)
3 I.D.S.T
4 Brick By Brick (Record Store Day limited edition only)
Label: Domino
Album: Suck It And See
Formats: 7″ Vinyl, 10″ Vinyl
Highest UK chart position: Number 28

THE HELLCAT SPANGLED SHALALALA

UK release: August 15, 2011
Tracks:
1 The Hellcat Spangled Shalalala
2 Little Illusion Machine (Wirral Riddler)
Label: Domino
Album: Suck It And See
Formats: 7″ Vinyl, Download
Highest UK chart position: Number 167

SUCK IT AND SEE

UK release: October 31, 2011
1 Suck It And See
2 Evil Twin
Label: Domino
Album: Suck It And See
Formats: 7″ Vinyl, Download
Highest UK chart position: Number 149

BLACK TREACLE

UK release: January 23, 2012
Tracks:
1 Black Treacle

2 You And I
Label: Domino
Album: Suck It And See
Formats: 7″ Vinyl, Download
Highest UK chart position: Number 173

R U MINE?
UK release: February 27, 2012
Tracks:
1 R U Mine?
2 Electricity
Label: Domino
Album: n/a
Formats: Download and vinyl (Record Store Day limited edition on 24 April 2012)
Highest UK chart position: Number 23

EPs

WHO THE FUCK ARE ARCTIC MONKEYS? (2006)
UK release: April 24, 2006
Tracks:
1 The View From The Afternoon
2 Cigarette Smoker Fiona
3 Despair in the Departure Lounge
4 No Buses
5 Who The Fuck Are Arctic Monkeys?
Label: Domino
Album: n/a
Format: Vinyl, CD
Highest UK chart position: Not eligible for UK chart but charted in Denmark at
    Number 2 and in Ireland at Number 5

Non-single (downloaded) songs that charted in the Top 30 singles chart

COME TOGETHER
Released: 2012
Label: Universal
Album: *Isles Of Wonder* (official soundtrack album of the 2012 Summer Olympics
    opening ceremony)
Formats: Download
Highest UK chart position: Number 21

DVDs

SCUMMY MAN

Released: October 1, 2006
Tracks:
1 Scummy Man
2 Just Another Day
3 When The Sun Goes Down
Label: Domino USA
Formats: DVD

AT THE APOLLO (SPECIAL LIMITED DVD BOX SET)

Released: January 1, 2008
Tracks:
 1 Brianstorm
 2 This House Is A Circus
 3 Teddy Picker
 4 I Bet You Look Good On The Dancefloor
 5 Dancing Shoes
 6 From the Ritz To The Rubble
 7 Fake Tales Of San Francisco
 8 When The Sun Goes Down
 9 Nettles
10 D Is For Dangerous
11 Leave Before The Lights Come On
12 Fluorescent Adolescent
13 Still Take You Home
14 Da Frame 2R
15 Plastic Tramp
16 505
17 Do Me A Favour
18 A Certain Romance
19 The View From The Afternoon
20 If You Were There, Beware
Label: Domino/Bang Bang Films/Warp Films
Formats: DVD